Practical
Handbook
for
Private
Investigators

Practical Handbook for Private Investigators

Rory J. McMahon

CRC Press

Boca Raton   London   New York   Washington, D.C.

Library of Congress Cataloging-in-Publication Data

McMahon, Rory J.
    Practical handbook for private investigators / by Rory J. McMahon.
      p. cm.
    Includes bibliographical references and index.
    ISBN 0-8493-0290-0
      1. Private investigators—United States—Handbooks, manuals, etc. I. Title.

HV8093 .M36 2001
363.28′9′068—dc21   00-052923
                                                                CIP

© 2001 by CRC Press LLC

No claim to original U.S. Government works
International Standard Book Number 0-8493-0290-0
Library of Congress Card Number 00-052923
Printed in the United States of America 1 2 3 4 5 6 7 8 9 0
Printed on acid-free paper

PREFACE

The book is designed for individuals studying to become investigators, as well as private investigators of all types and with all levels of experience. The author shares what his research and experience have taught him. He does not claim to have all the answers, as there is something new to be learned about investigations and people every day. From his perspective, this is one of the most attractive features of this career. This book is for use in the academic realm for the many private and community colleges offering classes in investigation and as a perspective that may be useful to private investigators in terms of their approach to working cases. It is certainly not meant to be the definitive thesis on how all investigations should be performed.

Most of the author's research on the various types of investigations was performed while he was a college teacher at a small private junior college in Fort Lauderdale, and during his 25 years as an investigator. Much has been borrowed from a wide variety of academic and professional sources over the years. It is hoped that the information will be useful to both students and professionals in the field of private investigation.

ABOUT THE AUTHOR

Rory McMahon has been an "investigator" of some sort for most of his adult life. In 1973, as a probation officer in Westchester County, New York, he investigated and supervised persons convicted of state crimes. In 1978, he was appointed a Federal Probation Officer in the Southern District of New York, which comprises New York City and the surrounding area, investigating and supervising persons convicted of federal crimes. He transferred to the Southern District of Florida in 1982, where he conducted presentence investigations on persons convicted of federal crimes in Miami, and subsequently supervised convicted career criminals—primarily organized crime members, major narcotics traffickers, and white collar offenders—as a member of the Special Offender Unit in Fort Lauderdale.

In 1990, he left government service to become a private investigator, working a wide variety of investigations. He became a Certified Legal Investigator (CLI) in 1997, specializing primarily in legal investigations. At the same time, he taught private investigation classes to college students pursuing careers as investigators. Based upon these experiences, he has written this book.

ACKNOWLEDGMENTS

I would like to thank Steve Mallon for hiring me to teach at City College in 1990, after I left government service. He helped me begin my career as an investigator and was an invaluable friend in those early days.

I would like to thank all of my students from 1990 to the present, who have been the source of inspiration for my writing, and for whom I hope this book will be the culmination of all the areas of learning from their City College careers. Special thanks to Gary Diehl, who provided his typed notes for use in classes; Celia Hochtman, who was one of my best students and became a lifelong friend; and Susan Henry, my recent student, who provided valuable input for several chapters in this book.

Finally, to my family, without whom I would be lost. Kelly, for her independence, loyalty to her friends and family, and dedication to her career. Tara, for her encouragement, her journalistic spirit and integrity, and her love and support; Conor, who is everything a ten year old son should be; Joseph Patrick, my beautiful newborn son; and my gorgeous wife, Fran, for her constant encouragement, support, and love.

CONTENTS

DEDICATION

To my mother, Patricia Maguire McMahon, whose death in July 1995 still leaves an incredible void in my life.

To my father, Judge Daniel F. McMahon, whose integrity and work ethic has been indelibly instilled in all of his six children.

1

INTRODUCTION

Since the trial of O.J. Simpson, the profession of private investigation has risen to a new level of respect among both the legal community and public at large. The success of O.J.'s "Dream Team" was largely a result of the brilliant work of the defense investigators.

The Dream Team found the witness who exposed Mark Furman's racism. They fashioned successful responses to everything that the prosecution witnesses testified about.

JOB OUTLOOK

According to the *Occupational Outlook Handbook* published by the U.S. Bureau of Labor Statistics, employment of private detectives and investigators is expected to grow much faster than the average for all occupations through the year 2005. Demand for investigators is expected to be generated by increase in population size, increased economic activity, and domestic and global competition. These forces are expected to produce increases in crime, litigation, and the need for confidential information of all kinds. As crime continues to increase, more firms will hire or contract for the services of private detectives. Additionally, investigators will be needed to meet the need for information associated with criminal defense and litigation for companies and individuals. Greater financial activity will also increase the demand for investigators. As competition becomes more intense, growing numbers of companies will hire investigators to control internal and external financial losses, and prevent industrial spying.

EARNINGS

Earnings of private investigators vary greatly depending on their employer, specialty, and the geographic area in which they work. According to studies done in 1994, private investigators averaged about $36,700 per year, earning an estimated $15,000 to 18,000 per year to start, with experienced investigators earning $20,000 to 35,000. Entry level corporate investigators earn $40,000 to 45,000, with experienced corporate investigators earning $50,000 to 55,000. However, a successful self-employed P.I. can earn $100,000 and more.

Investigators bill their clients $50 to 250 per hour to conduct investigations. Most investigators, except those working for law firms and corporations, do not receive paid vacation or sick days, health or life insurance, retirement packages, or other benefits. Investigators are reimbursed for expenses and receive pay for mileage.

In my experience in South Florida, intern investigators earn from $8 to 15 per hour. Investigators with two or more years experience earn from $15 to 35 per hour.

The potential earnings for those entering the field is unlimited. There has never been a greater need for these services than right now. Additionally, investigators are finally receiving the professional recognition that they deserve. Business is good, and the prospects for the future are incredible!

2

SKILLS NEEDED TO BECOME A SUCCESSFUL INVESTIGATOR

All investigations, regardless of type or purpose, depend on the gathering of factual information. Gathering factual information is the main purpose of any investigation, without which no case would be solved, no stolen property recovered, and no missing person located. Factual information in a concise written report is the product that we sell to our client.

Today's investigator must learn to think of himself as a highly sophisticated camera with the lens always open, recording and observing everything. Regardless of the case, the investigator wants answers to the questions who, what, when, where, how, and why. The private investigator is often the last hope for many people.

Three methods that investigators use to obtain information are:

1. Researching public records
2. Interviewing individuals with relevant information
3. Surveillance of individuals to learn about their behavior.

Investigators must use one, two, or all three of these methods in order to obtain the information needed by the client. To excel as an investigator, one must know how to do all three very well.

WHAT IS AN INVESTIGATOR?

An investigator is a professional researcher who uses observation, inquiry, examination, and experimentation to obtain evidence and factual information upon which sound decisions can be made. In order to achieve success as an investigator, certain basic guidelines must be observed.

Ask many questions when seeking information. Often, this means repeating questions in order to uncover discrepancies, and following up on initial questions with more detailed ones. You can never gather too much information. It is easy to eliminate nonessential information later on.

Recognize that suspects, criminals, and other subjects of investigation come from all walks of life and are represented by all races, both sexes, and an endless variety of lifestyles.

When investigating the crime scene, do not commit yourself to the guilt or innocence of anyone at the scene whom you may question. Remember, your purpose is to gather facts; judgments will come later.

Do not be overconfident. Be certain that you have gathered all the information. Before you conclude the investigation, ask yourself, "Is there more information I should attempt to obtain? Have I overlooked anything that could make a difference in the outcome of the investigation?"

Do not jump to conclusions.

Never take things for granted — make no assumptions about how much information is needed before you begin searching. False assumptions often lead to the loss of valuable information and evidence.

Work with evidence you find at the scene. Examine all evidence carefully; pieces of paper, documents, tools, fragments of cloth, or personal items belonging to a possible suspect or other person involved in the incident that you are investigating — any physical evidence can provide an important investigative lead.

Develop informants and sources of information before you need them. No investigator can get along without sources, because they can provide shortcuts to many investigative problems.

ATTRIBUTES OF A SUCCESSFUL INVESTIGATOR

The following attributes are the special qualities that will help you achieve success:

Suspicion

Be cautious of obvious things and wary of persons who are quick to provide alibis and identification. Demand verification whenever possible.

Curiosity

Develop your own curiosity and follow up on it. Have the desire to learn the truth. An inquisitive mind is essential to the investigator.

Observation

Your five senses are important tools of the trade. It may be important for you to remember unusual things about an individual (i.e., his manner and posture or the way he dresses). Learn to observe details.

Memory

The ability to recall accurately the facts and events or the physical characteristics of a suspect is a valuable skill.

An Unbiased and Unprejudiced Mind

Bias and prejudice will result in a poor investigation, unfairness to suspects, and clouding of facts that need to be uncovered objectively. Do not let personal likes or dislikes interfere with investigations.

Ability to Play a Role

This skill is especially important for private investigators who work alone most of the time. Using his own identity could expose the investigator to recognition and danger. The ability to assume convincing identities is particularly valuable in surveillance, undercover activities, and a variety of confidential inquiries.

Persistence and Capacity for Hard Work

Many times, you will find yourself working late into the night to follow-up a promising lead or question a particularly valuable witness.

Resourcefulness

An investigator must be able to adapt to all types of stressful situations that may demand technical skills.

Ability to Obtain the Cooperation of Others

In the course of your work you will make many contacts. Some will be clients, some will be witnesses, some will be suspects, and some will just be well-meaning citizens who can provide information. It is essential that you obtain cooperation from as many people as possible in order to secure the vital facts and information that you will need to conclude an investigation. You will need patience, courtesy, tact, and understanding.

A suspect or witness who has been intimidated, frightened, or angered by an impatient investigator is of no value.

Interest in Your Work and Pride of Accomplishment

True success in any profession is based on sincere interest and pride in a job well done. The knowledge that your efforts can bring a criminal to justice, locate a missing loved one, or save a business large sums of money can bring you immense satisfaction.

Street Sense

You should have an intuitive understanding of the way the world works and how people move through it. This can be developed and refined. The more time you spend on the street and the more attention you pay to detail, the sharper your street sense will become. This can be learned and sharpened as you work in the investigative field.

Good Listening Skills

You need to be a good listener in order to effectively communicate. In order to be a good interviewer, you must be able to understand the person who you are questioning. If you do not have good listening skills, you will never be an effective interviewer. Therefore, you will not be a successful legal or corporate investigator.

Ability to Put People at Ease

In order to convince people to submit to interviews, you need to be able to "schmooze," which means to make people feel comfortable talking to you. This is a very necessary skill to have in order to conduct successful interviews.

Ability to Speak at the Level of the Audience

There is nothing that turns a person off quicker than someone speaking down or using language that is difficult to understand. You must be able to speak to anyone from a high school dropout to a professional doctor in language that is appropriate and understandable.

Understanding of Body Language

To know if a person is truthful in an interview situation, you must be able to read body language. As a legal investigator, you may interview a potential witness for 30 minutes. At the end of that time, you must gauge that person's honesty and credibility as a potential witness.

Good Manners

There is no excuse for rude behavior — at any time!

Flexibility

You must have the ability to adapt to whatever situation presents itself.

Intuitive Understanding of Human Nature

People are people regardless of the circumstances you may be investigating. As investigators, we see people — our clients, subjects, and suspects — often at times of extreme emotional distress.

Self-Confidence

You need to have belief in your ability to handle any situation.

In my opinion, if you possess the above skills, you will be successful as an investigator and, more importantly, as a human being.

3

PRINCIPLES OF INVESTIGATION

Private investigation combines the skills of both science and art. Given the proper knowledge, tools, and money to operate, few cases exist that cannot be solved if the investigator devotes the time and energy necessary to complete the assignment.

Private investigators perform the following activities:

Criminal investigations
Matrimonial or domestic relations investigations
Negligence investigations
Security
Expert witness
Electronic countermeasures — also called communication security
    sweeps (i.e., debugging)
Corporate investigation
Shopping services
Skip tracing
"Day in the life" productions
Undercover investigation
Process service

TYPES OF INVESTIGATION

There are several types of investigation that will become part of your routine as an investigator.

Criminal Investigations

Private investigators work either for the victim or for the defendant or his attorney in criminal proceedings.

Serious crimes, which may lead to arrest and conviction of a subject, are the source of cases for the legal/criminal investigator. Burglary, theft, homicide, fraud, auto accidents, arson, kidnapping, and so on, are all examples of activities where violations of laws have taken place and you may be called to investigate. These cases typically fall into two categories:

1. Felonies — serious crimes which may involve punishment by death or imprisonment in state or federal prison in excess of one year.
2. Misdemeanors — lesser crimes usually punishable by a fine or imprisonment in a city or county jail, not to exceed one year.

Civil Investigations

This pertains to anything involving lawsuits in which questions of money or property must be settled. Violations of the law are usually not involved. Divorce, bankruptcy, personal injury and negligence cases, and lawsuits of various types are examples of civil matters that may require investigation.

Civil Actions

An attorney or client may hire an investigator to prove either one of the parties to the suit is liable. There are two terms an investigator must know.

1. The *plaintiff* is the party who brings a legal action; one who accuses other person of wrongdoing.
2. The *defendant* is the accused; the one who must defend himself against charges brought by the plaintiff. While he may be accused of wrongdoing, he is assumed innocent until proven guilty by the plaintiff and the plantiff's attorney.

Negligence Investigations

This type of investigation is conducted either for the plaintiff's attorney to prove liability or for the defendant's company or business to prove the absence of liability or absence of a permanent serious injury. This can be accomplished through the use of surveillance (often video or photo), locating and interviewing witnesses, or trying to establish that a pre-existing condition caused or was aggravated by the injury or that the defendant was at fault. A modest investigative fee often saves a client from a large monetary award.

Corporate Investigation

An investigator may monitor what is going on in a business, investigate fraud within or outside the company, and provide diligence investigations or pre-employment screening.

General Investigations

This category includes a wide variety of investigative activities. Included here are location of witnesses and missing persons, serving of legal process, skip-tracing, checks on employee dishonesty and fraud, security surveys, bodyguard work, surveillances, etc.

Personnel and Background Checks

This type of investigation is ordered by businesses, and is undertaken in order to determine whether the character, history, financial status, credentials of an individual make him a suitable candidate for a job, a position of public trust, a large loan, credit, etc. Insurance companies investigate applicants; banks check on individuals applying for loans and also check the applicant's credit rating.

Security

Many private investigative firms offer a range of security services, including:

- Security surveys — to determine vulnerability and to suggest corrective measures against theft.
- Celebrity protection.
- Event protection or security (i.e., concerts).

ASSIGNMENTS PERFORMED BY A PRIVATE INVESTIGATOR

Insurance Claims/Insurance Fraud

This is the largest and most complex category and includes inflated claims on vehicular accidents, phony claims by individuals and organized fraud rings, hit and run (multi-car) with phantom vehicle liability, staged accidents, phony and exaggerated personal injury claims, fraudulent income (disability claims), and paid or untruthful witnesses.

Witness Location

This involves researching public records (often the beginning of any investigation) and includes the use of the following:

- Telephone books, records, and listings.
- Cross reference books.
- Neighborhood and employment investigations.
- Postal records Freedom of Information Act (FOIA).
- Public records, including search of microfiche; voter registration lists; birth, death, and marriage records; real property records; fictitious business files; municipal, county, state, and federal civil court records; state and federal criminal records; corporate and partnership filings; Department of Motor Vehicle (DMV) records; church, medical, and dental records; credit history records; union records; state licensing boards; and law enforcement agencies.
- Trash (dumpster diving) — sometimes the best source of information about a person is found in the trash. It is legal to take the trash once it is put out on the street for pick-up.

Interviews and Statements

Witness, plaintiff, and defendant interviews are conducted, and statements and declarations are taken.

Service of Legal Process

Service of summons and complaint, service for civil subpoena for deposition, service for civil subpoena duces tecum, and service for civil subpoena for trial testimony.

Malpractice Defense

Investigation for medical, dental, and legal malpractice cases.

Bank Fraud

Investigation of all aspects of bank fraud cases.

Employment Investigations

Pre-employment screening, business partner thefts and fraud, employee theft, and business and industrial espionage.

Worker's Compensation Claims

Investigations include neighborhood and employment canvas, medical background and previous claims history, and surveillance and photography/videotaping.

Private Family Investigations

Investigations involving theft and embezzlement of family funds, theft and embezzlement of trust and estates, and the location of missing persons and runaways.

Homicide, Suicide, and Missing Persons Investigations

Death investigation including apparent death that may be staged for the collection of life insurance benefits.

Drug Investigations

Investigations of the transportation, purchase, and sale of illegal drugs using business and employment channels.

Reconstruction of Accidents; Vehicular and Personal Injury

Investigation of claims related to motor vehicle accidents and personal injuries claims.

Trademark and Patent Infringements

Investigation of protection of trademarks and patents.

Slip and Fall Accident Claims

Investigation of circumstances surrounding slip and fall accidents and resulting disability claims.

Domestic or Divorce Cases

Surveillance on cheating spouses, unfit parents, domestic abuse, and conducting hidden asset checks.

Shopping Services

Monitoring employees in stores to make sure that all the sales money is put in register; conducting drug screens on prospective employees. Also, spotters in bars, who monitor the restaurants/bars for theft by employees and constructive assessment of employee conduct.

Skip Tracing

Everyone is looking for someone.

"Day in the Life" Productions

Bodily injury or malpractice claims where the plaintiff claims total or serious disability. Photos or videos of a day or a week of activity often convince the plantiff to abandon the suit or at least settle for a substantially smaller award.

Undercover Investigations

This usually involves a business that tries to identify problems by hiring investigators to pose as employees.

SOURCES OF INFORMATION

Your effectiveness as an investigator will depend largely on your ability to obtain information from the following sources.

Physical Evidence

This includes identifiable objects and traces found at the crime and/or accident scene including fingerprints, clothing and personal effects, photographs, tire marks, notebooks, identification cards, credit cards, weapons, tools, etc. The types, nature, and importance of physical evidence varies with each case.

Scientific Examinations

This type of evidence may be provided by modern, well-equipped laboratories maintained by law enforcement agencies, private investigative agencies, universities, corporations, and medical centers. Any type of physical evidence from blood samples to metal scrapings can be analyzed. As an investigator, you may find yourself using such sources.

Records and Documents

A great deal of information concerning a suspect, missing person, or wanted man can be found in some of the records and documents of government and private agencies. In order to use these sources effectively, the investigator must know the type of information that a particular agency provides, and how to obtain that information. In some states, information is available under the public records law (see FS 119 in the State of Florida). Only active criminal record information is exempt. Law enforcement records would, in most instances, be unavailable, except following request for discovery information once the defendant has been arrested and charged with a crime. Two simple rules will help you in your search for information:

1. Take the time to learn the sources in your locality and strive to develop new ones. Browse through listings under city, county, state, and federal governments in your telephone directory. Become familiar with titles and functions of the various agencies listed. Visit a public library and become familiar with the various documents, references, and directories available. Help from a cooperative librarian can cut your search time in half.
2. Develop sources of information before you need them. Remember, nobody but the court can force any person to produce records or divulge information except for public records. A smart investigator develops his sources carefully so that he can obtain information on a personal basis when he needs it.

Information from People

Despite all databanks, libraries, volumes of documents, and reports available today, people remain our primary sources of information. Cab drivers, reporters, clerical personnel, court employees, as well as specialists and highly placed professionals have provided information that has led to the successful conclusions of many cases. The experienced investigator understands the importance of people as resources and devotes a great deal of time maintaining contacts and making new ones. As sources of information, people fall into two general categories: informants and clients.

Informants

Investigators classify their informants according to the type of information they are seeking. Informants are classified as victims, witnesses, or suspects, and are questioned for information concerning a specific event. Those classified as personal references are used to gather information in personnel investigations. Still another group, experts or specialists, are able to provide specific technical information about their fields of expertise. Investigators sometimes find it necessary to use paid informants who have connections with the underworld to gather information about criminal activities.

Personal References

Whenever an investigator is assigned to a personnel investigation, he will be interviewing personal references supplied by the subject. Naturally, the subject will select people who will give him good reviews. Such people generally tend to provide good news only. The investigator who does a thorough job will search for the neutral person, the one who will provide balanced information that points out the subject's weaknesses as well as his strengths. The best sources for such balanced information are professional people and former employers.

Experts

Anyone with special knowledge because of a profession or hobby is a potential expert. Biologists, psychologists, teachers, doctors, historians, and reformed criminals all qualify as experts. Success in getting information from such sources depends on the investigator. Specialists are usually people whose knowledge is in great demand. The investigator should do his homework before interviewing the expert. First, the investigator should outline the information needed and write out some important questions. The investigator should also come prepared with a note pad and a tape recorder. He should also acquire some knowledge of the subject so that he can talk intelligently to the source. Finally, he should be brief and to the point.

Paid Informants

These people can be useful in gathering first-hand information on underworld activities: gambling, prostitution, drug offenses, and organized crime. Information provided by professional informants has frequently been instrumental in solving crimes that otherwise would have remained unsolved. Paid informants are a dangerous source of information and are often misused. They are overly relied on as sources of information by law enforcement. Remember, credibility is a major factor in all investigations. Paid informants' credibility must be proven before they can be relied upon as witnesses. If you use paid informants, you must take precautions to protect yourself and to safeguard your source. First, determine the informant's motive. Is he talking because he wants money or a reward? Is his motive revenge against someone? Is he looking for some personal favor from you? Experienced investigators have learned that the informant who is primarily interested in money is the most reliable and can be used repeatedly.

After determining the informant's motive, you should plan on meeting privately with your informant. You should avoid close association in public.

Avoid calling paid informants by slang terms such as rat, stoolie, squealer, or snitch.

Finally, protect your informant from possible danger. Never reveal his identity or use any information the he gives you to his disadvantage. Offer privacy and protection, as well as money, in exchange for information.

Demeanor of the Investigator

Your success in obtaining information from a source will depend largely on your approach. Here are a few tips.

- Prepare for the interview by outlining the questions you want answered or the information you hope to get.
- Investigate the source and verify his identity and stability.
- Make an appointment if your source is a busy person and you need more information than you can obtain in a phone call.
- If you must go through a secretary, it is very important not to divulge the nature of your business to her.
- Identify yourself only to your source.
- Do not tell your informant too much. Never reveal any suspicions or personal feelings that you have about the case, because your attitude may slant the informant's answers.
- Conduct your business efficiently and politely.

Above all, remember that no one is required to give you information. Your own patience, tact, and determination will enable you to be successful in using people as sources.

RECORDS AND DOCUMENTS AS INVESTIGATIVE SOURCES OF INFORMATION

Public Library

For the investigator, the public library has a great deal of valuable information, primarily in the form of directories. With exception of city telephone directories, they are frequently overlooked. These sources are primarily professional membership directories and various employments listed by professional associations. The following is a brief list.

1. *American Medical Directory* both foreign and domestic, is issued by the American Medical Association (AMA). This provides names and addresses of all presidents and secretaries of all the county

medical associations listed. Listings of hospitals, sanitariums, related institutions, and names of doctors by states and cities are provided.

2. Directories of newspapers and periodicals provide a guide to newspapers and periodicals printed in United States and its possessions. These directories also provide descriptions of states, cities, and towns in which they are published. This source is useful for interrogations of out-of-town suspects.

3. *Lloyd's Register of Shipping* lists all sea-going merchant and passenger ships of the world and the owners. Similar publications are *Lloyd's Register of Yachts* and *Lloyd's Register of American Yachts*, which provide names and descriptions of yachts, their classification, and names and addresses of the owners.

4. *Who's Who* gives autobiographies of prominent people.

5. *Hotel Redbook and Directory* is published by the American Hotel Association. It lists hotels in the United States, Canada, Mexico, and other countries and is listed alphabetically according to cities, states, or countries.

6. *Baird's Manual of American Colleges and Fraternities* lists men's and women's organizations, professional fraternities, honor societies, local fraternities more than 50 years old, and inactive fraternities and sororities.

7. *Mastai's Classified Directory of American Art and Antique Dealers* lists persons and businesses involved in all phases of the antique business. Its listings are arranged by cities and business names.

8. National, state, city, and county guidebooks and directories are also helpful. Among the most useful are *Baedecker's Guides*, tourist guidebooks of all foreign countries, and congressional directories that provide biographical sketches of senators and representatives, listing of officers of the House and Senate, judicial and executive department personnel, foreign and diplomatic consular offices in the United States, and other valuable information.

Telephone Directories

Current and past telephone directories may be checked for variations in the spelling of a subject's name, and telephone listings of all persons with the same last name. In large cities, also check suburban and outlying directories.

Cross Reference Directories

These books have three separate types of listings. These listings include an alpha section that lists each party name (like a phone book). If the name is found, it will also give the subject's name and phone number. Polk directories will also list an occupation. In the address section, you can look up a listing if all you have is an address. It will tell you who lives there and the phone number. The number section lists all phone numbers by prefix. Once a number is located, it will give the name and address of the person to whom the number is listed. You may also use this directory to locate neighbors or parties nearby when trying to locate someone. As a rule, these directories do not contain unlisted numbers, but there are numerous exceptions.

Local Newspapers and Magazines

The daily paper is backed by an enormous behind-the-scenes operation and contains a potential gold mine for investigators within the various departments. The circulation department has available the names and addresses of subscribers and lists of professional subscription advertisers. The classified ad department keeps on file the names, addresses, and telephone numbers of classified advertisers and the date of each ad. Change of address for subscribers is on record as well. The newspaper morgue maintains a cumulative file on every person whose name has appeared in the newspaper. The library maintains all back issues of papers, many of which are stored on microfilm.

Become acquainted with local magazines published in your area. They report in depth on activities of prominent citizens in the community. Make the acquaintance of editors and investigative reporters who work for these publications because they will prove useful to you.

City and County Business Licenses and Permit Offices

These records contain the name, address, phone, owner, type of business, date filed, and expiration or renewal date on a license.

Local Police and Fire Departments

Local law enforcement may know the subject and may even run a check for you, if you approach them correctly. The fire department might tell you if they have ever received a fire zoning violation.

Fictitious Filings (DBA)

These records are kept by owner's name and cross-referenced by the business name. They will give you the name and address of any business the subject is involved in. Also, the names and addresses of all registrants and the date of filing are available. For a small fee, they will also certify this information for use as a court document.

Bureau of Vital Statistics

Records are maintained on deaths, births, and marriages. Aside from parties' names, it will also show addresses, relatives, and witnesses.

Court Records

A county criminal court contains records of traffic citations and all misdemeanor charges. A county civil court contains records of marriages, evictions, and all civil suits with a dollar amount usually under $10,000. The microfiche contains listings (alpha) of both plaintiffs and defendants. It will give you the date filed, case number, and nature of the action. The Florida Circuit Court is broken down into two categories: the circuit criminal that handles all felony cases and the circuit civil that handles all civil suits over $15,000, divorce cases, foreclosures, and probates.

U.S. Federal Courts are also separated into criminal and civil. They also contain the bankruptcy court. All courts contain files and records considered to be public records and available to the public. There may be records available to you from other government agencies (i.e., FBI, CIA, etc.). You must file a request under the Freedom of Information Act (FOIA). There are also agencies that will do research for you in Washington, D.C., and Canada.

City Hall

Property Assessor's Office

Maps of real property are on file, including dimensions, addresses, owners, taxable value of property, and improvements.

Street Department

Maps of the city are kept on file, showing widths of streets, locations of conduits, drains, sewers, and utility lines. Also listed are current street numbers, abandoned streets, and right of way.

Building Department

This department issues building permits, maintaining applicants on file, addresses of construction sites, amount and cost of construction, and the names of builders. Blueprints and diagrams showing construction details are also available.

Fire Marshal and Sanitary Engineer

These are the officials who conduct inspections on businesses to check for possible violations of code. They have the right to inspect all premises.

Health Department

Birth and death certificates are kept on file, as well as the records and statistics on outbreaks of communicable diseases, including VD and AIDS.

Sanitation Department

This department has access to all premises. Investigators may accompany them and search the contents of garbage (although you have to pay them something for this privilege).

City Attorney

This individual usually operates the consumer fraud division, which maintains files of complaints made by citizens against businesses suspected of fraud (State Attorney for criminal charges).

County Records

Most records in the courthouse are public and available to anyone. The trick is knowing where records are kept and what information they provide.

County Recorder's Office

This office maintains official index records. All instruments are required to be recorded; all papers pertaining to real estate transactions, marriage certificates, contracts (prenuptial), petitions for separation and divorce decrees (lots of information contained), notice of lien and attachment on real estate, certified copies of decrees and judgments of courts of record, official bonds, and, occasionally, birth and death records.

Also available in the County Recorder's Office is the General Index to Official Records. It is cross-indexed as to plaintiffs and defendants, grantors and grantees. The General Index shows the date that the instrument was filed, the defendants and the plaintiffs, the type of instrument, and the book and page of official records where the instrument may be found.

The value of information is exemplified by a death certificate, which contains the following information:

- Name, address, sex, age, race, birthplace, and birth date of the decedent.
- Place, date, and time of death.
- How long decedent has been in community.
- Hospital, if death occurred there.
- Social security number.
- Marital status, occupation, parents' names, including mother's maiden name.
- Death informant's name and address.
- Medical certificate, if under a doctor's care at time of death.
- Coroner's certificate which includes autopsy data, cause of death, and disposal of the body.

County Clerk's Office

This office may be checked for naturalization records, marriage license applications, petitions for divorce, and criminal files.

- *The Naturalization Records and Record Book* provides the names of applicants for citizenship, port and date of entry, manner of arrival, declaration of intent, and miscellaneous information relating to naturalization process.
- Marriage license applications provide pertinent information about applicants.
- Petitions for Divorce include information on the grounds or charges, place and date of marriage, children, and community property.
- Criminal files provide information about the complaint, the arresting officer's report, a description of preliminary proceedings, and other pertinent information.

County Auditor

This office lists all county employees, occupations, and rates of pay. Records of all fiscal business of the county are also available.

Property Assessor's Office

This office maintains plats or maps of real property in the county; with dimensions, address of owner, taxable value, and legal description. Files also include information on buyers and sellers of the property.

County Tax Collector

Records of names and addresses of property owners, legal descriptions of property are kept, as well as a record of the amount of taxes paid on real and personal property, and whether or not taxes are delinquent.

Registrar of Voters or Board of Elections

The affidavits of registration that include some biographical information on registrants are kept on file here. They have a file that lists registered voters according to precincts and, a roster of voters. Listings are maintained on microfiche and include subject's name, address, telephone number, date of birth, date registered, and voter registration number. This is free. Also on file are the nomination papers of candidates for public office.

Medical Examiner or Coroner's Office

Information is available on all deceased persons and include the name or description, date of inquest (if any), property found on the deceased, cause of death, and notes regarding disposition of the body.

STATE REGULATORY AGENCIES AS SOURCES OF INFORMATION

Examination of a subject's business, profession, or past or present employment may lead an investigator to one or more of these sources. For example, in the state of Florida, we have the following agencies.

Department of Motor Vehicles

Provides information regarding operator's licenses, verification of certificates of title, motor or serial numbers, license plate, and vehicle ownership.

Health and Rehabilitative Services

Social Service agencies and State Unemployment offices maintain information concerning individuals receiving assistance from these agencies. This information may be obtained for legitimate investigative purposes.

Professional and Licensing Bureaus (Department of State)

These bureaus set professional and vocational standards for the state and issue licenses or certificates to individuals who qualify. Professional and vocational groups licensed by such agencies include doctors, dentists, social workers, real estate agents and brokers, funeral directors, cosmetologists, contractors, pest control specialists, dry cleaners, chiropractors, accountants, teachers, architects, attorneys, and private investigators.

Florida Department of Law Enforcement (FDLE)

Maintains criminal records on all individuals who have been arrested in the state of Florida. Other states have State Police Agencies that keep criminal records of individuals arrested in that state.

State Comptroller's Office

Investigates all white collar and fraud crimes reported to state agencies.

State Bureau of Alcohol, Tobacco, and Firearms

Governs the issuance of licenses to establishments that sell alcohol, tobacco, and/or firearms. They are usually a valuable resource of information about such establishments.

FEDERAL SOURCES OF INFORMATION

Numerous agencies, bureaus, commissions, and boards of the federal government do not open their files or release information on request. However, as an investigator you may find it possible to get information from the following agencies.

U.S. Postal Service

The Postal Service will supply forwarding addresses. There are two methods by which to obtain change of address information. The first is to obtain a court order for the release of the information (e.g., when working a legal investigation). The second method (cheap and slow) of obtaining an address is to simply address an envelope to the last known address of the subject. Under your return address write, "Address Correction Requested." On the line below that write "Do Not Forward." When the Post Office receives this envelope, they will not deliver it, but will note the person's new address and return the envelope to you.

Most Post Offices can supply you with copies of applications on file for customers of postage meters, bulk-mail permits, and business reply permits. You can also obtain information concerning the holder of a P.O. box, provided it belongs to a business.

Bureau of Immigration and Naturalization (INS)

Records are maintained of all immigrants and aliens. Passenger and crew lists of all foreign vessels using U.S. ports are also kept on file.

Departments of the Army, Navy, Marines, and Air Force

Records are kept of all persons who are, or ever have been, in military service.

U.S. Coast Guard

A listing is kept of all persons serving aboard U.S. merchant ships.

Drug Enforcement Administration (DEA)

Records are maintained of all licensed handlers of narcotics and other drugs, such as physicians, pharmacists, and so on.

Bureau of Alcohol, Tobacco, and Firearms (ATF)

The alcohol tax unit keeps records of violations relating to the manufacture, storage, and sale of alcoholic beverages. This agency also enforces the National Firearms Act.

Federal Communications Commission (FCC)

Records are maintained of licensed holders for all broadcast communications media.

Federal Bureau of Investigation (FBI)

The FBI primarily serves as a clearing house for criminal identification records. On file are:

- Criminal records/fingerprints
- The national stolen property index, including stolen government property
- The national fraudulent check index
- Nonresident information on criminal offenses and subversive activities

Social Security Administration

The original social security applications are maintained and names are listed (maiden or married for women), along with address, sex, race, and parents' names and addresses, at time of application. Current records on cardholders show present employer.

Federal Aviation Administration (FAA) (Oklahoma City, OK)

Records of all licensed pilots, all aircraft, and aircraft parts are maintained here.

PRIVATE ORGANIZATIONS AND AGENCIES

The number of resources in this category are limitless. The experienced investigator knows just how significant these sources can be. Subjects under investigation do not abandon lifetime interests and associations. Frequently, they keep in touch with organizations that have always served them, and in so doing they leave behind various records. The following are examples of private sources that have proved valuable to investigators.

Telephone Companies

Local telephone companies publish geographical directories that list subscribers according to street address in addition to the regular telephone directories. They also maintain records of long distance phone calls.

Public Utility Companies (Gas, Electricity, and Water)

Applications for service usually contain the basic background information. Customers are usually filed according to address, rather than by name. Files include complete service history, number of meters in service, place of last service, and the names of persons who have had service at that address previously.

Credit Reporting Agencies

Most individuals and practically all businesses have credit reporting associations that maintain credit ratings and files on them. Attorneys, wholesalers, retailers, physicians, and so on, are among the many groups represented. The Retailers Credit Association is a national credit reporting organization that maintains files on individuals. On record are basic biographical and financial information on all individuals who apply for credit. Information on the credit rating and financial stability of businesses and individuals can be obtained only for a sound reason, because such organizations must protect privacy.

Insurance Reporting Agencies

Agencies serving insurance companies and underwriters gather information on policy holders. They have detailed records of bad risks in all types of insurance. Of particular value to investigators is the National Auto Theft Bureau. Maintained by auto insurance companies, this agency investigates abandoned and wrecked vehicles, wrecking yards, and junkyards. They also maintain files on professional auto thieves and theft rings and have a national teletype communications network.

Transportation Companies

Taxicabs, limousine services, auto rental companies, and so on, have very useful information which may include a complete record of a trip with time, location, destination, and stops enroute recorded. Drivers from limousine services frequently make useful informants.

Private Investigative Organizations

Many detective agencies are willing to sell specific information they have compiled during the course of an investigation.

Real Estate Agencies

Information can be provided on residents and former residents of property; former addresses of residents; business, social, and character references; and handwriting samples.

Hospitals

Records of patients, illnesses, operations, scars, wounds, injuries, and complications are kept. Such information is often useful in establishing descriptions and identifications of subjects.

School Records

These are good sources of information on behavior, scholarship, family background, disciplinary actions, and financial status.

Personnel Offices

Valuable employment information can be obtained concerning the subject's employment history, successes and failures, and financial standings.

Moving Companies

Information may be provided as to where a subject has moved.

Shipping Companies

Records are maintained on all passenger lists. Included are names, addresses, ports of embarkation and disembarkation, and stateroom numbers.

Travel Agencies

Information can be provided concerning a subject's travel, including departure times, itinerary, and insurance beneficiaries.

Jewelers

Repair records and invoices are maintained that might provide leads to stolen jewelry.

Funeral Directors

Information about families of the deceased is on file here.

MISSING PERSONS

Over one million people are reported missing each year. Many of these people are considered "skips" — a person who for whatever reason of his own chooses to leave a given area. You will find that no one disappears without a trace. If you, as the investigator, devote enough time and effort, and you follow the proper techniques and procedures, nearly everyone can be located. There are three major exceptions to this rule: the very rich, the very criminal, and the very dead. Usually, the longer a person is gone, the easier it is to find the person. Most skips or missing persons eventually leave either paper trails, verbal trails, or both.

Phase One — The Initial Interview

Every missing person case begins with an interview. The purpose of the interview is to develop a body of reliable information that is useful in an actual investigation. The client who is seeking the help of the investigator is likely to be emotionally upset and unable to provide accurate information without careful guidance from the investigator. The client may be thinking of the possibility of murder, kidnapping, serious personal harm to a loved one, and other unspoken fears. It is essential that your manner and approach be reassuring and professional. By remaining calm and comforting, you will be able to gather the vital information you will need to begin your investigation. See Figure 3.1.

Maintain an approach that helps the client remain calm. Project a personal image of professional competence. Allow the client time to relax before beginning a series of probing questions. Let him know that you will follow an orderly logical procedure.

Keep in mind that most missing persons leave situations that they consider unbearable. Your client may not recognize or want to reveal the nature of the circumstances that led to the disappearance. In practical terms, this means you should not accept at face value the initial statements made by the client such as, "everything was all right at home" prior to the disappearance. Get as complete a story as possible. Some clients may hesitate to divulge family problems because they are reluctant to "air dirty laundry" or because they fear that police action and/or publicity could result. You must assure them that all information will be treated in the strictest confidence. As a private investigator, you function much as an attorney does, for the benefit of your client.

Give your client a quick preview of the kind of information that you will be seeking and then proceed in an orderly fashion to interview him. You will be seeking information in three areas:

Has this person run away or disappeared before?
What was the motivating factor that caused the person to leave?
What does the missing person look like?

Previous Disappearances

A surprising number of runaways are repeaters. Clients may not readily volunteer information about previous disappearances for fear of embarrassment. Be sure to ask if the missing person has run away before. If so, then the client can provide valuable information about probable destinations. *Gather all the information you can about the previous incident.* Take the opportunity to check police reports about the disposition of any previous disappearances.

Motive

Determining the motive is perhaps the most important step in a successful investigation. The majority of people who run away do so for predictable motives: family arguments, inability to meet financial obligations, mental or emotional disturbances, inability to cope with severe stress, and so on. However, your client will not volunteer this information without your guidance.

Other motives for disappearances can be far more serious because they involve criminal activity. Some people run away with stolen money. Others leave because they have been threatened with physical violence. Some intend to collect insurance through fraud. When the interview reveals such serious motives, police involvement may be necessary, and further detailed investigation will have to take place.

Description

During the initial interview get a full, detailed description of the missing person. If possible, obtain a recent photograph. Keep in mind that the client may not be able to give you a satisfactory description because he is upset. Plan to get supplemental description from friends, associates, and schoolmates. A complete description includes the following elements:

> Physical appearance — height, weight, race, birthmarks, scars, characteristics, posture, manner of walking, and manner of speech.
> Clothing worn and personal articles carried at the time of the disappearance.
> Vehicle used — make, model, year, body style, license number, color, and condition of the vehicle used by the missing person.

Phase Two — The Investigation

After you have completed the initial interview, you are ready to begin the actual investigation. As you uncover additional information and clues, you will need to speak with your client many times. These follow-up interviews will enable you to eliminate inaccurate information initially provided and concentrate on following clues provided by new information. The three steps you will follow during the actual investigation include the following.

Check the Bad News Sources

Before going ahead with an extensive and costly investigation, you must determine if the missing person has already been found. This means checking area hospitals and jails. If you suspect suicide or other foul play, check the medical examiner's office. If these sources reveal the missing person, then the investigation is complete. If they do not, then you have the basis for further investigation.

Check Personal Belongings

The personal belongings of the missing person can provide important clues to the disappearance. This is especially true with juveniles. The personal effects should be examined including mail, clippings, items found in a purse or briefcase, items found in dresser drawers, and contents of an automobile glove compartment. With juveniles, notes scribbled in books and notebooks, sometimes passed to friends, can provide important clues.

Where foul play is suspected, the examination of personal effects is especially vital and should be pursued persistently. Remember, in cases involving possible criminal activity, your investigation will supplement or complement police efforts, and you will be expected to cooperate with the authorities.

Follow-up Investigation

Although you may develop sufficient information from the initial interview and check of personal belongings to successfully proceed, there may be times when you need to do additional investigation. Such follow-up investigation may involve people associated with the missing person and aspects of the individual's life.

It may be necessary for you to dig deeply into the missing person's social activities, medical history, family history, and employment record. Investigation into these areas may reveal patterns of unbearable stress that motivated the individual to run away. Membership in clubs, special interest groups, unions, and professional associations may provide clues about the individual's interests and associations. Financial records and credit ratings may reveal money problems, a frequent cause for desertion. Records of local government offices, such as state employment offices, relief agencies, and Department of Motor Vehicles may provide clues to temporary residences.

Comments made by a missing person's friends can be significant. You learn that the person missed his last class and friends add that he was acting strangely on the night he last attended. This can be an important clue in establishing the time of disappearance. Lifestyles are also significant. If the missing person is a gambler, pool player, gun collector, golfer, and so on, then his activities and associations provide additional clues as to his whereabouts.

Investigation into family history during the follow-up investigation may reveal serious marital difficulties. In the past, males made up the majority of those who deserted their families. Today, women are more frequently disappearing and leaving families and husbands. They are searching for a different kind of life. Frequently, deserters cannot be induced to return to their families if found. As an investigator, your role in such instances will be to determine their whereabouts and assure the client that the missing person is safe. Do not act as a marriage counselor. Reconciliation is a separate matter to be worked out between the involved parties.

RUNAWAY JUVENILES

Running away from home in search of adventure has always had a strong romantic appeal to many American kids. Many would-be Huck Finns took to the roads, not only to escape from home, but in search of adventure. In today's crowded world, running away offers none of the challenges it did in the past. Juvenile runaways can look forward to a life of extreme poverty, homelessness, crime, drug addiction, prostitution, and even early death. Parents, aware of the dangers the runaways face, are quicker to seek the help of private investigators in locating their children.

In dealing effectively with runaways, you need to know three things:

Who the runaway is.
What motivates the child to run away.
How to conduct an investigation involving juvenile runaways.

Today's Runaway — A Profile

Studies indicate that most of the runaways are from 14 to 16 years of age. Usually, the girls are older than the boys. The average juvenile runaway either goes home or is found in about one week. Knowing how to find the runaway rapidly is especially important because the longer the child is away, the more likely he is to commit crimes.

Psychological research shows runaways are likely to be hostile and defiant. They tend to behave impulsively and exhibit puzzling mood swings, extreme aggressiveness alternating with extreme passivity. Their behavior interferes with schoolwork where routine and discipline are required. Studies also show home atmospheres left by these juveniles are not conducive to happiness. Finally, police records indicate that juvenile runaways more than any other juveniles have been involved in delinquent activities prior to running away.

Motives

Although children leave home for many reasons including desire for independence, excitement, or adventure, the most common motive is desperation to get away from unbearable conditions. The following are the most common motives for running away.

Poor Home Conditions

Alcoholic/drug addicted parents, crowdedness, negative personalities of parents, step parents or others involved in running the household, physical or mental illness of family members, lack of affection, and so on may be contibuting factors.

Desire to Avoid Criticism or Punishment

Children who are reprimanded or are convinced they have disappointed or disobeyed their parents often run away to avoid dealing with the problem.

Rigid, Over-strict Home Discipline

Youngsters who do not feel close to their parents, owing to rejection or strict discipline, run away to escape parents' demands even though the infraction may be relatively minor.

Fear of Being Apprehended by the Police for an Offense

The crime may be relatively minor, such as petty theft, a fight, or broken windows, but the runaway fears the offense will be regarded as more serious.

Lack of Security in New Surroundings

Young people often find it difficult to adjust to the problem of establishing themselves in new communities or neighborhoods. They miss old friends and have difficulty making new ones.

Eloping

Many older juveniles, especially girls, run away from home to get married. In most cases, the marriages are valid.

Investigations

As with other missing person cases, investigating juvenile runaways involves initial interviews, examination of personal belongings, and follow-up investigation. The investigator who is successful in locating runaway juveniles builds a body of information through interviews with parents, friends, and relatives that focus on the runaway's home situation and on his involvement with friends and activities.

Home Situation

Keep the following questions in mind as guidelines:

> Is there hostility between parents and child?
> Are parents demonstrating marital instability, including violent scenes?
> Are other household members showing continuous conflict?
> Does anyone in household have physical/mental disorders, especially long-standing problems that could interfere with home life?
> Are there financial difficulties resulting in constant bickering or hardships that upset or humiliate family members, especially children?
> Is there alcoholism or drug addiction in family?
> Was there a sudden change in child's attitude, especially where his family was concerned? Did he or she suddenly become quiet or explosive, belligerent, or too submissive to be considered normal?
> Did his attitude towards studies, teachers, and so on, change recently?
> Did he stop talking about his friends? Did he suddenly abandon his old friends?

Friends, Activities, Etc.

Keep the following questions in mind as guidelines.

> Are the runaway's friends able to suggest clues to his activities, interests, previous behavior, or other details that would help you? An understanding attitude on part of an investigator can bring cooperation, especially if those friends believe you are trying to help a runaway.
> Did the juvenile frequent neighborhood video arcades, beaches, picnic grounds, parks, sports centers, or hamburger stands?
> Do the juvenile's friends have recent photos that would be helpful to you?

Locating Runaways

Most runaways can be located relatively near home, even though credit cards, family autos, or even their own ability makes it possible for them to go greater distances. As the runaway learns how to survive on his own (usually after several attempts), he is likely to be away longer and, thus, more difficult to locate. The following locations can be used as temporary hiding places (harbors or shelters).

A Friend's House

The runaway may be able to stay at a friend's house for several nights without arousing suspicion. The friend may tell his parents a convincing story about the visit. The home of a married friend is a more attractive shelter often used by a young female runaway.

All-Night Public Places

These include grills and coffee shops, railway and bus depots, airports, laundromats, and movie theaters. Runaways find them convenient first stops where their presence will not be noticed.

Lobbies, Vestibules, and Basements

These places serve as very short-term stops because food and bathroom facilities are not available.

Automobiles

It is not unusual to find exhausted runaways asleep in parked or abandoned cars.

Vacant Buildings

These may include apartments, commercial buildings, lumber yards, garden sheds, or unoccupied private residences.

Campgrounds, Parks, and Beaches

In mild weather these are common, pleasant stops for runaways. They can mingle freely with others without creating suspicion.

Skid Row

Local and out-of-town runaways often seek shelter in the rundown parts of town. They may share a "crib" with other runaways or derelicts, or flop in a cheap hotel.

Carnivals and Circuses

Kids still run away to join the circus. Carnival people are friendly and sympathetic, so these places are considered good choices by many runaways.

The Located Runaway

Assuming you have located a missing juvenile, the steps you should take are to notify parents or guardians of the child's location, because they may have special instructions and will be anxious to know about the child's status.

Determine if the child needs help. Does he display signs of illness or abuse? Attention to these needs puts you in a good position to talk to the runaway and get the complete story.

When speaking to the runaway, try to determine if he was involved in criminal activity (burglary, shoplifting, prostitution, etc.) or if he was victimized by adults in some way. Many young runaways have been seriously mistreated by sexual perverts and may need medical/psychological help. Others may have been persuaded to become members of gangs that commit serious crimes. At first, runaways may be unwilling to reveal details of their activities for fear of further punishment by parents or police, but with patience and skillful questioning you can get these details.

Watch for discrepancies in any story. Be cautious about accepting details of a supposed kidnapping. Check the story carefully and eliminate discrepancies to prevent you from falsely accusing someone.

UNDERCOVER OPERATIONS IN BUSINESS SETTINGS

Cover stories are an extremely important part of any undercover operation. The more complex the case and the greater the sophistication of the criminal suspects, the more attention must be given to the preparation of the cover story. An agent can only be as effective as his cover story is acceptable or believable. It must fit the role being played by the agent. There are three rules to observe on a cover story:

1. Keep it simple.
2. Keep it believable.
3. Keep it as close to the truth as possible.

Another trait that the good undercover agent would benefit from mastering is called "roping." The art of roping can be defined as the undercover agent's gaining the trust and confidence of a suspect to the point where the suspect will disclose past or present criminal acts or, at least, will not hide them from the agent's view. Techniques used to accomplish roping must steer clear of entrapment and areas of illegality. A mature thief would never reveal himself or herself to a newcomer (the undercover agent) until he feels that the agent can be trusted or, at least, is not a threat. Therefore, if the agent can create the impression that he, too, is dishonest, he will have neutralized some of the thief's defenses.

In any company setting, one can usually identify two main groups of employees — those who are relatively "straight" and free from dishonesty and those who care little about the company and take advantage of every opportunity to further their own ends either through company expense or outright illegality.

In the initial stages of an undercover investigation, it is often necessary for the agent to gain and keep the good will of the "straights." Members of this group often possess invaluable information about the illegal activities of persons in the group. During this time, the agent, in effect, must walk a tightrope between the two groups so as not to be identified too closely with either one to the detriment of a future relationship with the other. Eventually, the agent will have to decide to swing away from the "straight" group in order to become completely accepted by the thieves in the plant. This switching over from one group to the other is accomplished through the art of roping. It usually results in the alienation of the original group, which is loyal to the company and not interested in stealing.

The last (and most important) requirement for the supervisor in an undercover case is that he maintain an overall perspective on the entire case. The typical undercover case will involve the identification of various dishonest employees on the work force. This is usually done employee by employee. In other words, over a given time period, the undercover agent will gradually be able to identify more and more dishonest employees. It is up to the supervisor to ensure that the undercover agent does not become bogged down in a relationship with any one dishonest employee or group.

Subject Data File (addendum by line number)   Case#:_____

	THE SUBJECT
1	First: Middle: Last:
2	Maiden: Nickname(s):
3	Previous Legal Name:
4	Other Alias:
5	Primary or current address: Apt./Ste.:
6	City: Co. St: Zip: -
7	Phone: Pager:
8	Cell Phone: Fax:
9	Website: E-Mail: ICQ/UIN:
10	Computer: Password(s):
11	Internet Service Provider: Other "screen names":
12	Subject: Own/Rnt/Rsd From:_____ to _____ (Prm/Tmp) Cmp/Sb:
13	Owner (if not subj): o Listed on "Other Contacts"
14	Also lives here:
15	Complex Manager: Mgt. Co.
16	Address if diff: ICQ/UIN:
17	City: Co. St: Zip: -
18	Phone: Fax: E-Mail:
19	Cell phone: Pager: Website:
20	Other or prior Address (1): Apt./Ste.:
21	City: Co. St: Zip: -
22	Phone: Fax:
23	Subject: Own/Rnt/Rsd From:_____ to _____ (Prm/Tmp) Cmp/Sb:
24	Owner (if not subj): o Listed on "Other Contacts"
25	Also lives here:
26	Complex Manager: Mgt. Co.
27	Address if diff: ICQ/UIN:
28	City: Co. St: Zip: -
29	Phone: Fax: E-Mail:
30	Cell phone: Pager: Website:
31	Other or prior Address (2): Apt./Ste:
32	City: Co. St: Zip: -
33	Phone: Fax:
34	Subject:Own/Rnt/Rsd From:_____ to _____ (Prm/Tmp) Cmp/Sb:
35	Owner (if not subj): o Listed on "Other Contacts"
36	Also lives here:
37	Complex Manager: Mgt. Co.
38	Address if diff: ICQ/UIN:
39	City: Co. St: Zip: -
40	Phone: Fax: E-Mail:
41	Cell phone: Pager: Website:
42	Other Mailing Add: (for subject) This address re:

Figure 3.1   Assets Search Preliminary Data Sheet

43	Street (or P.O. Box)	Apt./Ste.
44	City: County: St: Zip: -
45	Sex: Age: DOB: ___/___/___ POB: Hosp:
46	SSN: Iss. Date: ___/___/___ Passport #: Issue Date: ___/___/___
47	DL #: Iss. Date: ___/___/___ PrsnlTaxID#:
48	Race: Height: Weight: Build: Eyes: Hair: (o Natural o Dyed):
49	Hair Style: Wig/Toupee?
50	Facial hair: Complexion: Teeth:
51	Jewelry:
52	Glasses: Hearing aids: Scars:
53	Tattoos: Piercings: Other marks:
54	L/R Handed Mannerisms/Tics/Movement: (see Med):
55	US Citizen?: Y/ N Nationality: US Citizenship Granted on: ___/___/___
56	INS Status: θ Student θ Resident Alien θ INS #: θ No INS Record
57	Other INS Status:
58	Accent: Languages Spoken:
59	Tobacco use: Brand: Alcohol use: Type/Brand:
60	θ Manner of dress: θ Sizes: Shoe___ Coat___ Neck:___
61	Pants___ Shirt___ Hat___ Blouse___ Bra___ Dress___ Ring___ Glove___
62	Favorite clothing: (specific items)
63	
64	®Miscellaneous data/items client or others may have on subject. Track everything collected on "Evidence Tracking Sheet".
65	θ Photos θ Videos θ Signature θ Handwriting θ Fingerprints θ Medical Records θ Dental Records θ DNA Sample
66	θ Resume θ Curriculum Vitae θ Journal / Diary θ Photo albums θ Bank statements θ Insurance Documents θ Wallet
67	θ Maps θ News Articles θ Official Reports θ Release Forms θ Financial, Business, Tax Documents θ Scrapbook
68	**EMPLOYMENT**
69	Employer: Frm: ___/___/___ To: ___/___/___ FT/PT Union Member?
70	Title: Lic.#: Salary:$___/___
71	Fired/Resigned Re:
72	Shift: ___to ___ am/pm, Days: Note:
73	Responsibilities: Travel? To:
74	Supervisor: Other Contact:
75	Address: Website:
76	City: St: Zip: - ICQ/UIN:
77	Phone: x Pager:
78	Cell Phone: Fax: E-Mail:
79	Employer: Frm: ___/___/___ To: ___/___/___ FT/PT Union Member?
80	Title: Lic.#: Salary:$___/___
81	Fired/Resigned Re:
82	Shift: ___to ___ am/pm, Days: Note:
83	Responsibilities: Travel? To:
84	Supervisor: Other Contact:
85	Address: Website:
86	City: St: Zip: - ICQ/UIN:
87	Phone: x Pager:

Figure 3.1 (continued) Assets Search Preliminary Data Sheet

4

INTERVIEWS, INTERROGATION, AND TAKING STATEMENTS

An interview is the questioning of a person who has knowledge of a subject that is relevant to an investigation. For the purpose of this book, this will be the working definition of an interview. Although the interview often resembles a conversation, it is a highly specialized form of conversation with a specific purpose.

INTRODUCTION TO INTERVIEWS

All information can be categorized into two areas: trivia (irrelevant information) and important information.

Important information is the who, what, when, where, why, and how (the five W's and H). Important information includes unusual observations at the scene, other unusual observations, and the interviewer's gut feelings about the subject noted during the interview.

Interviews, whether formal or informal, always involve a relationship between two people: the interviewer and the person being questioned (the interviewee). The interviewee must be convinced that talking to the investigator is the most important thing at that point in time. Investigators must convey interest in the interviewee without appearing forced or contrived, providing undivided attention and the appearance of listening thoughtfully and with consideration to what the interviewee says.

There is considerable controversy about taking notes, tape recording, and using prepared notes during the interview. Too often note taking interferes with the flow of the interview and observation of the significance of pauses, facial expressions, and body movements that will tip off the investigator to the believability of the person interviewed. Note taking versus recording statements will be discussed later in this chapter. In my opinion, it is better to record a statement than to take notes, providing the interviewee will permit the recording. However, when needed, note taking should be confined to facts that are more difficult to remember, such as family names, addresses, dates, telephone numbers, and so on.

Interviews need to maintain focus. It is necessary to keep the interviewee focused on the issue under discussion and not to allow rambling thoughts and comments. This can be accomplished by asking relevant questions to bring the focus of the interview back to the matter at hand. When possible, you should organize the interview questions in advance. You should have an outline of the material you wish to explore and the information you need to obtain and have a series of questions firmly fixed in your mind.

STRATEGIES

Ask the interviewee to relate the series of events in his own words. The interviewee should be allowed to tell the entire story once without interruption. If he stops, nod your head or repeat a phrase that was used to stimulate him or her into continuing. It is not productive to ask questions that require only a yes or no answer. However, questions should be kept simple and easily understood by the interviewee.

Investigators should analyze the interviewee's behavior and body language for clues to truthfulness and honesty. Does the interviewee maintain eye contact or act fidgety? These clues to truth or deception will be discussed further in the section on body language.

The investigator also must strive to convey understanding and empathy with the interviewee. A nod or smile will help convey connection with the interviewee. Remember never to talk above the level of understanding of the person. Defining the purpose of the interview at the beginning of the conversation will help get the relationship off to a good start.

The presumption of every interview should be that the interviewee has information and material that is pertinent to the case. The investigator's task and intent should be to obtain all that information.

Role Playing

The investigator must be willing and able to play the role that is required, depending on the circumstances, in order to promote the most open response to the interview.

During the early stages of the interview process, an investigator may realize that the witness, victim, or suspect has some personal problem (defense mechanism, fear, or other more conscious reaction) that prevents him or her from cooperating in the investigation. Some witnesses and victims are reluctant to cooperate because they fear for their personal safety or they fear their involvement will create an undue burden (time and/or money) on their families. In these instances, the investigator may attempt to calm the person by playing the role of a protector or benefactor. As a concerned listener, the investigator plays the role of an understanding stranger.

Common Interviewing Errors

Although there are many interviewing errors, these are the two most common:

1. The interviewer does not allow the interviewee to tell his own story.
2. The interviewer talks too much.

Interview Guidelines

The following strategies are important interview guidelines:

1. The investigator must **control** the interview.
2. Prior preparation is essential. Review the facts of the case and all available records and data before commencing the interview. Know what you are talking about.
3. Carefully evaluate the subject of the interview.
4. Play whatever role is required to facilitate the free flow of information.
5. Tactfully select the best combination of strategies to use.
6. Do not automatically discredit information that is unfavorable to your position.
7. Remember that you responsibility is to gather the facts.

Empathy

Empathy is the feeling associated with emotional identification with another person. When used correctly, the mutual concern (real or imagined) that results will ensure the free flow of information. The interviewer should follow these guidelines: appear sincere, use a very understanding approach, have a nonjudgmental attitude, and be careful to disguise negative feelings or lack of compassion for the interviewee.

CRIMINAL INVESTIGATION TECHNIQUES

Questioning is divided into two broad classifications:

1. *The interview* is conducted to learn facts from persons who may have knowledge of the wrongful act but are not themselves implicated.
2. *The interrogation* is conducted to learn facts and to obtain an admission or confession of wrongful acts from persons who are implicated in them to obtain a a written, signed, and witnessed statement, and to establish the facts of a crime or develop information which will enable the investigator to obtain physical or other evidence to prove or disprove the truth of an admission or confession.

Purpose of an Interview

An interview is an informal questioning to learn facts. The successful investigation of facts regarding criminal acts requires that the investigator be able to learn, through personal questioning, what the person interviewed has observed through his five senses: *smell, sight, hearing, touch,* and *taste.* Effective interviewing requires that the investigator make full use of his knowledge of human nature so that the interviewee will disclose all that he knows about the matter in question.

Preparation for an Interview

Interviews should be planned carefully and thoroughly to prevent repetition. The investigator must review thoroughly all the developments in the case prior to the interview. He must also consider the relationship of the interviewee to the investigation, that is, complainant, victim, witnesses, or informant. The effective interviewer combines his knowledge of human nature with available information about the person to be interviewed such as education, character, reputation, associates, habits, and past criminal record. The investigator also should prepare by noting pertinent facts to be developed to detect and evaluate inconsistencies and discrepancies in the statements of the persons interviewed, and to require clarification of the statements as necessary.

Control over Interviews

An investigator must maintain absolute control of the interview at all times. If the interviewee becomes so evasive as to obscure the purpose of the interview, effective results may be obtained by a more formal type of questioning, taking notes, or by aggressiveness of the investigator. Although an investigator has no legal power to force a person being interviewed to disclose any information, he may, if clever, induce the interviewee to disclose whatever he knows.

Attitude and Demeanor of the Investigator

The investigator must establish a cordial relationship with the interviewee. The investigator should be friendly. The interviewee should be permitted to give an uninterrupted account while the investigator makes mental notes of omissions, inconsistencies, or discrepancies that will require clarification by later questioning. The investigator should avoid a clash of personalities, acts of undue familiarity, the use of profanity or violent expressions (kill, steal, murder), improbable stories, or distracting mannerisms like pacing the floor or fumbling with objects.

Types of Approach

The indirect approach in interviewing consists of discussions carried out in a conversational tone that permit the interviewee to talk without having to answer direct questions. The direct approach consists of direct questioning as in an interrogation. The use of interrogation techniques often succeeds when the person interviewed fears or dislikes police officers, fears retribution from a criminal, desires to protect a friend or relative, or is unwilling to cooperate with the investigator. The talkative person should be allowed to speak freely and to use his own expressions, but should be confined to the subject by appropriate questions.

Interviews of Complainants, Victims, and Witnesses

In interviewing complainants, the investigator should be considerate, understanding, tactful, and impartial regardless of the motive for the complaint. When interviewing a victim, the investigator must consider his or her emotional state, particularly in crimes of violence. Frequently, victims have unsupported beliefs regarding the circumstances connected with the crime.

When interviewing a witness, the investigator must frequently assist them to recall and relate facts exactly as they observed them. The emotions of witnesses before, during, and after the incident, and when interviewed, greatly affect their recall of events as they occurred. A frightened witness may recall events differently than a calm, unruffled person. *Credibility of a witness is usually governed by his character and is demonstrated by his reputation for truthfulness.*

During the interview, the investigator must continually evaluate the mannerisms and the emotional state of the interviewee in terms of the information developed. The manner in which a person relates his information or answers questions may indicate that he is not telling the truth or is concealing something. Evasiveness, hesitation, or unwillingness to discuss certain situations may signify a lack of cooperation. The relation of body movement to the emotional state of the person must carefully be considered by the investigator.

Purpose of the Interrogation

Interrogation is the questioning of a person suspected of having committed the act under investigation. The purpose of the interrogation of a suspect is to obtain an admission or confession of wrongful acts and to obtain a written, signed, and witnessed statement. The interrogation should only be conducted after sufficient information has been obtained and the background of the subject has been thoroughly explored.

The investigator should base his plan for interrogation on background data, information, or direct evidence received from victims and witnesses, physical evidence, and reconstruction of the crime scene. The plan, which should be written, should take into consideration the various means for testing the truthfulness of the suspect and gaining a psychological advantage over the suspect through the use of known facts and the proper use of time, place, and environment.

The Interrogation

No time limit should be placed on the duration of the interrogation except that it should not be so long and under such conditions as to amount to duress. Questioning for many hours without food, sleep, or under glaring lights has been held to constitute duress and, thereby, may invalidate the confession. Obviously, investigators who are not law enforcement officers have much more latitude in this area.

An interrogation usually should be conducted in complete privacy. Witnesses to a confession may be called in to hear a reading of the statement and declare that it is indeed the subject's statement, to witness the signing by the subject, and to affix their own signatures.

Attitude of the Investigator

Owing to the importance of an admission or confession, the investigator must become skilled in the art of interrogation. The investigator must master a variety of questioning techniques, learn to judge the psychological stress or weaknesses of others, and learn to take advantage of his own particular abilities in questioning any suspect or reluctant witness.

Types of Approach

The Direct Approach

This is normally applied where guilt is reasonably certain, that is, "Why did you steal the money?"

The Indirect Approach

This is applied in interrogating a person who has knowledge of the crime (when you do not have enough evidence to point the finger), that is, "Do you know who was involved in stealing the money?"

The Emotional Approach

This is a method designed to play upon the emotions of a person, i.e., "You know that Mr. Smith has suffered severely from the theft of the money from the company. Is there anything you can tell me about who may have been involved?"

Subterfuge

This approach is applied to induce guilty persons to confess when all other approaches have failed. For example, a hypothetical story, signed false statement, the cold shoulder, playing one suspect against another, and contrasting personalities (good cop/bad cop).

Persons who have been interviewed may later be interrogated. An interrogation is not confined to individuals suspected of criminal acts but may include persons who may have been accessories or may have knowledge of the crime which they are reluctant to admit. When an interview or interrogation develops information which will have value as evidence, it must be recorded in a written, signed, and witnessed statement, or a tape recorded statement.

Reading Body Language

An estimated seventy percent of communication occurs on the nonverbal level. The nonverbal physical actions of the lying suspect may be characterized as follows.

Gross Body Movement

Examples are posture changes, movement of the chair away from the interrogator; an indication of being about to stand up or perhaps leave the room.

Grooming Gestures

This would include rubbing hands; stroking the back of the neck; touching the nose, earlobes, or lips; picking or biting finger nails; shuffling, tapping, swinging, or arching of the feet; rearrangement of clothing or jewelry; dusting; picking lint or pulling threads on clothing; adjusting or cleaning glasses; straightening or stroking hair.

Supportive Gestures

Gestures such as placing hands over eyes or mouth when speaking, crossing arms or legs, holding forehead with hands; and placing hands under or between legs are characterized as supportive gestures.

Summary of Body Language Skills

The investigator should vary his expression to fit changes in the emotions expressed by the interviewee. Make polite and friendly use of the social smile but do not overdo it. Use facial expressions to show interest as a listener and to be interesting as a speaker. Avoid undue use of facial expressions — especially a blank stare, which may be seen as showing hostility or lack of interest. Avoid fixed, frozen expressions that do not vary with changes in the situation. Avoid weak expressions that are badly timed and appear insincere. Failure to use expressions to accompany your own speech, or to reflect what the speaker is saying, may also convey lack of interest.

Eye Contact

The general rule is to maintain eye contact broken up by definite looks away. Look more while listening, less while talking. Look away when taking up the conversation, look back when handing it back. Maintain eye contact with serious expressions when trying to gain control of a situation. Avoiding eye contact, at one extreme, conveys nervousness and lack of confidence. Staring, on the other extreme, conveys hostility and intrusiveness.

Distance

Keep an appropriate distance and adjust to cues to compensate when too close or too far away. Too much eye contact, leaning forward, and close proximity can give an intrusive or domineering impression. Too much distance, too little eye contact, or turning away can convey a cold impression.

Touch

A brief touching on the hand, arm, shoulder, or other acceptable area of the person's body can convey warmth and emotional support, or can be used to draw attention to an important point that you are making. Sudden and uninvited touching can be seen as too intimate. Too many touches to control direction and attention can make you appear domineering.

Use of Voice

Aim for moderate volume, a resonant tone, varied pitch, and varied pace. High volume, a booming tone, and an over varied, or low pitch make you seem domineering. Low volume, a thin tone, and unvarying pitch and pace, especially a slow pace, convey a submissive, depressed attitude. Stuttering and some other speech disturbances convey anxiety.

Posture

For an attentive posture, lean forward with a straight spine and arms open, turned toward the speaker. For a relaxed posture, lean back with your head up and let your limbs take a symmetrical position. Avoid slumped shoulders, bowed head, folded arms, and deflated chest. Do not turn your body away. These cues convey submissiveness, depression, and lack of interest.

Gesture

Use gestures of emphasis to make your speech livelier and easier to follow. Use gestures that clarify meaning (such as pointing), and that convey meaning of their own (such as nodding to show agreement). Do not overuse gestures when trying to secure a speaking turn, this appears aggressive. Fidgeting and hand wringing conveys anxiety. Foot tapping conveys irritation.

Appearance

To create a positive impression, dress to conform to the situation you expect to meet. Looking attractive is an advantage in almost any situation. The following points are important to remember about the use of body language:

1. Posture — how you hold your body can reveal feelings about events or people, and your degree of interest.
2. Eye contact — most of us respond unconsciously to the eye signals of others, but with greater awareness, we can learn to control situations more effectively and access moods and motives of others more reliably through eye contact.
3. Reading facial expressions — faces convey our most expressive body language. Reading faces tells us how we are getting along. Spontaneous smiles and frowns are especially informative, but just as sincere words can be selected, so can sincere facial expressions.
4. Language of touch — how, when, and where we touch others can make or break relationships. If the message conveyed is appropriate, most people will respond positively to being touched.
5. Making conversation — the art of conversation involves intricate skills. Showing interest, starting and ending conversations, taking your turn or interrupting, bring all our resources into play.
6. Detecting insincerity — research has revealed principles for detecting lies and deception. Facial expressions may be the least revealing; the rest of the body may reveal signs of insincerity, as do some speech patterns, tone of voice, and even reduction in blinking.

Postures of Agreement and Disagreement

When people disagree with what is being said, they tend to have "closed" postures, holding head and trunk straight, and folding the arms. If they are seated, they are likely to cross their legs above the knee. A more neutral attitude is conveyed by folding your hands on your lap and crossing your legs at the knee. When people agree, they are more likely to have "open" postures — leaning the head and trunk to one side and leaving their legs uncrossed.

An interested listener leans forward with legs drawn back. When interest fades, the head begins to lean and requires support by a hand. When completely bored, people let their heads drop and the body has a backward lean with legs stretched out. People who are concerned about what their bodies might be signaling try to lean forward.

Posture provides a system by which conflicts can be avoided through signaling acceptance of another's dominance. If you do not want to challenge someone's authority or do not want to reveal a challenge before the time is right, avoid expansive arm gestures and turn both head and body in a show of attention, rather than the head alone. However, when you do need to assert authority, hands on hips and attention that is confined to turning the head will demonstrate that you are in charge.

Even in one-to-one conversations or in some small groups, you sometimes need to penetrate the polite reactions of the listeners to be an effective speaker. Unconscious shifts in the positions of bodies and limbs can be early warning signals that you need to find something more interesting to say or you need to overcome objections.

Eye Contact

Eyes are usually thought of as receivers of information. We use our eyes to see the world around us, but they also transmit signals that play a vital role in everyday social interaction. How we look at other people, meet their gaze, and look away can make the difference between an effective encounter or one that leads to embarrassment or even rejection. Looking into the eyes of another is such a powerful act of communication that it must be carefully controlled.

As soon as the conversation begins, eye contact will usually be broken as the speaker looks away. Usually, the person who is listening will look more than the person who is talking. To show responsiveness and interest as a listener, you need to look at the other person's face for roughly three-fourths of the time, in glances lasting from one to seven seconds. On other occasions, you might be faced with a person who will not let you get a word in edgewise. The speaker avoids your eyes at the very moment you want to signal that you are going to say something. There is a way to remedy this. First, switch off the support that you give by looking at the speaker. Look to one side, but in such a way that you can tell when you are looked at.

Looking away during the conversation can be self-revealing. If you ask someone a question, they will meet your eyes and then look away.

Some will look away to the left, others to the right. It seems to depend on the anatomy of the brain. Those who look away to the left are likely to be more artistic or religious and those who look to the right are more scientific minded. In most people, the left hemisphere of the brain deals with verbal questions (such as how to spell a word), and such questions prompt them to look right. The right half of the brain deals with spatial questions (such as how to get somewhere), and these are associated with looking to the left.

Pupil Signals

We find it difficult not to look at people who arouse our emotions. When the person is a stranger we usually look less often and more briefly in an effort to mask our real feelings. Along with any emotional response comes a widening of the pupils of the eyes, even though the light falling on them remains constant. This is an involuntary reflex, originally an evolutionary adaptation to let more light into the eye, so more information is available to the eyes in an emergency, but it also acts as a mood signal. The sight of dilated pupils unconsciously triggers an emotional response and a corresponding pupil-enlargement response in the person being looked at.

Reading Facial Expressions

Usually, people's facial expressions seem to be better guides than their words about what they are feeling. It is possible to read emotions and attitudes from people's faces. Smiles and frowns are often spontaneous expressions of happiness and anger. Universally, people express and recognize four basic emotions. There are two other emotions — fear and surprise — distinguished by everyone except remote populations in New Guinea. Also, three independently expressive regions of the face — the eyebrows, the eyes, and the lower face — are used. The following six facial expressions will help you determine another person's emotions:

1. Happiness — appears in a smiling mouth and wrinkles around the eyes.
2. Sadness — raised brows, lowered eyelids, and a down-turned mouth.
3. Anger — gives the eyes a penetrating stare and causes the lids to tense. The lips of the angry mouth are pressed together or opened and pushed forward.
4. Disgust — shows itself in a wrinkled nose and raised upper lip. The lower eyelids are pushed up and the brows are lowered.

5. Surprise — raises the brows, the eyes are wide open, and the jaw drops, opening the mouth.
6. Fear — raises and draws together the brows. The eyes are open and tense and the lower lids are raised. The mouth is open and lips may be drawn back tightly.

Detecting Insincerity

The ability to deceive others is thought to be a characteristic genetically selected through human evolution. There are many occasions in everyday social encounters when people, for one reason or another, want to avoid expressing their true feelings. The ability to do this varies, and success breeds success. Those who lie effectively will tend to lie more often, perfecting their deception skills in the process. Those who fail are deterred from future attempts and get less practice.

The way in which deceit oozes from our bodies is referred to as nonverbal leakage — a series of body language cues that indicate insincerity. Controlled observation has revealed just what these cues are. One of the most reliable is the way we speak. People who are deceptive make fewer factual statements, preferring instead more general sweeping remarks. They frequently leave gaps in the conversation to avoid mistakenly saying something that would give them away. They speak with a higher pitch when lying, and at a slower rate. They hesitate more and are more likely to stutter or to make other speech errors.

A more difficult cue is facial expression. People are better at controlling this than any other aspect of their body language. In general, people smile less when lying and they are slower to respond to what you are saying with facial expressions and other body language. The eyes, in particular, are hard to control. Pupil dilation and reduced blinking are among the most consistently observed nonverbal leakages.

Tip-Off Movement of the Body

The hands are especially reliable cues for detecting deceit. A noticeable mannerism of deceptive people is a decrease in simple hand movements. To curtail the messages of the hands, they keep them still or out of sight. Fewer head movements are also very common. When the hands are allowed to move, they display an above average frequency of auto-contact behaviors. These self-touching movements are strongly related to high levels of arousal and nervousness, which is essentially what lie detectors measure. In everyday encounters you need to be aware of people's hands as they touch their noses, stroke their chins, or brush their hands across their mouths.

Postural cues are also important. Liars tend to make more postural shifts than nonliars. Information about nonverbal leakage should help you detect deception and insincerity more easily. The question is, what should you do about it? It all depends on the situation and the motive the person has for deceiving you.

TAKING STATEMENTS

A witness is anyone who has some particular knowledge of a given situation or occurrence. It is not necessarily an eyewitness. The three purposes for taking statements from witnesses are preservation of the recollection of an occurrence, to aid in the possible settlement of a matter without proceeding to trial, and impeachment of an untruthful witness in the event of a deposition, court hearing, or actual trial. The three different types of statements are the signed, handwritten, or printed statement, the in-person or telephone recorded statement, and the typed legal declaration under penalty of perjury.

One major problem with the phone interview or recorded statement is that you cannot see who you are interviewing. Often, if your client is an attorney or an insurance company representative, he will rely on you to provide him with a detailed description of your impression of the witness, including appearance, attitude, demeanor, attentiveness, quickness of response, and general body language.

The most common form of statement you will use will be the in-person or telephone-recorded statement regarding a car accident and/or personal injury claim. Most personal injury (plaintiff) attorneys require that investigators have the witness write the statement in his own hand. This is done to protect the investigator from being deposed by opposing counsel. However, it is preferable that the investigator print the statement to ensure that it is accurate and legible and then have the witness read and sign it.

The most common method of beginning a statement is the identification and qualification of the witness. This gives your client the witnesses' name, address and phone number, place of employment, date of birth, and social security number. Next, you state the purpose of the statement by identifying the accident or incident. Ask for a very detailed description of the location including all landmarks, points of interest, and individuals or vehicles present. Based upon the information presented by the witness, draft the main body of the statement showing the sequence of events (as a witness recalls, whether they are right or wrong), up until the time the witness departs the area.

Remember, once you have submitted the signed statement to your client, it may be read or reviewed by insurance companies, attorneys, and/or judges. It is therefore incumbent upon you to make it as clear and descriptive as possible. In other words, if the person reading the statement has never been to the area in question, he should thoroughly and totally understand the condition at the accident site, including the locations of all individuals both before and after the incident, and who said what to whom.

The ending of the statement is also important, both in your discussion with the witness and the documented statement. Once the witness has indicated that he has given all of the facts he can remember, you can conclude in the following manner. If the witness is friendly and cooperative, simply show him or her the statement, ask him or her to read and sign each page (one at a time). Once he has finished, ask the witness if there is anything you might have left out or anything he wishes to add. If the witness indicates the statement is adequate, then simply add the final two sentences required by law: (1) "This statement is free and voluntary," and (2) "No threats or promises have been made in connection with this statement." (Figure 4.1, 4.2.) You may want to have the witness sign and Acknowledgment of Interview (Figure 4.3).

Admissions, Confessions, and Written Statements

Obtaining written statements can serve four specific purposes:

1. To provide a written record for the case file.
2. For use at the trial to refresh recollection, impeach witnesses, and monitor testimony.
3. To discourage a witness from wrongfully changing their testimony at trial.
4. To assist the attorneys in planning their presentation by reducing the elements of surprise that unforeseen testimony would produce.

Admissions

An admission is a self-incriminating statement by the subject falling short of an acknowledgement of guilt. It is an acknowledgement of a fact or circumstance from which guilt may be inferred. A simple statement that the subject was present at the scene of the crime (or event) may be an admission.

Confessions

A confession is a direct acknowledgement of the truth of the guilty facts as charged or of some essential part of the commission of the criminal act itself. To be admissible in court, a confession must be voluntary and trustworthy. Examples of circumstances which would render a confession inadmissible are threats of bodily harm, illegal detainment, deprivation of necessities or necessary privileges, and physical oppression.

Furthermore, the investigator should be able to show that the confession was voluntary as evidenced by one of the following:

> The statement was not obtained by urging or by request, but was a spontaneous or self-induced utterance.
>
> The statement was obtained without coercion and not during an official investigation or while being detained.

Depositions

A deposition is testimony of a witness reduced to writing under oath or affirmation, before a person empowered to administer oaths, in answer to questions submitted by the party desiring the deposition and the opposing party. A deposition is ordinarily used to take the testimony of a witness who may be unavailable at trial (criminal or civil). Ordinarily, a deposition is taken by an attorney, not an investigator.

Written Statements

Whenever possible, important statements of witnesses and suspects should be reduced to writing. Written statements should be taken from subjects and suspects, recalcitrant and reluctant witnesses, key witnesses, any witness who gives an indication of a tendency to change his mind, and witnesses who will not be available at legal proceedings.

Contents of Statements

The investigator should consider first what information the witness may possess and could be expected to give at testimony and, second, what information is needed to support the case. The common grounds of these two considerations should be the substance of the statement given by witnesses.

The statement of a suspect should substantiate the elements of the charge or contain any information relevant to the issues of the case. In addition, it should include any details of extraordinary circumstances or explanations offered by the suspect.

Finally, the investigator should apply the criteria used to judge a report of investigation. The purposes of such a report are:

1. To provide a permanent record of information.
2. To present clear, direct, complete, and accurate information.
3. To present information that can form the basis of additional investigation.
4. To present information that can form the basis of charges and/or specifications.

Methods of Taking Statements

The following methods may be used when taking statements.

1. The subject may write his own statement without guidance. A statement of this nature, which is sufficiently complete, is usually a desirable form.
2. The subject may dictate to a stenographer without guidance.
3. The investigator may give the subject a list of essential points to be covered in the statement and suggest that he include these matters and add whatever other pertinent information that he may wish.
4. The subject may deliver his statement orally in his own way to the investigator, who writes the statement.
5. The subject may deliver the statement orally to the investigator or stenographer in response to questions put to him or her by the investigator. The answers are recorded verbatim.
6. The investigator may assist the subject, indicating which statements will express the subject's intended meaning. Naturally, great caution must be exercised by the investigator to protect himself or herself from a charge of influencing the subject. Tape recording the statement would be useful.
7. The investigator may prepare the statement by writing the version of the information provided by the subject. The investigator must use the expressions employed by the subject and submit the statement to the subject for corrections and changes.

Form of Statement

Identifying Data

The first paragraph of a statement should contain the date, place, identification of the maker, name of the person to whom the statement is made, plus a declaration by the maker that the statement is made voluntarily.

The Body

The body of the statement can be given in narrative form. It is of great importance, particularly in a confession, that the statement include all the elements of the crime and the facts associating the suspect to these elements. The words of the subject should be used, but the scope of the confession should be guided by the investigator. The investigator may write the statement himself to ensure the inclusion of all the necessary details. The subject should then be requested to read the statement and initial each page at the bottom. Each page should be numbered by writing in the lower right corner, i.e., page ___ of ___ pages.

Conclusion

The concluding paragraph should state that the subject has read the document of so many pages and has signed it. The subject should then request to initial any corrections made on the statement.

Witness to a Confession

The presence of witnesses will provide a defense claiming that duress in the form of threats and promises were employed by the investigator. After the investigator has prepared the statement for signature, witnesses may be introduced so that they can testify to the following:

1. The subject read and revised the entire statement with the investigator.
2. The subject objected to certain words, phrases or statements.
3. The subject corrected certain words and phrases, and initialed the corrections.
4. The subject evidently understood the contents of the statement.
5. The subject was in his right senses, knew what he was doing, and acted voluntarily.
6. The subject acknowledged the statement to be true and correct.

Each person witnessing the signature should sign as a witness. The signature should indicate the name and address. If the witness is a member of a law enforcement agency, it should be accompanied by his grade, title, and assignment.

Admissibility of Confessions

A confession that was obtained under duress or by compulsion or without the presence of constitutional safeguards is inadmissible in court. The investigator who obtains a confession through the employment of illegal practices renders inadmissible not only the suspect's statements but very likely the evidence which might be developed subsequently from the leads contained in the statement (the fruit of the poisonous tree). Great caution and sound judgment must be exercised in obtaining a confession to avoid casting a shadow on its legality. The investigator should have a thorough knowledge of the court requirements for admissibility and of the procedures, safeguards, and standards of conduct.

The test for admissibility employed by the federal and state courts is that a *confession must be trustworthy and voluntary.*

Forms of Duress

Coercion

The direct application of illegal physical methods. This refers to beatings or forms of assault such as hitting with a rubber hose, punching, forms of torture, and so on.

Duress

The imposition of restrictions on physical behavior. This includes prolonged (six or more hours) detention in a dark room, deprivation of food or sleep, and imposing conditions of excessive physical discomfort and continuous interrogation over extraordinarily long periods of time.

Psychological Constraint

The free action of the will may be unlawfully restrained by threats or other methods of instilling fear. Suggesting the prospect of harm to the suspect, his relatives, or his property can be interpreted as psychological abuse even though the suggestions are not in the form of explicit threats.

MCMAHON & ASSOCIATES

<u>Witness Interview Protocol</u>

1. Introduction and identification of interviewing Investigator (show and explain ID, leave a business card).

2. Go over the "Witness Interview" Statement of interviewee's rights with the interviewee.

3. Ask permission to record the interview.

4. With recorder on, state date and time of interview, name of interviewer and interviewee, reiterate purpose of interview, and produce affidavit.

5. Fill out of witness data sheet recording verbal answers to data and personal information questions.

6. With recorder on, ask the following while the interviewee fills out the affidavit:

   A. Do you understand the purpose of this interview?

   B. Have you been promised any kind of reward whether it be cash or any other promise of favor in exchange for the information you are about to give?

   C. Have any threats or insinuation of negative action been made to entice you into giving the information you are about to give?

   D. Have any promises of favor or threats of negative action been made by others in an attempt to have you alter the truth of your Statements with us here today?

   E. You are about to give the following truthful information of your own free will?

   F. Have any promises of favor or threats of negative action been made against you by persons or parties opposed to you talking with us today?

   G. Do you understand that both parties in this situation may, under certain circumstances, be privileged to the information you are providing today?

7. Q & A session

8. With recorder on, ask: Is there any information you feel that is pertinent to this case that I have not asked you? Is there any information that you have provided today that you wish to correct or retract?

Signed: _____   Date: _____
                    Witness

Figure 4.1 Witness Interview Protocol

MCMAHON & ASSOCIATES

<u>Witness Interview</u>

If you are in receipt of this document, you have been asked to participate in an interview concerning a situation to which you have direct knowledge.

The purpose of this interview is for us to ascertain the truth of a particular situation. As they say in the courts, we want the truth, the whole truth and nothing but the truth. We represent our client in this matter and wish to gather as much information as possible relevant to the situation so that our client and any legal representatives they may have, will be able to determine the viability of their claim.

As an interviewee, you should be made aware of the following:

1. We make no promise of reward of any kind whether it be cash, property, tangible items, or promise of favors in return for the Statement(s) you are about to make.

2. You are not required to talk to us. However, as you have been identified as having specific information relevant to this case, you may be subpoenaed to testify under oath in court. (One of the purposes of interviews such as ours is to find the truth in a matter so that court may not be necessary).

3. You have the right, if you feel uncomfortable speaking with us, to bring someone to the interview with you. It can be a friend or relative, your own legal representative, or even a tape recorder or video camera of your own so that you have direct record of what it is discussed.

4. The information gathered here today will be kept privileged amongst the parties involved in this matter. This includes our client and their legal representatives as well as the matter's opposition and their legal representatives. No part whatsoever of your Statements will be made publicly associated with you without your express permission.

5. Your photo (if one is taken) will not be used for any purposes other than to identify you to our client. Your photo will not be published or used to identify you to anyone not privileged to this information without your express consent.

Investigator:_____
                (print)

_____   Date:___/___/___
             (signed)

Figure 4.2 Witness Interview Form

MCMAHON & ASSOCIATES

Witness Acknowledgement

I _____ certify by signature below that the information I am providing is, to the best of my knowledge, complete, truthful, and unbiased. By my signature below I further affirm the following that:

1. I understand the purpose of this interview.

2. I have not been promised any kind of reward whether it be cash, tangible items, or any other promise of favor in exchange for the information I am about to give.

3. No threats or insinuations of negative action have been made to entice me into giving the information I am about to give.

4. No promise of favor nor threats of negative action have been made by others to have me alter my statements.

5. I am about to give the following truthful information of my own free will.

6. I have given permission for this session to be tape-recorded.

7. I have read the written notes taken by the interviewer and acknowledge that they are an accurate depiction of the answers I have given.

8. I have given my permission to be photographed for the purposes of identification by the client.

Agent: _____ Signature: _____ Date: _____

Interviewee: _____ Signature: _____ Date: _____

Witness: _____ Signature: _____ Date: _____

Page # ____

Figure 4.3 Witness Acknowledgment Form

5

LEGAL INVESTIGATIONS

THE LEGAL INVESTIGATOR

Anthony Golec, in his bible for legal investigators entitled *Techniques of Legal Investigation*, defines a legal investigator as "the trained professional who searches out the facts to which the attorney can apply the law." He further goes on to describe the purpose and functions of the legal investigator as:

- To interview prospective witnesses and prospective parties to the litigation
- To find and interview prospective experts in the technical areas of the litigation
- To search for pertinent evidence, be it physical, testimonial or documentary
- To assemble a complete factual picture of all the events surrounding the events under litigation.

In order to become a legal investigator, knowledge of the Constitution and the court systems is required. Obviously, in one chapter of a book, all the necessary information to accomplish that task cannot be provided. However, what can be provided is an overview from which one see the perspective needed in order to become an legal investigator.

STRUCTURE OF THE CONSTITUTION

The Constitution is divided into seven parts, or articles.

Article I

The first article sets up the structure and function of Congress, which is comprised of two houses, the Senate and the House of Representatives.

Article II

The second article sets up the executive branch of government. It provides that the executive powers of the United States shall be vested in the President.

Article III

The third article vests the judicial power of the United States in the Supreme Court and in such lower courts as Congress sees fit to establish.

Article IV

The fourth article spells out some of the duties which the states owe to each other, including the duties extending full faith and credit to the laws of sister states, and granting equal privileges and immunities to citizens of other states and of interstate extradition.

Article V

This article defines two procedures for amending the constitution:

1. The Constitution may be amended when three-fourths of both houses shall propose amendments, and these are ratified by three-fourths of the states or by state conventions in three-fourths of the states.
2. The Constitution may be amended by application of the Legislators of two-thirds of the states. Congress shall call a convention for proposing amendments which shall be valid when ratified by the Legislators of three-fourths of the states.

Article VI

This article contains the "supremacy" clause, which provides that the Constitution, laws, and treaties of the United States shall be the supreme law of the land, and that state judges are to be bound by it regardless of their state constitution and laws to the contrary.

Article VII

This historical article provides that the Constitution shall become effective when ratified by nine states and shall be operative for those states which ratify it.

Limitations on State Powers

The Constitution prohibits the states from entering into treaties, alliances, or confederations; coining money; passing a bill which inflicts punishment without a trial; and enacting ex post facto laws.

Powers Retained by the State

Under the case *District of Columbia v. Brooke* (214 US 138), states have passed laws defining crimes, regulating traffic, and providing for criminal procedural rules.

The Bill of Rights

The Bill of Rights, or the first 10 amendments to the Constitution, was not intended to establish any new principles of government but simply to include certain guarantees which the colonists wanted to maintain. The specific provisions of the Bill of Rights provide a broad framework that would mean little without court interpretation.

The First Amendment

Prohibits Congress from making any law establishing a religion or prohibiting freedom of religion. It also provides freedom of speech, freedom of the press, and the right of the people to assemble and petition the government for redress of grievances.

The Second Amendment

Provides that the right of the people to keep and bear arms shall not be infringed.

The Third Amendment

Provides that no soldier during peace time shall be quartered in any house without the consent of the owner.

The Fourth Amendment

Provides against unreasonable searches and seizures.

The Fifth Amendment

Provides safeguards to persons accused of crimes. It provides that a person cannot be held for a capital crime without a Grand Jury indictment; that no person shall be tried twice for the same offense; that no person shall be compelled in any criminal case to be a witness against himself; that no person shall be deprived of life, liberty, or property without due process of law; and that no person shall be deprived of his property for public use without just compensation.

The Sixth Amendment

Provides for speedy and public trial by an impartial jury of the state in which the crime was committed, the right to confront witnesses, the right to be informed of the nature of the charges, the right to have compulsory process, and the right to have an attorney represent you.

The Seventh Amendment

A safeguard of property rights. It provides for the right to a jury trial in property controversies exceeding a specified amount.

The Eighth Amendment

Restricts both the legislative and judicial branches of government and guarantees certain rights to individuals including guarantees against excessive bail, excessive fines, and cruel and unusual punishment.

The Ninth Amendment

Provides that certain rights contained in the Constitution do not deny others retained by the people.

The Tenth Amendment

States that "powers not delegated by the Constitution nor prohibited by the states are reserved by the people."

Due Process of Law

Included in the Bill of Rights is the provision that "no person shall be deprived of life, liberty, or property without due process of law." This provision as it appears in the Fifth Amendment is a restriction only upon the federal government. It was not until 1868 that a federal constitutional provision concerning due process applied to the states. In that year, the Fourteenth Amendment was ratified. That amendment stated in part, "Nor shall any state deprive any person of life, liberty, or property without due process of law."

In the early decisions of the Supreme Court, the judges decided that certain rights such as free speech were so fundamental that they must "be protected against abuse by state officials." In applying the "fundamental rights" theory, these judges justified making these rights applicable to the states by way of the Fourteenth Amendment's due process clause. These rights, such as freedom of speech, were so fundamental that a state in violating these rights failed to comply with the demands of the Fourteenth Amendment.

In 1925, the Supreme Court in *Gitlow v. New York* (268 US 652) expressed the opinion that the rights protected by the First Amendment are fundamental personal rights protected by the due process clause of the Fourteenth Amendment.

Habeas Corpus

The *Writ of Habeas Corpus* (Latin for "you have the body") is used to question the legality of the detention of a prisoner. Its sole function is to release petitioners from unlawful imprisonment. When a defendant is charged with violating state statute in a felony case, after a preliminary hearing in a lower court, he is tried in an intermediate court, often called a circuit court. If convicted, he may appeal to a State Court of Appeals and then to the Supreme Court of the state. Finally, on constitutional questions, he may appeal to the U.S. Supreme Court. This may be done by the appeals process through state and federal courts or by a *Writ of Habeas Corpus*. This writ sets up a hearing on the constitutional issues of a defendant. Habeas corpus proceedings in federal court determine the issues of whether the defendant was provided with his fair full constitutional rights and safeguards in state proceedings.

CRIMINAL AND CIVIL PROCEDURE

Types of Law

There are two types of law, public law and private law.

Public Law

This type of law concerns the structures, power, and operations of a government; the rights and duties of citizens in relation to government, and the relationships among nations. It can be subdivided into four sections.

Constitutional Law

The fundamental law of a nation is derived from the Constitution, which records the body of rules in accordance with which the powers of government are carried out. Constitutions may either be written or unwritten; America's is written, England's is unwritten. In some nations, courts have the power of judicial review, whereby they declare unconstitutional, and therefore void, laws that go against the provisions or arrangements of the constitution.

Administrative Law

Includes laws governing the organization and operation of agencies of the Executive Branch of government, the substantive and procedural rules that these agencies create and apply pursuant to their regulatory and other administrative functions, and court decisions involving public agencies and private citizens.

Criminal Law

Consists of laws that impose obligations to do or refrain from doing certain things, the infraction of which is considered to be an offense against the victim as well as society. Most laws are backed by sanctions (punishments), which are applied in the event of conviction. Major breaches of criminal law, usually defined as punishable by imprisonment for more that one year are called felonies; less serious crimes, called misdemeanors, are punishable by imprisonment for up to and including one year or by fines or both.

International Law

Concerns the relationships among nations including the use of the high seas, international trade, boundary disputes, warfare methods, and so on.

Private Law

Unlike public law, private law does not involve governments directly but rather indirectly as a mediator between disputing parties; private law provides rules to be applied when one person claims that another has injured his person, property, or reputation, or has failed to carry out a valid legal obligation. Private law is subdivided into six main categories: tort law, property law, contract/business law, corporation law, inheritance law (probate or wills), and family law. These will be discussed later in the book.

Sources of Law

Laws can also be subdivided on the basis of the sources from which they derive. Some of the major sources are constitutions and administrative rules, legislative statutes, judicial precedents (also known as case law), and customary practice.

Statutes are now outnumbered by the numerous administrative rules and regulations that have accompanied the growth of administrative government in modern times. Judicial precedents are recognized as valid law that later courts must follow in common law but not in civil law systems. Judicial precedents are prior cases decided by the courts.

Customary practice is a minor source of law in the legal systems of advanced nations but is the primary, if not only, source in primitive legal systems.

Civil Procedures

Each of the state and federal judicial systems has rules of civil procedure that govern the conduct of most noncriminal judicial proceedings. Procedural law exists so that substantive law can be implemented. The principle objective of procedural law is to give the parties to a dispute an equal and fair opportunity to present their cases to a nonprejudicial and convenient tribunal. If procedural rules are correctly drafted and implemented, both parties to the dispute should feel that they have been fairly treated. It should be understood that the federal government and each state has established procedural rules for its court systems.

Civil Trials

A trial is a legal procedure available to parties who have been either unwilling or unable to resolve their differences through negotiations, settlement offers, or mediation attempts. Trials involve the staging of a confrontation between the plaintiff and defendant as contradicting witnesses, and arguments collide in the courtroom in accordance with procedural and evidentiary rules. The trial process may, as a result of appeals, take many years, but will result in either a dismissal of the complaint or a judgment.

In some cases, parties with a right to present their evidence to a jury prefer instead to try their case before a judge. This is called a bench trial. The right to a federal jury trial is provided by the Seventh Amendment to parties involved in a common law civil action. The right to a civil jury trial in the state judicial system is determined by state law. The judge is responsible for making sure that:

- The jury is properly selected in a jury trial
- Due process requirements for a fair trial are satisfied
- Proper rulings are made with respect to admissibility of evidence
- The rules of procedure are followed by the parties
- The judgment is awarded in accordance with the law.

Criminal Procedure

Criminal procedure is that area of the law that deals with the administration of criminal justice, from the initial investigation of a crime and arrest of a suspect, through trial, sentence, and release. The goal of criminal justice is to protect society from antisocial activity without sacrificing individual rights, justice, and fair play. The procedures used to apprehend and prosecute alleged criminal offenders must comply with the requirements of law. One objective of using the adversary system, involving prosecutors and defense attorneys, is to ensure that procedural justice is afforded the defendant. The judge umpires the dispute between the litigants and tries to ensure that both parties receive a fair trial; one that meets the requirements of substantive and procedural law. The judge or jury determines the guilt or innocence of the accused by properly evaluating the facts presented in open court.

State and federal courts protect the accused from lengthy imprisonment prior to trial, prevent long delays that could impair the defense of the accused person through the loss of evidence, and prevent or minimize public suspicion and anxiety connected with the accused, who is yet untried. The right to a speedy trial starts when the prosecution begins, either by indictment or by the actual arrest. How much time must elapse to result in an unconstitutional delay varies with the circumstances. The accused has the burden of showing that the delay was the fault of the state and resulted in prejudice.

Basic Components of a Criminal Offense

A criminal offense includes the following components: the wrongful act, the guilty mind, concurrence, and causation. Proof of each element is required beyond a reasonable doubt for a conviction.

The Wrongful Act

The wrongful act, or *actus reus*, is the unjustified actions against someone's person or property. There are special rules that govern the wrongful act. For instance, the law recognizes the existence of a legal duty, whereby the failure to act is equivalent to a criminal act. The duty to act can be imposed by statute (i.e., filing income tax returns), by contract (such as between parents and a daycare center), by one's status (parent/child or husband/wife), or because one has assumed a responsibility (taking care of a disabled person).

Another exception to the requirement of a physical act is recognized in possession offenses in which the law treats the fact of possession as the equivalent of a wrongful act. Possession can be actual, as when the accused is found with the contraband on his person, or constructive, as when the contraband is not on the suspect's person but is under his control.

Criminal State of Mind

The second requirement of a criminal offense is that the alleged criminal offender possess a criminal state of mind (*mens rea*) at the time of the commission of the wrongful act. This is called a concurrence of a wrongful act with a wrongful state of mind. Concurrence is required because some people who commit wrongful acts do not have a wrongful state of mind. A specific intent crime requires proof of the commission of an actus reus plus a specified level of knowledge or additional intent, such as the intent to commit a felony. Criminal negligence results from unconscious risk creation.

Causation

There are some criminal offenses that require proof that the defendant's conduct caused a given result. The prosecution must establish causation beyond a reasonable doubt when it is an element of a crime. A key to establishing causation is the legal concept of "proximate cause." Criminal liability attaches only to conduct that is determined to be the proximate or legal cause of the harmful result. This includes both direct and indirect causation. Often the legal cause is the direct cause of harm.

Proximate cause is a flexible concept. It permits fact finders to sort through various factual causes and determine who should be found legally responsible. In addition, the accused is only responsible for the reasonably foreseeable consequences that follow from his act. The law provides that an accused is not responsible for consequences that follow the intervention of a new and independent causal force.

The Concept of Crime

Crime is a wrong against the public interest to which a governmental jurisdiction has attached a penalty. It is an act that has been committed or omitted in violation of a public law either prohibiting or commanding it. The law may prohibit the commission of overt acts such as robbery, rape, burglary, speeding, or disorderly conduct. It may also require that acts be done. Thus, an individual's failure to act may constitute a violation of criminal law (i.e., failure to file tax return).

Crime is classified by grades, generally in accordance with the degree of penalty attached to it. The three usual classifications of crime are treason, felony, and misdemeanor. Treason consists of waging war or giving aid and comfort to the enemy. A felony is a crime that carries a penalty of death or imprisonment for more that one year in a state prison. A misdemeanor is a crimes that carries a penalty of less than one year to be served in a city or county jail.

The Effective Limits of Criminal Law

The concept of security of the person and the right of enjoyment of personal property appears to be the fundamental basis of criminal law. Crimes of aggression, such as murder, assault, rape, burglary, and theft of person or property are considered *mala in se*, immoral or wrong by their very nature.

A second category of crime can be described as regulatory, which is designed to provide a degree of conformity for the purposes of safety, efficiency, and convenience (i.e., traffic laws). These crimes are *mala prohibita*, bad only because the legislature has prohibited them.

A third category of crime promotes honesty and morality. These laws prohibit such acts as sale of impure food and drugs, pollution of the environment, obtaining property under false pretense, and so on. These crimes are classified as protective crimes.

A fourth category of crime regulates personal morality. These are referred to as vice crimes and include adultery, sodomy, prostitution, pornography, and so on.

The final category of crime involves the use and sale of narcotics and alcohol. The addict and alcoholic are psychologically and physically dependent and, unlike vice criminals, can seldom voluntarily terminate their continuous offenses.

The Authority to Arrest

The general requirements (elements) of an arrest by a police officer are the following:

- There must be an *intent* on the part of the officer to make an arrest, intent to deprive a person of his liberty, and intent to restrain him physically if he does not peacefully submit.

- The officer must inform the individual of his intention to place him under arrest and the reason or cause for the arrest.
- The officer must identify the authority under which he acts. If the officer is clearly uniformed, this requirement is normally met.
- The individual must be placed under the officer's actual control. If the officer communicates his intention, authority, and reason for the arrest, and the individual submits to the officer and obeys his commands, an arrest is made.

Investigative Detention Short of Arrest — Stop and Frisk

In 1968 the issue of a police officer detaining (stopping) and conducting a cursory search (frisking) was raised before the U.S. Supreme Court in *Terry v. Ohio*. In this case, the facts clearly indicated the good faith and reasonable judgment of the police officer and substantial motivation for his actions.

Searches

The Fourth Amendment prohibits unreasonable searches. Until 1914, the court had no authority to exclude evidence obtained from an illegal search from being admitted into evidence. In the U.S. Supreme Court case, *Weeks v. United States*, the court created the exclusionary rule. It provides that evidence obtained as a result of an unreasonable search is inadmissible in any federal criminal prosecution. In 1961, in *Mapp v. Ohio*, the Supreme Court held that all evidence in violation of the Constitution is inadmissible in a state court.

Interrogating the Accused

Historically, the primary test for the establishment of validity of a confession admitted into evidence at a criminal trial was whether the confession was voluntary and trustworthy. Voluntary meant that no physical force was used to obtain the confession. Trustworthy meant that the circumstances under which the confession was obtained were unlikely to induce an innocent person to confess.

In 1943, in *McNabb v. United States*, the Supreme Court expanded the voluntary–trustworthy test for federal cases and established an additional test requiring civilized interrogation standards.

In 1957, in *Mallory v. United States*, the court held that before a confession may be admitted into evidence it must be voluntary, trustworthy, obtained under civilized standards of interrogation, and not obtained during any unnecessary delay between time of arrest and taking the accused before a magistrate. (These rules only applied to federal cases.)

In 1964, the Supreme Court in *Escobedo v. Illinois* held inadmissible a confession obtained after police failed to advise a prisoner of his absolute constitutional right to remain silent and refused to honor his request to consult with his attorney.

In 1966, *Miranda v. Arizona* the court extended the Escobedo doctrine further and established a series of procedural requirements that must be met before any interrogation of the arrestee could occur.

THE TRIAL

Preliminary Proceedings in the Trial Court

Pleas

The defendant may enter a plea of guilty, not guilty, *nolo contendere*, stand mute, or make a motion to invalidate the indictment or information. After entry of the plea, the defendant may be asked to choose to be tried by jury or by judge without a jury. The court will then docket the case for trial. In approximately one-half of the states and in federal courts, the defendant may enter a plea of *nolo contendere*. By entry of this plea, the defendant indicates that even though not guilty, a decision has been made not to contest the charges. The defendant may choose to stand mute or not enter a plea. When this occurs, the judge will enter a plea of not guilty and proceed accordingly.

Motion to Suppress State's Evidence

A motion to suppress the state's evidence may be filed prior to the time of trial and frequently is filed during arraignment (the formal reading of charges) or shortly thereafter.

The motion alleges that the evidence that the state plans to use at trial was obtained unlawfully through violation of the defendant's rights. Normally, this motion is filed in an attempt to exclude evidence obtained as a result of a search or wiretap, or to challenge the validity of a confession.

Motion for a Bill of Particulars

To be technically correct, the indictment or information must contain a statement of the act constituting the offense. The accusations must be certain and direct concerning the particular circumstances of the offenses charged. It is possible for the accusation to meet these requirements and yet be drawn in such a way that the major issue is not clearly defined. Under such circumstances, a defendant may file a Motion for a Bill of Particulars. A Bill of Particulars is a supplementary document prepared by the prosecution, which presents more elaborate details of the charges.

Motion for Discovery of Evidence

A Motion for Discovery is a procedure by which the defendant is permitted to examine certain evidence possessed by the prosecutor prior to trial. Because of the defendant's privilege against self-incrimination, the prosecutor does not have a similar right of discovery. However, the prosecution may be entitled to notice of the defendant's intention to use an alibi or insanity as a defense and may obtain the names of witnesses to be used for this purpose.

Motion for a Change of Venue or Judge

If it can be established that a fair and impartial trial cannot be obtained in the county where the crime was committed, the defendant is entitled to have the trial moved to another county. This is accomplished by filing a Motion for Change of Venue. A Motion for Change of Judge, or a recusation, may be used to request the assignment of another judge to try the case, based upon grounds of bias and prejudice or other disqualifying circumstances.

Motion for Continuance

The court may grant a continuance, at its own discretion, when valid reasons are presented by the defendant, some of which are unavailability of important witnesses, illness of the defendant, need for more time to prepare the case adequately, or recent discharge of the defendant's attorney.

The Motion for Continuance is the most frequently filed motion by the defense.

Pretrial proceedings should be concerned with assuring the defendant's constitutional rights and correcting any defects in previous proceedings, thereby avoiding a reversal of the case on appeal and the expense of a retrial.

The Guilty Plea

In felony cases and in some serious misdemeanor cases, the plea occurs after an initial appearance and a preliminary exam, normally at the time of arraignment before the trial court. The acceptance of the plea by the court is usually a brief ritual at which the judge learns from the defendant whether he is fully aware of the charges pending against him or her; the extent of the punishment that may be assessed upon conviction; and the defenses available to the charges. The judge is also responsible for determining whether the plea is entered freely, intelligently, and voluntarily. The court is not required to accept a guilty plea if it feels injustice will result.

Limited resources of prosecutor's offices and the court, and the desirability of avoiding the time-consuming and expensive process of trial by jury, have led to the universal practice of plea bargaining. Plea bargaining consists of negotiations between the prosecutor, the accused, and the defense attorney to exchange prosecutorial concessions for a plea of guilty. Prosecutors may make a broad array of promises in exchange for these pleas. The promises may include such action as:

- Recommendation of a specific sentence
- Reduction of charges
- Dismissal of other pending charges
- Agreement not to charge the defendant with additional offenses for which adequate evidence is available
- Recommendation for probation
- Similar recommendations.

The courts generally recognize that the practices engaged in during plea bargaining, under proper conditions, constitute lawful exercise of prosecutorial discretion. The sentencing practices of the courts seem to reinforce plea bargaining and generally encourage entry of guilty pleas.

Jury Trial and Jury Selection

After the arraignment and necessary hearings on motions, the case is docketed for a specific trial date. When the case is called for trial, the first action is selection of the jury. In all jurisdictions, the jury is viewed as the instrument for determining the facts. It is given broad discretion in exercising its decision making powers. It is allowed to deliberate in secret and reach a decision that it is not required to justify. Traditionally, the jury in a felony case consists of 12 jurors who must reach a unanimous decision concerning the defendant's guilt or innocence. However, in a 1970 case, the Supreme Court in *Williams v. Florida* held that there was no constitutional requirement to seat 12 jurors and that a state could establish a procedure requiring a different number.

Selecting the Jury Panel

State statutes or court rules will normally specify the procedure for selecting the jury panel (venire). Designated officials (i.e., jury commissioners, sheriffs, clerks of the court, etc.) will compile a list of prospective jurors within the court's jurisdiction. This list will normally be taken from voter's registration lists or the tax rolls. For normal operations, the court may specify 50 prospective jurors (venire persons) be called. The clerk randomly draws the prescribed number of names and prepares court summons ordering the prospective jurors to appear for jury duty. In selecting a jury panel, the Supreme Court has made it clear that the Constitution bars conscious discrimination in jury selection by reasons of race, national origin, religion, sex, or economic status.

Qualifying the Jury Panel

The prospective jurors report at the time and place designated in the summons. The judge usually meets with the panel and explains the operation of the court system and the responsibility and function of the jurors. The judge also explains that under law certain individuals are not qualified for service as jurors. Such exclusions may include:

- A person who cannot read, write, or understand the English language
- A person with unsoundness of mind or a physical defect such as deafness or blindness
- An individual convicted of a felony.

The judge explains that certain venire persons, because of special conditions, may not be required to serve as jurors, even though they possess proper qualifications. Individuals who fall under these special conditions may exercise an exemption and choose not to serve as jurors. Some examples are physicians, clergymen, news media personnel, college students, and women with small children.

The judge instructs the clerk to draw the jury. The clerk draws 12 (or 6) names from the receptacle containing the names of qualified venire persons. Those selected are seated in the jury box. Through a process known as *voir dire* examination, the individual jurors are questioned to establish their qualifications for service in the particular case. Before such qualification begins, the jurors are placed under oath to answer truthfully all questions concerning their qualifications. The *voir dire* begins by either the judge, the prosecutor, or the defense attorney introducing the parties in the case and making general inquiries relating to a juror's qualifications. After completing general opening questions, counsel may ask specific questions relating to qualifications. If during questioning a prospective juror indicates that he has knowledge, attitudes, opinions, or relationships that clearly indicate a bias or prejudice toward either party, counsel may challenge the juror for cause. In some cases, grounds for challenge for cause are established by statute. Counsel directs challenge for cause to the judge. The judge then makes a ruling concerning the challenge. The judge may question the juror further if there is insufficient information upon which to base a decision. If the judge finds sufficient evidence to warrant dismissal, the juror will be dismissed, and the clerk will draw another juror. All that is required is that the juror have no fixed opinion that will prevent him or her from rendering a fair and impartial verdict based upon the evidence admitted in the trial and the law presented by the judge.

After 12 (or 6) jurors have been tentatively accepted, counsel may then exercise peremptory challenges. Using a peremptory challenge, counsel may excuse a juror without stating any cause whatsoever. The number of peremptory challenges available to each side is regulated by statute or court rule. Each time a peremptory challenge is exercised, the clerk draws a new juror who is then subjected to questioning to determine whether a challenge for cause applies to him. The process continues until all challenges are exhausted or waived. The 12 (or 6) individuals remaining constitute the jury for the case. Some states permit the selection of alternate jurors. If one of the principle jurors becomes ill or a personal emergency arises, the juror may be released and an alternate juror substituted. When the principle and alternate jurors are selected, the jury panel is sworn in.

The Trial

Although a relatively small percentage of total criminal cases are adjudicated by juries, the right to a trial should be recognized as a significant constitutional guarantee. The Sixth Amendment provides that the defendant in a criminal prosecution has a right to a public trial. Furthermore, the defendant has a constitutional right to be present in the courtroom during every stage of the proceedings from arraignment through sentencing, and to confront witnesses against him.

Opening Statements

After the jury has been empanelled, the indictment is usually read. The prosecution then makes an opening statement. The purpose of this statement is to inform the jury of the general nature of the case, the facts as the prosecution views them, and the significance of witnesses and physical evidence that will be presented to prove the alleged facts. The opening statement must be restricted to the specifics of the case being tried. After the prosecutor's opening statement is concluded, the defense attorney may make an opening statement or request permission to defer or reserve the statement until the prosecution's case has been concluded. If the defendant chooses, the opening statement may be waived.

The State's Case

After the opening statement, the prosecution must present its proof by calling its witnesses. The Sixth Amendment provides that "in all criminal prosecutions, the accused shall enjoy the right to be confronted with witnesses against them." All courts agree that the defendant's right to confrontation and cross examination of the witnesses are essential, fundamental requirements of a fair trial and due process.

If physical evidence is to be introduced, there must be a witness to identify it, testify to its relevance, establish that it is in approximately the same condition as it was at the time it was obtained (or adequately explain why it is not), show that there was no opportunity for anyone to tamper with it (chain of custody), and state that it was not obtained in violation of the defendant's constitutional rights (if challenged by the defense). Physical evidence is introduced during the course of the regular testimony subject to approval of the judge for admissibility.

The prosecutor begins the presentation of evidence by direct examination of the first witness. (See Figure 5.1 for a sample Witness Evaluation Form.) In response to the prosecutor's questions, the witness relates information about the case. Upon the completion of direct examination, the defense may conduct a cross examination of the witness. With this, defense counsel attempts to clarify or enlarge upon testimony of the witness and, on occasion, to impeach credibility of the witness by attempting to discover any bias, prejudice, or interests in the defendant's conviction.

Upon completion of cross examination, the prosecutor may conduct a redirect examination limited to those matters discussed during cross examination. Additional examination may be conducted by the attorneys, but they are generally limited in nature and scope to those matters related during the preceding examination. After the testimony of the first witness, the prosecutor calls subsequent witnesses, who undergo the same process. When the testimony of the State's final witness is concluded, the prosecutor announces that the State rests its case.

Motion for Judgment of Acquittal

At the close of the State's case, the defendant may enter a motion for a judgment of acquittal. Such motion challenges the sufficiency of the evidence to sustain a conviction and asks the court to rule, as a matter of law, that the State has not met its burden of proof. If the State has clearly failed to meet its burden, the judge may grant the motion and acquit the defendant. If the possibility of conviction exists, the motion is overruled.

The Defense's Case

The defense attorney presents his case following the same format as that of the prosecution. In most instances, the only investigation conducted by the defense will be the work of the criminal defense investigator hired by the defendant, or the attorney, or appointed by the court in cases of indigence. The defense will call witnesses and conduct direct examination followed by cross examination by the prosecutor. The defendant may waive presentation of witnesses and submit the case based only on the State's evidence. If the defendant presents witnesses, the defendant is not required to testify. If the defendant refuses to take the witness stand, neither the prosecutor nor the judge is permitted to call this lack of testimony to the attention of the jury. To do so would constitute reversible error by the judge. However, once the stand is taken, the defendant is subject to the same cross examination as other witnesses, including disclosure of prior criminal convictions, for the purpose of attacking personal credibility. Upon completion of testimony of the final witness for the defense, the defense rests its case.

Rebuttal and Surrebuttal

After the defense rests its case, the prosecutor is given the opportunity to call additional witnesses for the special purpose of refuting or rebutting the evidence presented by defense witnesses. If the prosecution calls rebuttal witnesses, the defense may conduct surrebuttal and disprove points raised or established during rebuttal.

After receipt of all the evidence, the defense may again enter a motion for acquittal which challenges the sufficiency of the evidence and requests the court to rule as a matter of law that the state has not met its burden of proof.

Instructions to the Jury

The judge is responsible for instructing the jury clearly, fully, and accurately on all issues that have been raised during the trial. The instructions traditionally include a definition of the crime with which the defendant is charged, the State's burden of proof, the presumption of the defendant's innocence, instructions relating to specific evidence in the case, and procedures for electing a foreman and returning a verdict.

During the progress of the trial, usually in chambers, the judge will give both attorneys the opportunity to submit suggested or requested instructions. In the absence of specific request, the judge may use a standard form or pattern instructions that apply to all cases of a specific type, or, if there are special circumstances in the case, the judge may require one of the counsel to draft a suggested instruction on the point in question.

Prior to the formal instruction to the jury the judge prepares the set of instructions to be given. Both counsel review them. If there is a disagreement, there may be a conference between the judge and the attorneys. Subsequently, the judge prepares the final instructions and both counsel are given an opportunity to record any objections to them for possible appeal.

In some jurisdictions, along with giving the instructions, the judge may summarize the evidence, analyze it generally, and emphasize what are considered to be significant aspects.

Closing Arguments

After instructions to the jury, the prosecutor and defense attorney present closing arguments. The primary purpose of the closing arguments is to give counsel an opportunity to summarize the evidence, comment upon it in relation to theories on the case, and attempt to persuade the jury to accept particular inferences and deductions.

The attorneys are generally given liberal freedom in their range of discussion, use of illustrations, and the employment of persuasion, as long as they confine themselves to discussion of evidence presented and normal deductions arising therefrom.

Jury Deliberations

Following the closing arguments, the jury retires to the jury room for deliberations in an effort to arrive at a verdict. Many jurisdictions do not permit the jury to separate once deliberations begin. This restriction may require that the jury stay overnight (or longer) in a hotel (sequestered).

If the jury reports back to court that it is unable to reach a verdict after considering all the circumstances involved, the judge may send them back to the jury room for further deliberations and encourage them to reach a verdict. When the jury has arrived at a verdict or finds itself hopelessly deadlocked, they return to the courtroom. If a verdict has been obtained, it is received and announced. If a verdict has not been obtained and all reasonable methods of obtaining it have been exhausted (hung jury), the judge dismisses the jury and declares a mistrial. After the jury has returned a verdict, counsel may request that the jury be polled. The judge or the clerk then asks each juror individually whether the verdict announced is the individual's verdict. This process is designed to determine whether each juror is acting freely, according to conscience, or is the subject of group domination by fellow jurors. If the poll discloses it was not a unanimous verdict, the judge may direct the jury to return for further deliberations or be dismissed and a mistrial declared.

If the verdict is not guilty, the defendant is discharged and the case permanently terminated, except in two states (Connecticut and Wisconsin) which permit the state to appeal a not guilty verdict. If the verdict is guilty, the judge will set a sentencing date and remand the defendant to jail or permit a release on bail. If a mistrial is declared, the parties are in the same position as if no trial had occurred, and proceedings may be reinstated against the defendant.

Motion for a New Trial

After receipt of a guilty verdict, in most jurisdictions the accused may file a motion for a new trial with the judge of the trial court within a specified time period (usually 10 to 30 days). The motion requests that the judge set aside the verdict and grant a new trial because during the trial the defendant was deprived of a substantive right or the conduct or circumstances of the trial resulted in a prejudicial verdict. The grounds for a new trial may include the following:

- The trial was held in the defendant's absence.
- The jury received (and probably considered) evidence other than that properly presented in court.
- The jury was guilty of misconduct (a juror was intoxicated, a juror communicated with a third party, etc.).
- The court erred in a decision on a question of law during the trial (admission of tainted evidence, overruling a proper objection, etc.).
- The court gave an improper instruction to the jury.

Before a new trial can be granted, the defendant must establish that the error caused (or had a potential for causing) substantial prejudice, especially in cases where the defendant's guilt is clear and convincing. On occasion, a new trial may be granted because of newly discovered evidence of a substantial nature.

Sentencing

After a guilty verdict, the court sets a sentencing date for pronouncing formal sentence. At the appointed time, the prosecutor, defense attorney, and the defendant are present in open court before the judge. Unless there is good cause shown, the court pronounces sentence.

The Sentencing Decision

Sentencing alternatives available to the judge, depending on jurisdiction, may include the payment of a fine, probation, imprisonment, confinement in a nonpenal facility, a combination of the above, or death.

Depending on the nature of the case, the court may order the defendant to make restitution to the victim or forfeit the property used in the commission of the crime. If the crime is one involving addiction to drugs or alcohol or one in which insanity or sexual psychopathy are involved, the court may order the defendant to be confined in a specific treatment facility.

Probation

Probation is a privilege the court may extend to selected offenders which permits them to avoid incarceration by conforming to prescribed conditions of good conduct during the probationary period. In granting probation, the judge may present a number of conditions that the probationer must meet. If the probationer fails to comply with the conditions of probation, he is subject to revocation followed by imprisonment.

Incarceration

If the judge decides against probation in a case, the alternative is incarceration. Depending on law of particular jurisdiction, the judge may have two other decisions to make:

1. Location of incarceration — work camp, reformatory or prison.
2. Length of sentence — the penalty for a particular offense is established by statute. The statute may provide for a minimum or a maximum sentence. Some states provide for an intermediate, which is a sentence that is not stated in a specific number of years. When the defendant is convicted of more than one offense during the same term or court, or the defendant is already serving a prison sentence, judges have the option of imposing either concurrent or consecutive sentences.
   a. Consecutive sentences — time served does not apply to the second sentence until the first sentence is completed.
   b. Concurrent sentences — the term served by the defendant applies to both sentences at the same time.

Appeals

The primary function of defendant's appeal is to review alleged errors of law and defects in the trial process. Re-arguing the facts of the case is not permitted in an appeal. On rare occasions, appellate courts will reverse a conviction based upon insufficient evidence. Appeals are based on the written record — in order to raise procedural defects as grounds for reversal, the court normally requires that objections must be raised at the time of the alleged defect and at subsequent opportunities, such as at a motion for a new trial. Before appellate courts will reverse a decision, the court must find the error to have substantially affected the defendant's rights and to have had the potential of affecting the results of the trial. The court may find that a procedural error was committed, but conclude that it was harmless and affirm the conviction.

The Appeal Process

After notice of appeal, the defendant must file a petition with the appellate court specifying those errors and issues upon which appeal is based. The transcript containing pertinent court documents and relevant portions of trial testimony or ruling will be submitted with the petition. Supporting data in the form of a brief is also submitted. Things that the brief shall contain are an abstract of the case, presenting the questions involved and manner in which they are raised (objections and how they come about). A copy of the defendant's brief must be served on the official representing the State in appellate court. The prosecutor or Attorney General may file an answering brief opposing the arguments presented by the defendant. Appellate court may make a decision based upon briefs, or the court may request that the attorneys involved present oral arguments to a formal session of the court. After oral arguments, the case is submitted to members of the court for disposition. The decision of the court will be subsequently announced in a written opinion. The court will:

- Affirm the lower court decision.
- Reverse trial court; order a new trial.
- Reverse based on insufficient evidence or other cause; defendant released.

Writ of Certiorari

Petition for a Writ of Certiorari specifies the nature of the case, errors alleged, and previous court's disposition of a case. It is a petition for a review of a case by U.S. Supreme Court.

Executive Review

Governors of individual states and the President of the United States possess the power to pardon an individual convicted of a crime, to commute the sentence to one less severe, or to grant a reprieve that orders a delay in execution of a sentence. These powers are vested exclusively in the chief executive and may be exercised at discretion.

LEGAL INVESTIGATIONS

Within the field of legal investigation there are several specialties, including criminal investigations and civil investigations. See the Law Firm Case Assignment Form shown in Figure 5.2.

Criminal Investigations

Investigation of serious crimes, which may lead to arrest and conviction of a subject. Burglary, theft, homicide, fraud, auto accidents, arson, kidnapping, etc., are all examples of activities where violations of laws have taken place.

Civil Investigations

Pertains to anything involving lawsuits in which questions of money or property must be settled. Violations of the law are usually not involved. Divorce, bankruptcy, and lawsuits of various types are examples of civil matters that require investigation.

CIVIL ACTIONS

An attorney or client may hire an investigator to prove that either one of the parties to the suit is liable. There are two terms an investigator must know, plaintiff and defendant.

Plaintiff

The party who brings legal action; one who accuses another person of wrongdoing.

Defendant

The accused, or one who must defend himself or herself against charges brought by the plaintiff. While he may be accused of wrongdoing, he is assumed innocent until proven guilty by the plaintiff and the plaintiff's attorney.

Role of the Legal Investigator

In essence, the role of the legal investigator is to assist the attorney in whatever task is deemed necessary to best defend the client. Whether you are working directly for the attorney or for the plaintiff/defendant, your job is to help the attorney win the case. In most instances this will involve locating and interviewing potential witnesses, both for and against your side; reviewing the evidence of both sides and finding additional evidence that either helps your case or refutes the evidence in favor of the other side; conducting background investigations on all potential witnesses and parties in the case; and, in criminal investigations, supplying examination diagrams and photographs of the crime scene. An outstanding investigator is proficient in his ability to analyze a situation and achieve the results necessary for his side to win the case. I define winning as achieving the best results possible for the client. That does not always mean that the client actually wins the case.

Evidence

Evidence may be defined as anything that is legally seized and submitted to a court of law for consideration in determining the truth of the matter. Throughout the investigative process, the investigator will be seeking evidence to identify and connect the suspect to the commission of the crime, as well as any documentation tending to expose a possible motive. Evidence, regardless of form or type (business records, photographs, sketches, incendiary devices, etc.) must be identified, collected, and correctly packaged throughout the case-building process.

Direct Evidence

Evidence with such individualized or identifying characteristics that it tends to prove the fact without the support or corroboration of evidence of any other fact. This evidence can be positively identified as having come from a specific source or person if sufficient identifying characteristics or microscopic or accidental markings are present (i.e., fingerprints, palm prints, teeth, certain ballistic materials).

Circumstantial Evidence

Evidence with class characteristics only. This evidence, no matter how thoroughly examined, can be placed into a class, but a positive source cannot be identified (i.e., soil, blood, hair, flammable vapors). Circumstantial evidence tends to prove the fact only with the intervention of evidence of other facts. It is evidence which falls into the logical progression of events and from which inferences can be drawn.

Evidence that substantiates a motive for arson includes:

- Lack of inventory, empty shelves, and so on, in a commercial retail business
- Business books and records that when audited identify an arson for profit insurance fraud scheme
- Files and office cabinets left open to expose records to the ravages of the fire
- Accelerant residue on the charred remains of a homicide victim showing that the fire was set to conceal a murder

Chain of Evidence

The term *chain of evidence* refers to the chain of custody (possession) of an item of evidence from the point in time that it was first discovered until the time that it was offered as an exhibit in court. Any break in the chain of custody will prohibit the use of the item as evidence in any court presentation. Every time a piece of evidence passes from one person to another, the identities of the individuals involved must be documented. Legal investigators might use a form similar to the one shown in Figure 5.3 if the proper procedures were not followed.

In order to account properly for evidence from the time it is found to the time it is produced in court, an investigator must adhere to strict guidelines during each stage of the evidential procedure. The stages are:

1. Discovery — the date, place, and time of the discovery must be documented in your detailed notes.
2. Collection and identification — photograph the evidence where it is found, mark the evidence carefully with an identifying mark, and then remove the evidence from the scene.
3. Packaging — place the evidence in an airtight bag or cardboard box marked with the date, place, and time of the discovery along with some identifying information about the collector. When possible, it should be packaged in front of witnesses.
4. Vouchering and transmittal — a form on which the investigator lists all of the physical evidence that has been collected, who has examined it, and where the evidence has been up until presentation to the court.
5. Laboratory analysis.
6. Court presentation.

The investigator must decide which items will be removed from the scene for transport to the laboratory and which should be photographed and remain at the scene. The size of the samples to be taken and the areas within the scene from which they are removed are important issues which must be considered.

The Five-Step Sequence: Documenting the Crime Scene

1. Visual inspection — i.e., read the observable burn patterns.
2. Note taking — keep a written record of observations and impressions at the scene.
   - Give observations in chronological order.
   - Avoid indiscernible codes and cryptic observations.
   - Be clear and concise.
   - Make decisions as to what is really important. Be sure to include the following

     Time of investigator's arrival

     Exact address

     Weather conditions

     Identity of persons present

     Statements made, verbatim if possible

     Odors at the scene

     Extent of damage and description of location

     Anything unusual

   Keep your original handwritten notes in the case file. *Do not destroy!* If recorded on a cassette tape, keep the original tape.
3. Photography — photograph the scene thoroughly. Long, wide shots of the area followed by close-ups for detail are preferable. Use color and black and white if possible (especially where there is evidence of blood and a color photograph is inadmissible). Sequences should be chronological entering the building, and from room to room. Indicate in your notes the number of each frame and the subject of picture.

   Mark the back of each developed photograph with date, location, name of photographer, and type of camera used.
4. Sketches — thorough and accurate drafting of a crime scene sketch is the next essential step in documentation. The purpose is to provide orientation, showing the relationship of objects to each other. Give the overall view of the scene, eliminating clutter and items not important to the scene. Clarify issues and refresh the memory of witnesses during interviews; avoid unnecessary and legally prohibited return trips to the scene.
5. Search for evidence.

Throughout my ten years as a legal investigator, I have worked on many criminal and civil cases. The majority of my work on these cases involves locating and interviewing witnesses. I have been fortunate to have worked with many skilled attorneys and experience first hand the thrill of victory when the jury returns with a not guilty verdict or a large monetary judgment for the client. I have also experienced the disappointment at juries finding clients guilty in cases where we felt strongly that the state had not proven guilt. It is a very humbling and frustrating job on those occasions. However, like most jobs, you have good days and bad days. I can definitely say that working as a legal investigator is never dull.

WITNESS EVALUATION

Name:

Home Address: **Home Phone:**

Employer:

Work Address: **Work Phone:**

Occupation:

DOB: **SSN:**   **CDL:**

Close Relative: **Address:**   **Phone:**

Marital Status: **SPOUSE:**

Educational Background:

Military Experience: Branch_____; **Rank**_____; **Type Discharge**_____
                        Court Martials_____; **Time Period in Service**____

Criminal History:

Driving History:

Drug/Prescription Medication/Alcohol History:

Attitude Regarding Case:

Relationship to Case:

Personal Appearance: Ht:____**Wt**____**Hair**____**Eyes**____**Glasses**_____
                        Scars/Marks/Tatoos_____

General Impression:

Interviewer: **Date:**

Figure 5.1 Witness Evaluation Form

Your Company Name Here
Address
Telephone

Law Firm Case Assignment Form

Date _____ Due Date _____   Attorney/Contact _____

Law Firm _____   Phone _____

Address _____   Fax _____

City, State, Zip _____   E-mail _____

Your Case Caption _____

Your Client _____

Court Case Gen. No. _____   Your File No. _____

Date of Incident _____

Location of Occurrence _____

Services Requested
(Please check all that apply)

☐ Activity Checks/Canvas		☐ Serve Legal Documents
☐ Asset Search	☐ Disability	☐ Misc _____ ☐ Sexual Harassment
☐ Background Check	☐ Domestic/Custody	☐ Missing Persons ☐ Skiptrace
☐ Contract Matter	☐ Eavesdropping Sweep	☐ Obtain Records/Reports ☐ Surveillance
☐ Coverage Matter	☐ Employment Matter	☐ Personal Injury ☐ Traffic Collision
☐ Criminal Defense	☐ Interview Witnesses	☐ Photographs ☐ Video
☐ Death Investigation	☐ Malpractice _____	☐ Product Liability ☐ Worker Compensation

Subject/Search Request
(Complete if applicable)

Last Name/Company _____   First Name _____ Middle Initial _____

DOB _____ SSN _____   DLN _____ State _____

Address _____

Telephone _____ Spouse _____   Minor Children Y / N

Employment _____   Occupation _____

Address _____

Telephone _____   Vehicles _____

Physical Description: M / F Race _____ Height _____ Weight _____ Hair _____ Eyes _____ Glasses? Y / N Beard? Y / N Moustache? Y / N

Distinguishing Characteristics (Scar, Tattoos, Birth Mark, etc.) _____

Injury Description _____

Represented? Y / N   **Please use reverse side for comments, instructions, detailed information or additional names or parties to this matter.**

Figure 5.2 Law Firm Case Assignment Form

MALPRACTICE DATA SHEET

FILE#: _____ DATE: _____ TYPE: _____

CLIENT: _____ ATTORNEY: _____

CLIENT TEL: _____ ATTY. TEL: _____

CLIENT ADDRESS: _____

PLAINTIFF: _____

ADDRESS: _____ TEL: _____

DOB: _____ SS#: _____ MARITAL STATUS: _____

OCCUPATION : _____

DATE OF INCIDENT: _____ LOCATION: _____

GENERAL SUMMARY OF SITUATION:

_____

_____

_____

_____

DEFENDANT (1): _____

ADDRESS: _____ TEL: _____

OCCUPATION: _____

DEFENDANT (2): _____

ADDRESS: _____ TEL: _____

OCCUPATION: _____

STATUTE RUNS: _____ ATTY/ PARALEGAL: _____

IMMEDIATE ASSIGNMENT: _____

_____

_____

_____

Figure 5.3 Malpractice Data Sheet

6

FRAUD INVESTIGATION

The investigation of fraud is a logical inquiry which requires some training but is not as difficult as one might imagine. Common sense is the most important tool for any investigator. Certain attitudes and approaches on the part of the investigator are necessary to accomplish a professional and thorough investigation. One must have a focused sense of direction, patience, and determination to properly gather all the evidence needed.

Fraud is defined as a false representation or the concealment of a material fact with the intent and result that it be acted upon by another to his loss or detriment. It is making a false statement of a past or existing fact with knowledge of its falsity or with reckless indifference as to its truth with the intent to cause another to rely upon it, resulting in his injury.

1. Knowledge — the maker of a statement knows it is false
2. Intent — the statement is made with the intent to gain a benefit
3. Reliance — the other party relies upon the false statements
4. Injury — the victim suffers a financial loss owing to relying on the false statements

Three main reasons for fraud investigations are to recover funds, to prevent repetition and deter others, and to clear innocent people. Three important rules of fraud investigators are:

1. Whenever possible, inquiries should be concentrated around the central issue or hub of the fraud.
2. Investigators should not seek the most complex solution to the case. The rule is to examine the most obvious answer and only when that has been eliminated go on to more complicated solutions.

3. If concealment is difficult to unravel, investigators should "follow the money" — determine who benefited at the end of the fraud and work backwards.

It is not possible to provide a planned outline applicable to all investigations of fraud. However, these are the steps that would generally be followed:

- Selection of statutory violations, that is, which laws have been broken. Carefully identify the elements of proof for each statute and the method required to obtain the evidence desired; that is, documents, witnesses, and so on.
- Identification of the documentation required to prove fraud. The best evidence rules require that original documents be submitted when available.
- Identification of witnesses who can authenticate records and define actions taken by the suspect that constitute fraud.
- Identification of the appropriate investigative techniques to be used to obtain the desired evidence, that is, witness interviews, use of technical investigative devices, and so on.
- Determination of the desired outcome for the client early in the investigation. Is criminal prosecution the goal, or is he looking for identification of the subject, restitution if funds are found, and termination from the company in the case of corporate fraud by an employee?

CORPORATE FRAUD

Fraud is a deliberate (intentional) deception practiced on another to serve an unfair or unlawful gain. A survey by *Fortune* magazine revealed that a total of 117 of America's largest and most prestigious corporations committed at least one federal criminal offense since 1970. The social cost of white collar crime has been estimated to be between 400 million and 40 billion dollars per year.

Embezzlement is the fraudulent appropriation of property by a person to whom it has been entrusted, or to whose hands it has lawfully come.

Corporate fraud is any fraud perpetrated by, for, or against a business corporation.

Financial fraud is a material misrepresentation of a financial fact intended to deceive another to his economic detriment.

FINANCIAL FRAUD AUDIT

Financial investigations are built on paper, although now are being quickly replaced by the computer. Thorough analysis of all financial transactions will reveal the fraud.

In order to determine whether a fraud has been committed, the amount of money taken, and the mechanism for the fraud to have occurred, an audit must be conducted. There is a fixed and orderly routine followed in a typical financial audit; that is, a set of predesigned tasks, procedures, and tests for the verification of business transactions and evaluation of the adequacy of the account system to reflect fairly, accurately, and consistently the financial condition of a business at a point in time. In essence, the auditor takes a snapshot of the business and that picture should represent the reality of the company's financial situation at that time.

The financial auditor's purpose is to dissect and rebuild a structure by using infinite details. Auditors begin where a loss of something of value or a suspicion of property loss exists. Fraud auditing is unlike financial auditing in that it proceeds from a theory that is based more on investigative notions that on financial auditing notions.

The usual method of employee theft, fraud, and embezzlement executed within the accounting system involves the creation of a fake debit which, in turn, will be offset by a credit to an asset account or expense account, fake debits and phony credit memos, phony invoices, phony employees, phony expense vouchers, and so on. In frauds within the system, there is usually evidence altered, forged, or fabricated, or missing documents. In frauds outside the system, transactions may have bypassed the accounting system completely.

Corporate Fraud Investigations

An accounting system consists of records that provide both detailed information of business transactions, which are called journals, and summary information of account balances, which are called ledgers. The most commonly used journals are for recording cash receipts and disbursements. Other journals used include those in which sales and purchases are recorded. Ledgers can be subclassified into general ledgers, which reflect current balances in asset, liability, revenue, and expense accounts in a summary form (i.e., total debits and credits posted), and subsidiary ledgers, which reflect the specific details of transactions between the firm and its customers and suppliers. These subsidiary ledgers are kept on the basis of individual customer or vendor name and/or account number. All books and records should be handled with care.

Audit Trail

The audit trail is made up of paper documents that support each step in a regular business transaction (purchase, sale of goods, etc.) from requisition to purchase, to receipt of goods and payment; or from billing a customer to receipt of his payment on account and deposit in the bank. An effective audit trail is one that provides an auditor with an opportunity to trace any given transaction backward or forward from an original source of the transaction to a final total.

Analysis of the suspect's financial transactions, what he received, where and how the money was spent will reveal if there is money remaining and where it is located.

Corporate Fraud Detection

Fraud uncovered during internal audits tends to involve lower level officials of the company. Fraud by senior management is more difficult to find and document. Corporate fraud requires M.O.M.M.:

> **M**otivation
> **O**pportunity
> **M**ethods
> **M**eans

The fraud audit purpose is to determine the state of mind or mental disposition of employees toward fraudulent behavior. Fraud is committed by people, not by computers or accounting systems.

Detection Techniques

The primary rule in all fraud investigation is to follow the assets. There are ten basic rules:

1. Never overlook the obvious!
2. Look for deviations. Never seek the most complex solution.
3. Always concentrate on the weakest, most simple point in the fraud. Most frauds have three elements:
   a. Theft act
   b. Concealment
   c. Conversion
4. If accounts have been manipulated or records destroyed, the person whose guilt would otherwise have been the most obvious should be treated as the prime suspect.

5. If after an investigation of all available facts guilt appears to point toward a particular person, chances are he is the responsible party.
6. Fraud detection and prevention is not an occasional exercise but rather a routine aspect of business. Fraud detection is a continuous management function.
7. It is not necessary to detect all frauds at any one time. A deterrent is established with each case detected and investigated.
8. To detect fraud, resources must be allocated specifically to that task.
9. Detecting fraud is hard work.
10. Fraud usually escapes detection because nobody is made accountable for the task. An auditor is a watchdog, not a bloodhound. Police investigate fraud, they seldom detect it.

Individual Net Worth Investigations

An individual net worth investigation is simply the difference between what the person owns and what they owe at a given point in time. It is useful to use the net worth format when a suspect systematically acquires assets such as money, stocks, bonds, certificates of deposit, real estate, cash value life insurance, and luxury items (jewelry, furs, automobiles, and antiques), and he systematically reduces his liabilities, such as loans and mortgages. A typical net worth computation encompasses four complete years financial records, preferably the years prior to and including the suspected fraud time frame.

Bank records and business financial records are the most important source available for net worth analysis. However, traditional investigative techniques should also be used to develop additional information. These techniques include physical surveillance to document lifestyle, spending habits, and possible criminal activity; that is, drug use, prostitution, gambling, and so on. Additionally, searching through the suspect's garbage (dumpster diving) may reveal a wide range of useful information including bank accounts and other indications of where the money may be located.

ECONOMIC CRIME SCHEMES

Advance Fee Scheme

These schemes are devised to obtain fees in advance for services the promoter has no intention of providing. They may be practiced in any type of financial dealings, but usually occur when an offender claims to have the means of obtaining buyer's for one's business, property, securities, or other assets, or to have access to sources of loan financing.

The granddaddy of all economic crime schemes was the advance fee scheme. While a Federal Probation Officer in Fort Lauderdale, Florida, I supervised Phillip Morell Wilson, who is credited with being one of the founding fathers of the advance fee scheme. He created a bank, The Bank of Sark, on the island of Guernsey, off the English coast. He created a phony set of books showing millions of dollars in assets, which then issued letters of credit to a host of South Florida con men. The deal was so complicated that he was offered a reduced sentence to help federal prosecutors unravel the scheme and testify against his co-conspirators. This incident was given much attention in Jonathan Qwitney's book, considered the bible on economic crime, *The Fountain Pen Conspiracy.*

Pyramid Scheme

An investment fraud in which an individual is offered a distributorship or franchise to market a particular product. The investment contract also authorizes one to sell additional franchises. The promoter of a pyramid scheme represents to the buyer that the marketing of the product will result in profits; however, he emphasizes the potentially quicker return on investment by the sale of franchises. Attempts to sell the product usually fail because the actual product is overpriced and there have been no real efforts by the promoters to market the product.

Ponzi Scheme

This is basically an investment fraud. The Ponzi operator solicits investors in a business venture, promising extremely high return on dividends in a short period of time. The dividends are never paid. The Ponzi operator never actually invests the money in anything. The Ponzi operator actually does pay dividends to the investor, but in reality he is simply returning some of the investor's original money. The return, paid promptly and cheerfully, is used to induce the investor to put up additional funds. In some cases the phony dividend is used to encourage the investor to solicit friends and associates to invest in the scheme. The Ponzi operator, when he has accumulated sufficient funds, concludes his scheme by fleeing with all of the investor's funds.

Planned Bankruptcy Scheme

A merchandising swindle based upon the abuse of credit, which has been legitimately or fraudulently established. The scheme consists of over-purchasing of inventory on credit, sale or other disposition of merchandise obtained, concealment of the proceeds, non-payment of creditors, and filing of a bankruptcy petition, either voluntarily or involuntarily. This scheme is referred to as a planned bankruptcy, or in more common terms a "bust out," because getting out is the ultimate goal of those operating the scheme. Planned bankruptcies can be extremely lucrative, and organized crime has been particularly active in this type of fraud.

Chain Referral Scheme

This involves the sales of grossly overpriced products through false representations that the cost will be recovered by commissions the promoter will pay on sales made to the purchaser's friends.

Merchandising Schemes

While many economic crimes are hidden and difficult to detect, some of the more visible and blatant offenses are committed by retail stores. These frauds are based on twisting the truth for increased profits.

Bait and Switch

This is advertising a product with no intent to sell it as advertised. These ads are designed to bait or lure customers into the store. Once the consumer is in the store, the advertised product is criticized by the salesman, who then tries to switch the customer to a higher priced variation of the same product.

Phony Sales

A going out of business sales, fire sales, liquidation sales, and so on.

Deceptive Sales Contest

Using this technique, a dishonest business through direct mail, TV, or newspaper advertising, promotes a contest in which the victim is led to believe that chance of winning a valuable prize is much greater than it actually is.

Short Weighting

When the producer at the packaging stage of production fills containers of the product to 9/10 capacity and then charges retailers or consumers for the full capacity.

Home Improvement, Debt Consolidation, and Mortgage Loans

Home owners already heavily burdened with debt are the victims. An individual whose home is in need of repair, whose debts need to be consolidated, or who needs a mortgage loan, is offered a loan sufficient to pay off all debts or finance home improvements. The one monthly payment, the victim is told, will be less, or at least no larger than the combined payments that are currently being made. The large amount of the loan offer stems from the promoter's intention to quickly sell the note at a discount to a finance or mortgage loan company. To do so profitably, he knows that the amount must sufficiently exceed the cost of the home improvement work so as to offset the discount. In this type of scheme the promoters rely on the confusing terms of the signed documents and numerous put-off tactics to delay serious consequences when home improvement work falls in arrears, is poorly done, or is not done at all.

Credit Card Fraud

Several distinct crimes are included under the classification of credit card fraud. An individual may falsely acquire a credit card by misrepresentation made on the application. Once the card is obtained, the individual uses the card to defraud merchants and other providers of service. Finally, professional credit card rings often deal in counterfeit, lost, stolen, or misdelivered credit cards. They generally know exactly how long they may use an invalid credit card without detection, and they also know the dollar amounts they may charge before detection is likely.

WHITE COLLAR CRIME

The essential characteristic of a crime is that it is behavior prohibited by the state as an injury to the state, and against which the state may react by punishment. White collar crime is described as the intent to commit a wrongful act or to achieve a purpose not consistent with law or public policy. It is the disguise of purpose through falsehoods and misrepresentations employed to accomplish the scheme, and conceal-ment of a crime. These illegal acts characterized by deceit, concealment, and violation of trust that are not dependent upon application or threat of physical force or violence. Such crimes are committed to obtain money, property, services, or to secure personal or business advantage. White collar crimes are deliberate and organized. Businessmen are organized formally for the control of legislation, selection of administra-tors, and restriction of appropriations for the enforcement of laws, which may adversely affect them.

The Watergate Scandal in 1972 and the prosecution that followed clearly marked a high point in public awareness and concern for crimes of the rich and powerful. Illegalities perpetrated by individuals and businesses make innocent victims of the public through the use of cover ups, deception, and violation of trust and power. Computers and other forms of high tech record keeping have been viewed as a vehicle to wealth and have made white collar crime a major public problem.

Corporate Crime

One frequent objection to the criminological study and call for greater legal control of corporate crime is the argument that these crimes are not as serious as other forms of crime, particularly street crimes. Even though the great economic cost of corporate crime is recognized, it is argued that these crimes are nonviolent and, therefore, less important. The notion that these crimes are nonviolent or less serious is then used to justify their exclusion from greater legal controls. The most controversial issue in the study of corporate crime is whether it really is a crime. White collar crime is real crime, but it is not treated as such by the criminal justice system.

Cost of Corporate Crime

Except in cases of fraud, the victim of ordinary crime knows that he has been victimized. The victims of corporate crime, on the other hand, are unaware that they have been victimized. Government experts estimate that violations of antitrust, tax fraud, bribery, pollution, and other federal laws by the nation's largest corporations cost the economy billions of dollars. A U.S. Senator estimated that faulty goods, monopolistic practices, and other violations annually cost consumers between $174 and $231 million per year.

Difficulties in the Use of Criminal Sanctions

Some actions of corporate executives are more likely to be regarded as criminal in nature, that is, bribery of officials, price fixing, and manufacture and shipment of harmful products.

The use of criminal sanction against corporate officers is limited by the fact that they project certain profiles and are unlikely to be judged harshly except where they are responsible, for their faults are undeniable. The argument is often presented that corporate executives should not be subject to criminal sanctions for violating legal regulations because they are responsible for advances in the industry that have raised living standards and the caliber of life in our society.

Difficulties involved in investigations leading to criminal prosecution have been and remain biased in favor of the corporate offender. The study of white collar crime has attempted to do two things:

1. To present evidence that persons of the upper class commit many crimes to get there and these crimes should be included within the general scope of theories of criminal behavior.
2. To develop theories that may explain all criminal behavior — both white collar and other.

The first of these objectives has been realized in that a large number of corporations have been found to have violated laws with great frequency. The theory that crime is due to personal and social pathologies does not apply to white collar crimes. Therefore, such pathologies are not essential factors in crimes in general.

The RICO Act

The Racketeer Influenced Corrupt Organization Act (RICO) of 1970 was initially designed to flush out crime and white collar criminals who have no connection to organized crime. State and Federal RICO Laws provide remedies to organizations which have been victimized by fraud. Under the RICO Act, organizations which have been victimized can sue for three times their losses plus attorneys' fees and costs.

Management Fraud

Management fraud goes beyond the narrow legal definition of embezzlement, fraud, or theft. It is made up of all forms of deception practiced by managers to benefit themselves to the detriment of the enterprise. It is usually covered up by its victims to avoid the adverse effects of publicity.

Environment of Corporation

Management should clearly set forth in written policies its commitment to fair dealing, its position on conflicts of interest, its requirement that only honest employees be hired, its insistence on strong internal controls that are well policed, and its resolve to prosecute the guilty. Management negligence or refusal to be realistic can generate a climate for fraud to expand.

Federal and State Fraud Statutes

The five Federal fraud statutes are:

1. False statements (18 USC 1001)
2. False claims (18 USC 287)

3. Mail fraud (18 USC 1341)
4. Conspiracy (18 USC 371)
5. Wire fraud (18 USC 1343)

In the state of Florida there are four fraud statutes:

1. Computer related fraud (FS 815)
2. Fraudulent practices and credit card fraud (FS 817)
3. Forgery and counterfeiting (FS 831)
4. Worthless checks/drafts (FS 832)

Types of Violations

The violations of the corporation studies showed great range and varied characteristics. The following six main types of corporate illegal behavior were found:

1. Administrative violations involve noncompliance with the requirements of an agency.
2. Environmental violations include incidents of air and water pollution.
3. Financial violations include illegal payments or failure to disclose such violations.
4. Labor violations fall into four major types: discrimination against race, religion, national origin, and sex.
5. Manufacturing violations involve three government agencies: the Consumer Product Safety Commission, the National Highway Traffic Safety Administration, and the Food and Drug Administration.
6. Unfair trade practices involve various abuses of competition (monopolization, misrepresentation, price discrimination, credit violations, and other abuses that restrain trade and prevent fair competition).

Business crime is an illegal act, punishable by a criminal sanction, which is committed by an individual or corporation in the course of a legitimate occupation or pursuit in the industrial or commercial sector for the purpose of obtaining money or property, avoiding the payment of money or the loss of property, or obtaining business or personal advantage. A corporate crime is an act committed by corporations that is punished by the state. Corporations, unlike individuals, cannot be jailed, only fined. White collar crimes involve monetary offense not ordinarily associated with criminality until recent years. Objectives for investigation into suspected fraud are:

1. First and foremost, protect the innocent, establish facts, and resolve the matter.
2. Determine the basic circumstances and stop the loss.
3. Establish essential elements of the crime to support a successful prosecution.
4. Identify, gather, and protect the evidence.
5. Identify and interview witnesses.
6. Identify patterns of action and behavior.
7. Determine probable motives which will identify potential suspects.
8. Provide accurate and objective facts upon which judgments concerning discipline, termination, or prosecution may be based.
9. Account for and recover assets.
10. Identify weaknesses in control and counter them by revising existing procedures or recommending new ones and by applying security equipment where justified.

STEPS IN THE INVESTIGATION PROCESS

The first step in the investigation process is to establish that a loss has occurred and an asset lost. The process should determine that the asset was accountable at some point and then definitely missing at another. Once the time frame has been bracketed, it is relatively simple to determine which employees could have been involved in the loss.

Most frauds are discovered by accident, rather than by audit or accounting system design. Fraud detection is more of an art form than a science. It requires creative thinking as well as science, persistence, and self-confidence. Every fraud is unique.

The police should be informed if the loss is substantial, the evidence is strong, and the employee either appears to be untruthful or makes an admission or confession. Once charges are filed, the company should not withdraw its complaint without a recommendation from the prosecutor. Charges should not be dropped in lieu of restitution, for the company will lose the confidence of the police, the prosecutor, and the court in future cases.

The second step is to establish the facts. Get as much information as possible from informants. Interview all those who may have been involved in the control or access to the asset during the bracketed period. Gather documents, organize data, examine documents for forgery, and look for "out of balance" conditions. Do not stop at the documents themselves, look behind them to the facts they are supposed to establish and look for relationships — things that do not make sense.

The third step, interviewing, is a significant part of the investigative process. Interviewers should speak calmly and avoid accusatory attitudes. They should show compassion and interrupt the suspect only to clarify points. If the suspect elects to be silent, the interviewer should not threaten or intimidate, however, an employee should not be allowed to return to the work area, because valuable evidence may be lost.

Once serious wrongdoing is suspected and the evidence obtained, the suspect will have to be confronted and interrogated. However, suspected employees have certain Common Law and statutory rights. If these rights are infringed upon, whether or not the employee is guilty, he may have the right to sue the interrogator and the company. An accused employee can file a civil action if the employer has made defamatory statements. Liable is a written defamation. Slander is an oral defamation.

An employer can be sued for false arrest or false imprisonment when he unreasonably restrains an employee's freedom of mobility. The restraint need not be physical touching or locking a person in a room. Intimidating employees or telling them they cannot leave the room or the city has been held to constitute false imprisonment.

Interrogation

Only a trained and experienced investigator can tell whether the person he is interrogating are lying or telling the truth.

> Unusual or specific indicators in response to **hot** questions may suggest that the subject is less than truthful. These may include dry mouth and lips that result in a clicking sound when speaking; avoiding eye contact or staring at the interviewer, then dropping the eyes down and away to the side as the question is answered; an unusual high pitch to the voice or rapid speech patterns; restlessness and shifting in the chair, crossing both the arms and legs with elbows kept tucked into the side. Also watch for abnormal eye blink rate, biting the lips or tongue, tightly squeezing the lips together, looking at or playing with fingernails, crying at inappropriate times, claiming memory failure or having a remarkably keen memory, and smiling at inappropriate times or phony over smiling. Other key nonverbal signals include rounding the shoulders with the elbows at the knees, dropping the head to look downward at the floor, and deep sighing that may indicate an admission is forthcoming. An experienced investigator will be aware of these signals and press the line of questioning accordingly.

Compounding a Felony

The laws in the United States provide that the right to punish or to forgive a criminal is reserved to the state. Defrauded employers who have been the victim of fraud cannot take those rights upon themselves. Agreeing for a consideration, not to prosecute, is itself a crime. It is called compounding a felony and can result in legal punishment for the employer, investigator, or both.

Controlling Crime/Accountability for Asset Protection

Protection and preservation of a firm's assets (human, capital, technological, and informational) from the foreseeable consequences of acts of public enemy (property theft, fraud, embezzlement, sabotage, information piracy, and commercial corruption) and human errors and omissions (employee negligence) are the responsibility of firm officers, directors, and agents by a host of federal, state, and local laws.

Proving Corporate Fraud

A fraud audit is the result of two events; finding of accounting discrepancies, and allegation by some person that a fraud has been committed. When fraud is found, an investigator is needed. Where a discrepancy is found, an auditor is needed. The two principle types of auditors are internal and external.

Reasons for Leniency in Corporate Frauds

The reasons for leniency in corporate fraud situations. are the wealth and prestige of the businessmen involved, their influence over the media, the trend toward more lenient punishment for all offenders, the complexity and invisibility of many business crimes, and the existence of regulatory agencies and inspectors who seek compliance with law rather than the punishment of violators.

APPENDIX 1

LEGAL ASPECTS OF INVESTIGATIVE WORK

Even when suspected, defendants and claimants are protected from:

1. Defamation (slander and liable)
2. False imprisonment
3. False arrest
4. Trespass
5. Assault and battery
6. Negligent use of a firearm
7. Invasion of privacy
   a. Surveillance conducted in an unreasonable or obstructive manner
   b. That which disturbs the sensibility of the average person
   c. Surveillance conducted for other than a legitimate purpose
8. Wiretapping and eavesdropping
9. Disclosure of communications and documents generated in the course of the investigation

APPENDIX 2

CORPORATE FRAUD

Corporate Fraud Classification System

Crimes Against the Company

Theft, fraud, and embezzlement.

1. Input scams
      Cash and petty cash diversions (thefts)
      Cash and petty cash conversions (check kiting, check raising, and signature endorsement forgeries)
      Payables manipulations (lapping fake credit memos)
      Payables manipulations (phony vendor invoices, benefit claims, and expense vouchers; overcharges by vendors, suppliers, and contractors)
      Payroll manipulations (phony employees and altered time cards)
      Inventory manipulations (bogus reclassification of inventories to obsolete, damaged, or sample status)
2. Throughput scams
      Salami slicing, trap door, Trojan Horse, time bomb, and super zap techniques (bypassing controls in systems and application programs)
3. Output scams
      Destroying exceptions reports and logs
      Stealing files, programs, reports, and data (customer lists, research and development results, marketing plans, etc.)

Crimes for the Company

1. Smoothing profits (cooking the books)
      Inflating sales
      Understating expenses

Not recording sales returns
Inflating ending inventory
2. Balance sheet window dressing
 Overstating assets
 Not recording liabilities
3. Price fixing
4. Cheating customers
 Short weights, counts, and measures
 Substitution of cheaper materials
 False advertising
5. Violating governmental regulations, that is, EEO, OSHA, environmental standards, securities, and tax
6. Corruption of the customer — personnel
7. Political corruption
8. Padding costs on government contracts

Corporate Fraud Typology

Internally generated corporate frauds are the subject of investigation of corporate fraud.

For the Company

1. Regulatory violations
 OSHA, EEO, ERISA, EPA, FTC, FDA, ICC, OFCC, Wages Hour, Antitrust, SEC, IRS, FCPA, Building and Fire Codes, State Sales, U.S.E, Extraction and Property Taxes, Rate Regulation, Padding Government Contracts, etc.
2. Consumer and customer frauds
 False labeling, branding, advertising, and packaging
 Short weights and counts, defective products, and substitution of inferior goods
 Price fixing
3. Stockholder and creditor frauds
 False financial statements and representations
 False or forged collateral
 Stock manipulation, insider trading, and related party transactions
4. Frauds against competitors
 Theft or compromise of competitor's trade secrets or proprietary information
 Predatory pricing and other forms of unfair competition.
 Copyright and patent infringement

5. Corruption of customer's and competitor's personnel and/or regulatory authorities or union leaders

Against the Company

1. By executives
   False claims for bonuses, benefits, or expenses
   Commercial bribery by vendors
   Sales of proprietary information or trade secrets to competitors
   Theft or embezzlement of corporate assets
   Fabrication of operational or financial performance data
2. By nonmanagement employees
   Pilferage
   Sabotage of company property
   Theft or embezzlement of corporate assets
   False claims for bonuses, benefits, or expenses
   Intentional waste
   Falsifying time, attendance, and productivity reports

Frauds from Within the Accounting System

1. False input scams (creating fake debits)
   False or inflated claims from vendors, suppliers, benefits claimants, and employees, or false refund or allowance claims by customers
   Lapping on receivable payments or customer bank deposits
   Check kiting
   Inventory manipulation and reclassification
   - Arbitrary write-ups and write-downs
   - Reclassification to lower value — obsolete, damaged, or "sample" status
   Intentional misclassification of expenditures
   - Operational expenses vs. capital expenditure
   - Personal expense vs. business expense
   Fabrication of sales and cost of sales data
   Misapplication and misappropriation of funds and other corporate assets (theft and embezzlement)
   Computerized input and fraudulent access scams
   - Data manipulation
   - Impersonation and imposter terminal
   - Scavenging
   - Piggybacking

- Wiretapping
- Interceptions and destruction of input and source documents
- Fabrication of batch or hash totals
- Simulation and modeling fraud (fraudulent parallel systems)

Forgery, counterfeiting, or altering of source documents, authorizations, computer program documentation, or loan collateral

Overstating revenues and assets

Understating expenses and liabilities

Creating off-line reserves

Related party transactions

Spurious assets and hidden liabilities

"Smoothing" profits

Destruction, obliteration, and alteration of supporting documents

Exceeding limits of authority

2. False throughput scams

Salami slicing, trap doors, Trojan Horse, and logic bombs

Designed random error during processing cycle

3. Output scams

Scavenging through output

Output destruction, obliteration

Theft of output reports and logs

Theft of programs, data files, and systems programming and operations documentation

Frauds from Outside the Accounting System

1. Confidence schemes by outsiders
2. Fraudulent misrepresentations by current and prospective vendors, suppliers, customers, and employees

7

COMPUTER CRIME

The Internet is becoming the vast new frontier for most private investigators. Computers are not simply useful tools to make the job of an investigator easier, they are a necessity in order to remain in business. In the future, those who do not operate on the World Wide Web will become as extinct as the dinosaur.

In the United States all financial institutions report incidents of frauds committed against them to the Securities and Exchange Commission (SEC). The amount of computer fraud as a product of the increasing use of computers will grow unless computer security can eliminate traditional frauds by employees.

COMPUTER CRIMES

A computer crime is defined as an illegal act in which knowledge of computer technology is used to commit the offense. According to the FBI, 21 states have enacted laws dealing with computer crime, but there is little consistency from state to state, and several have failed to deal with hackers who enter the systems for fun rather than profit. Computer manipulation crimes involve changing data to create records in a system for the specific advancement of another crime. Virtually all embezzlement in financial institutions requires creation of false accounts or modification of data in existing accounts. The perpetrator does need not need to know computer programming, but he must have a good sense of how to operate the system.

The FBI categorizes computer crime into five groups, and not all involve financial transactions. Computer thieves can also steal goods and services, college degrees, and titles to properties as well as negotiable securities. The five categories of computer crimes are system deceit/unauthorized transactions, system alteration, physical destruction, theft of information, and time theft, that is, the unauthorized use of the computer.

It is estimated that 85% of computer fraud cases are never reported because of embarrassment, loss of public confidence, false arrest concerns, and overall difficulty of prosecution.

Institutions are heavily dependent on automated systems and electronic transfers of funds for various business activities and are exposed to the possibility of significant fraud in the computer area because computer records are in electronic form and computer processing of accounts and transaction data may be performed by a group of persons outside the financial institution. Additionally, transactions may be initiated from remote facilities by various employees, customers, and external parties.

Maintaining the security of a computer system and electronic transactions involves checking:

- Adequate physical security to prevent accidental or intentional damage to the computer system and related equipment
- Software and data file security to ensure computer programs and data files are not altered accidentally or deliberately
- Techniques for maintaining transaction data controls and for analyzing the reasonableness of transactions to detect and report possible crime attempts
- Use of customer identification methods to restrict unauthorized individuals from initiating transactions to customer accounts
- Secure communications networks to prevent unauthorized interception or alteration of electronic data
- Adequate internal controls to prevent, detect, and correct computer crime and other concerns

COMPUTER FRAUD

Any incident involving computer technology in which there is a victim who suffered (or could have suffered) a loss and a perpetrator who by intention made (or could have made) a gain is the defined as computer fraud.

An indicator of possible problems is present in some or all of the following elements of a vulnerable computer system (five tip-offs of computer related fraud).

1. The computer generates negotiable instruments or is used to transfer credit, process loans, or obtain credit ratings.
2. Employee relations are poor; dismissed data-processing personnel remain on the job until their termination date; a computer programmer is overqualified for the job with the possible result that bottled up creativity will seek undesirable outlets.

3. Separation of key personnel is inadequate, either in terms of responsibility or physical access.
4. After hours data processing operations are loosely supervised.
5. Auditors have little expertise or background in computer operations.

Indicators that require follow-up investigation include situations in which:

■ Computer reports or carbons of pertinent forms are inside the trash bins
■ Auditors are not involved in the development of application programs resulting in the absence of built-in checks and balances
■ The industry is depressed, yet computer-generated data indicates record sales for the company
■ Frequent violations are reported of the rule that requires that at least two people should be present when data processing equipment is operated
■ Computer operations, including storage of output data, can be viewed by the general public
■ System components are near open windows, next to outside walls, or in front of open doors (easily accessible)
■ The personnel department submits candidates for data processing positions with only routine screening. The chief weakness of computer systems is people
■ Data preparation equipment is easily available and loosely controlled
■ Access to computer facilities is not limited to those with a need to be there
■ Transactions are rejected by the system because they did not pass one or more control points or were put aside, ignored, or deliberately overridden
■ Increase is noted in employee complaints about overwithholding by the computer or about inaccuracies in the year-end earning statements
■ There is a surge in customer complaints about delays in crediting their accounts
■ Key forms such as purchase orders, invoices, and checks are not numbered sequentially
■ Continuous form checks are not stored securely
■ The bill for use of computer time is much larger than the computer time logs seem to indicate
■ Access to central processors is attempted from a remote terminal whose exclusive user is on vacation
■ Payments are sent to new suppliers, but they are not listed in company directories

THE COMPUTER CRIME INVESTIGATOR

The computer crime investigator is a specialist in criminal investigation, data processing, auditing, and accounting. His knowledge of data processing should include computer operations, systems design and analysis, programming, and project management.

A primary element in a computer crime investigation course is the manner in which it is structured and whether it contains all the vital areas of required knowledge. A computer crime investigation curriculum should include the following:

1. The types of threats and vulnerabilities to which a computer is susceptible
2. Data processing concepts relative to software (programming) and hardware (the equipment itself)
3. Types of computer crimes
4. Investigative methodology including investigative procedures, forensic techniques, review of technical data systems, investigation planning, interview/interrogation techniques, information gathering and analysis, and case presentation techniques

THE INVESTIGATIVE PROCESS

Most computer frauds are complex, hidden, and extensive. The detection of wrongdoing is usually first noticed by the internal auditor. The investigator must then establish essential elements of the crime to support successful prosecution; identify, gather, and protect evidence; identify and move closer to suspects; identify patterns of action and behavior; determine probable motives, which will often identify potential suspects; provide accurate and objective facts upon which judgments concerning discipline, termination, or prosecution may be based; and identify weaknesses in control and counter them by revising existing procedures or recommending new ones, and by applying security equipment where justified.

The first step in the investigation of computer fraud is to establish that loss of asset occurred; the process should determine that an asset was accountable at some point and definitely missing at another point. The second step is to establish the facts. Get as much information as possible from everyone involved. Interview anyone who may have had control or access to the asset during the established time frame. Finally, gather evidence, organize data, examine documents for forgeries, and look for "out of balance" conditions.

AREAS OF COMPUTER ABUSE

The following are the most likely areas where computer abuse will occur.

Payroll

Fictitious personnel can be created.

Inventory

Fictitious accounts can be created and records falsified to show bills were paid, while inventory was delivered to fictitious persons and locations.

Accounts Receivable

This information can be mismanaged by a loss of computer records of monies owed to the firm.

Disbursements

Through manipulation of data, a company may be tricked into paying for goods and services that were never received.

Operations Information

This data can be very valuable to a firm's competitors, especially in the areas of growth plans and new designs.

TELECOMMUNICATION CRIMES

Telecommunication crimes involve the illegal access to or use of computer systems over telephone lines. A hacking program tries to find valid access codes for a computer system by continually calling the system with randomly generated codes. Use of a hacking program constitutes unauthorized access to a system, and access codes generated by a hacking program are stolen property. Misuse of telephone systems also falls into the telecommunications crime group. Phone phreaking and BBSing are terms used to describe telephone frauds in which stolen or false telephone access cards are used to pay for long distance telephone calls.

Computer Manipulation Crimes

These types of crimes involve changing data or creating records in a system for the specific advancement of another crime, usually theft. Virtually all embezzlements in financial institutions require the creation of false account or modification of data in existing accounts to perform the act.

Hardware and Software Thefts

These thefts characterize the illegal use of a computer. Software piracy involves the duplication of programs without authorization and or payment. Virtually millions of dollars are lost by software developers to this type of crime each year, even though vendors are now attempting to safeguard their programs through the use of copyright protection devices.

Computer Losses

In an American Bar Association survey of 283 large companies, 48% admitted they had suffered from computer crime; 72 of them assessed their losses at between $145 and $730 million. The U.S. Chamber of Commerce estimates that computer crime losses total around $100 million per year; other estimates are closer to $500 million. The average computer crime loss is $500 thousand.

Methods of Attack

There are many ways to compromise a computer. Some are technical attacks, while others can be accomplished with only a basic understanding of computer operations. The following are the most common methods of attack.

Data Diddling

This is the simplest, safest, and most common method used by insiders. It involves putting false information into the computer. The data is changed before or during input from a computer, such as fraudulent payroll information.

Trojan Horse

The computer criminal can alter the computer circuitry or a computer program by adding instructions unknown to the owner. As a result, the computer performs unauthorized functions, for example, it deletes accounts payable or receivable.

Salami Slicing Techniques

Typically, this involves a money crime; it is an automated form of stealing small amounts of assets from a large number of sources.

Trap Doors

In the development of large application programs and computer operating systems, programmers often develop debugging aids that provide breaks in a code. These programs are made deliberately to change or alter existing programs legitimately. These programs, called trap doors, provide computer abusers with the ability to alter data without detection.

Logic Bombs

These are illegal instructions given to a computer that operate at a specific time or periodically. They are often dependent upon date, time, and/or another operation for execution.

Trashing (Dumpster Diving)

This practice, also known as scavenging, is the surreptitious obtainment of information from discarded printouts, manuals, tapes, and disks. It often involves searching through trash bins for discarded computer listings or carbon sheets from multicopy forms.

Piggybacking and Impersonation

Physical piggybacking is a method for gaining access to controlled access areas through the use of stolen or fraudulent cards. Electronic piggybacking involves gaining access to secured data through the use of someone else's password or identification sign-on. Compromise of the security system takes place when the computer verifies the sign-on but not the person. Impersonation is simply the process of one person assuming the identity of another, either physically or electronically.

While most of the attention regarding the misuse of computers is given to criminal aspects of computer abuses, it is likely that civil actions will have an equally important effect on long term security problems. The issue of computer crimes draws attention to the civil and/or liability issues in the computing environments. In the future, there may be more individual and class action suits against businesses and employers. All of these give rise to a bright future for the investigator who specializes in computer related investigations. This area is just beginning, but promises to be the fastest growing area of need for the investigative industry. Not only is there a need for detection of events that occurred on the computer; likewise, there is a need for an analysis of computer operations to prevent, as much as possible, and safeguard the business community from outside abuse, misuse, and hacking. Systems security will be a need in all business communities that conduct business through a computer.

APPENDIX 1

INVESTIGATION OF COMPUTER FRAUD

When investigating what appears to be an insider computer crime, the following factors should be considered.

1. Opportunities
   - Familiarity with operations
   - Position of trust
   - Close associations with suppliers and other key people
2. Situational pressures — financial
   - High personal debt
   - Severe illness in family
   - Inadequate income or living beyond means
   - Extensive stock market speculation (losses)
   - Loan shark involvement — owing money on gambling loans
   - Excessive gambling
   - Heavy expenses incurred from extramarital involvement
   - Undue family, peer, company, or community expectations
   - Excessive use of alcohol or drugs
3. Situational pressures — revenge
   - Perceived inequities (e.g., low pay or poor job assignments)
   - Resentment of superiors
   - Frustration, usually with the job
4. Personality traits
   - Lacks personal moral honesty
   - No well defined code of personal ethics
   - A wheeler–dealer, that is, someone who enjoys the feelings of power, influence, social status, and excitement associated with rapid financial transactions involving large sums of money
   - Neurotic, manic depressive, or emotionally unstable
   - Arrogant or egocentric
   - Psychopathic

- Low self-esteem
- Personally challenged to subvert a system of controls

Investigators should also construct a personal biography of suspects composed of three factors: a criminal history, a list of associates, and references.

APPENDIX 2

COMPUTER CRIME

Profiling the Computer Criminal

Profiles on computer criminals should include the following items:

- Tools or devices used
- Computer or other skills demonstrated in the crime
- Orientation as to politics, religion, or interest in pop culture which forms a subtext of the crime (i.e., reference to religion, gangs, political movement, etc.)
- Files may provide a clue as to information a suspect is looking at and how that information would be used (who would benefit from having that information?)
- Evidence as to the criminal's personality and way of thinking (i.e., well organized or impulsive, planned in advance with meticulous detail or random haphazard event?)
- Do crimes occur in any logical pattern (day, date, time of day) or random times and days?
- Unusual qualities in the method of attack on software or hardware, or the altering of information on the computer

Investigative Procedures on Malicious E-mail

- Preserve the evidence
- Trace the e-mail's path through your system with the help of the network administrator. Be on the lookout for any bypasses of e-mail security
- Obtain complete e-mail records of individuals involved for the preceding 30 days
- Review all personnel files
- Interview the individuals involved. Get their version on the record. Who had access to their computers? Why?

- Interview co-workers, witnesses, supervisors, and so on
- Follow the audit trail
- Inspect the computers involved for signs of tampering, unauthorized access, and so on
- Compare stories, events, and evidence against all other records, access logs, terminal logs, and so on

Indications of Suspicious Behavior by Employees

- People who never take a vacation
- Workers with excessive overtime, living at the job, and who are always around the job site
- Employees with a criminal record, history of substance abuse, or gambling problems
- Employees with constant financial problems
- Workers with extreme political views or radical lifestyles

Examine the elements of the crime and analyze what is necessary to commit the crime, such as knowledge of software used, knowledge of how to create a logic bomb, an accomplice in accounts payable, a mail drop to receive the checks, dummy businesses to act as vendors, fake IDs to open bank accounts, and bank accounts to negotiate the checks.

Analysis of these elements gives the investigator new avenues to explore and leads to follow, for example, an accomplice within the company. Physical evidence of penetration of computer security includes broken glass, cut wire fences, picked locks, cut locks, jimmied doors, disabled security cameras, changed locks, security gurads unable to access the computer area, holes cut in walls or doors, and disabled alarm systems.

In cases of embezzlement, you need to analyze the flow of data and documents through the financial processing system (FPS). Determine:

> What steps are required to issue a check?
> Where are the checks printed? Who has access to that area?
> What steps are necessary to have someone added to the payroll?
> Is it possible to change information within the FPS programs? How?
> Is there a FPS paper or audit trail? How does it work?

Conducting Internal Investigations

The Risk Matrix

The risk matrix includes opportunity factors as well as means, motive, and high risk factors. Included in opportunity factors are events that occurred on suspect's shift, or just before or after; whether or not the suspect is knowledgeable about the work involved; whether or not the suspect had the necessary skills to commit the event; whether or not there is a relationship between the suspect's actions and the event; and whether or not the suspect has an alibi.

Included in the means factors are whether or not the suspect had access to the area, whether or not the suspect possessed access materials to the area, and whether or not the suspect had the ability to bypass security to obtain access to the area. Motive factors include the suspect having high risk factors, the suspect having resentment against the company, and the suspect having political grievances. High risk factors include family problems, financial problems, a lifestyle beyond salary means, co-workers suspicious of the suspect, the suspect acting defensive during interviews, substance abuse or gambling problems, and other suspicious lifestyle factors (extramarital affair, cult activity, etc.). Anyone who exhibits characteristics within the risk matrix should undergo the following investigation.

- Review of personnel records.
- Interview previous co-workers and supervisors.
- Review the suspect's work product.
- Extensive background check of the suspect.
- Interview current associates.
- Make asset searches.
- Provide surveillance of the suspect after work.
- Interrogate the supect once incriminating evidence is found.

Conducting External Investigations

The investigator should cooperate with police or any other investigative agency, preserve evidence and the crime scene, obtain the dollar loss and provide documentation, obtain intelligence information, identify and interview witnesses and suspects, and question vendors, suppliers, and visitors.

Report Writing

Your report should include a summary of the incident, a description of the evidence establishing a *corpus delicti* (body of the crime), a description of how the crime was committed and the suspect's motive, the financial impact of the crime, and a review of the evidence identifying those responsible.

If the crime was committed by an employee of the company, your report should provide the employee's history with the company, any previous disciplinary problems, criminal history, family background, amount of gain from the crime, and the suspect's financial resources.

If the crime involved a vendor, supplier, or contract worker, your report should provide a history of the relationship with the company, the compensation received, background on the suspect, criminal history, profit from the crime, and the insurance coverage and financial stability of the employer.

If the crime was committed by another company, your report shold provide a background of the other company and its officers, a criminal background check of the officers, profit from the crime, and the applicable insurance.

If the crime was committed as part of an ongoing criminal enterprise (RICO), your report should provide a pattern of criminal activity, the types of crimes involved in the pattern, and the evidence proving the crimes.

APPENDIX 3

THE INTERNET AND THE WORLD WIDE WEB

The Internet is a world-wide network of computers that allows a multitude of types of computers to communicate with each other. There are two ways of communicating: information may be *sent* or it may be *received*. The Web, or World Wide Web, is part of the Internet. The World Wide Web may be accessed to use text, graphics, sounds, and animation; for commercialization purposes, there are unlimited "pages" or Web sites, and the Web provides hypertext on links. According to a 1998 study, 100 million people went online because the Web is fast, easy, and inexpensive. An Internet user needs at least a 486 or Pentium computer with 16 MB RAM, and a modem (phone line) with at least 28.8K, preferably 56K. The user also needs the following software: a Windows OS (operating system), a browser, an Internet service provider (ISP), and virus scan software.

Commercial service providers, such as AOL, Compuserve, and others provide a gateway to the Internet. The Internet is easy to learn and use and provides restricted access for the user. ISPs provide a direct connection to the Internet, and the average cost is $20 per month for unlimited use. In this case, the system may be slightly more difficult to operate with less support, but provides unrestricted access. There are different types of Web accounts, including a browser, e-mail, newsgroups, and search engines. Browsers use a point-and-click method of navigating the Web. Some common Web browsers are Netscape Navigator, Microsoft Explorer, and Mosaic.

E-mail is noted for its ease of use, speed, and its multiple addressing capability. E-mail is an inexpensive method of communication.

Search engines are convenient methods of finding information; they are home page locators that provide various searching methods when you register with the search engines. There are over 40,000 newsgroups. One well known newsgroup is Usenet, also called net news. E-mail messages may be posted to newsgroups such as Alt.private.investigator.

The Universal Resource Locator provides information page addresses. Users only need to type in an address or click to link. This is the most common hypertext transfer protocol that directs users to home pages.

There are approximately 1000 search tools with broad-based search engines containing subject directories, meta search engines, and specialized search tools. The top search engines include Hotbot at www.hotbot.com, AltaVista at www.altavista.digital.com, Excite at www.excite.com, Infoseek at www.infoseek.com, Lycos at www.lycos.com, and Webcrawler at www.webcrawler.com. There also are subject directory engines like Yahoo at www.yahoo.com, Magellan at www.mckinley.com, Needle in a Haystack, and Virtual Reference Desk at www.refdesk.com.

To structure a search, review search engine techniques. Read the FAQ of the search engine and focus the search using primary and secondary words.

Meta search engines are useful to search several engines at same time. Remember to keep search terms simple. Metacrawler at www.metacrawler.com, Dogpile at www.dogpile.com, Metafind at www.metafind.com, and Inference Find at www.inference.com/infind/ may also be used.

If you cannot find the results you are seeking, reconsider search terminology, check the spelling and truncation, use specialized search engines, post your inquiry to discussion groups or listservs, and contact the local librarian.

8

CRIMINAL INVESTIGATION

THE INVESTIGATIVE FUNCTION

A criminal investigation is the systematic process of identifying, collecting, preserving, and evaluating information for the purpose of bringing a criminal offender to justice. Successful investigations are based upon a systematic plan which proceeds in an orderly and logical manner. Without such a plan, relevant and highly significant evidence may be overlooked and improperly or inefficiently gathered, and incorrect conclusions may be drawn. Everything piece of information relating to a crime is subject to use. Examples include the testimony of an eyewitness, fingerprints left at the crime scene, or a forged traveler's check.

BASIC ELEMENTS OF THE INVESTIGATIVE PROCESS

The basic elements of the investigative process include recognition, collection, preservation, and evaluation of information.

Recognition

Information relating to a crime must be recognized as such by the investigator. Examples include drops of blood at an assault scene, a neighbor who viewed a burglary, and the bank records of a drug dealer.

Collection

Relevant information must also be collected by the investigator. Examples include scraping the dry blood, interviewing the neighbor, and reviewing the dealer's bank records.

Preservation

The information must be preserved to ensure its physical and legal integrity. Examples include sealing the blood scrapings in an evidence bag, obtaining a sworn statement from the neighbor, and obtaining copies of the dealer's bank records.

Evaluation

The information must be evaluated by the investigator to determine its worth. Examples include recogniztion that blood of a common type is of little value, the ability of the neighbor to pick the offender from a lineup, and bank records that clearly indicate deposits of money far in excess of the suspect's salary.

ROLE OF THE CRIMINAL INVESTIGATOR

The criminal investigator carries out the investigative function and will perform five different tasks. See Figure 8.1 for a sample investigation check list.

Determine that a Crime has been Committed

Conduct which does not violate any statute is not a crime. Crimes are defined by written penal codes, and conduct that does not fall within the definition may not be illegal. Agency jurisdiction may be limited. The investigator needs to conduct a preliminary investigation to determine in which jurisdiction the violation has occurred. There is also the possibility of a false report. For a variety of reasons, a person may falsely report that a crime has occurred. The legal concept of *corpus delicti* (body of the crime) establishing the existence of a crime is important, because the prosecution is required to prove the existence of a criminal act.

Identify the Offender

The primary task of the investigator is to identify who committed the crime. The true name of the offender is not required. The identity concept means individualizing a particular person as the offender, not necessarily determining the suspect's true name. Specific identification may not be possible until arrest and fingerprinting. Identification of the offender must be assured in an arrest warrant. The law requires that an arrest warrant contain the name of the accused or, if unknown, some description by which the accused can be identified with reasonable certainty.

Locate and Apprehend the Accused

The Constitution requires the presence of the accused. A criminal suspect has the right to be present at his own criminal trial (*Illinois vs. Allen*, 397 U.S. 337). Most offenders are not actively hiding or avoiding the police. The majority rely on the possibility of not being identified as the offender.

Success in locating fugitives normally depends upon assistance from relatives and associates. Many fugitives are apprehended while committing another criminal act.

Presenting Evidence of Guilt

Assuming an offender can be identified and arrested, evidence of guilt must be provided at trial. The responsibility for collecting such evidence rests with the investigator. Two basic legal principles greatly affect this task.

Legally Admissible Evidence

Information which may logically prove a person guilty of the crime is not necessarily admissible in court.

Proof Beyond a Reasonable Doubt

The prosecution must produce evidence which leads to no other reasonable conclusion than that the accused committed the crime as charged. Evidence sufficient to arrest a suspect may be insufficient to convict.

Recover Property that is Wrongfully Held

In many cases, an investigator has the responsibility for recovering stolen property. More than 90% of all serious crime involves the taking of property from its rightful owner. An object which may not lawfully be possessed is called contraband. The investigative mission may also include suppression and collection of such items.

REASONS FOR INVESTIGATING CRIME

The investigative process has four social goals.

Future Deterrence

The identification and punishment of a criminal offender will deter him from misconduct in the future.

Deterrence of Others

Identification and punishment of an offender may deter others from engaging in similar undesirable activities.

Community Safety

The investigative process promotes public safety by identifying and bringing to court those persons who pose serious threats to the safety of the community because of violent or other antisocial behavior.

Protection of the Innocent

Accurate investigations help ensure that only criminal conduct is punished and that innocent parties will not be subject to prosecution.

LIMITATIONS ON SOLVING CASES

Not all crimes can be solved. Factors over which investigators have little control will greatly affect solvability of a crime. These factors include the following.

Unknown Crime

The commission of some crimes may never be known to police (e.g., the murder and disposal of a derelict).

Unreported Crime

Some crimes are never reported to the police even though someone knows they occurred. This failure to report may be due to personal embarrassment of the victim, the pettiness of the offense, or skepticism concerning the ability of the police to solve the crime.

Lack of Ability to Solve a Crime

Clearance-by-arrest figures indicate that crimes which lack witnesses or in which the property taken cannot be identified have low solution rates.

In crimes against persons, investigators arrest a suspect in almost one-half of the cases. In property based crimes, less than 20% of the cases are cleared by arrest.

Petty Offenses

Other crimes remain unsolved because they are too petty to justify the expense of police resources to identify the offender.

INVESTIGATIVE THEORY AND METHODS

Crime and Information Theory

Every crime generates information signals. Systematic interpretation of these signals can help solve crimes. Types of information include sensory forms, written forms, and physical forms.

- Sensory forms — the outward signs of a criminal event that can be perceived by the five senses
- Written forms — any written material produced by a criminal act
- Physical forms — a physical object which proves, upon evaluation, to be a clue in the investigation

Some information generated by criminal activities may be time critical, meaning that failure to retrieve the information at the right time will cause it to be lost forever.

Types of Evidence

All criminal evidence fits into one of the following categories.

Testimonial Evidence

This is the most common form of evidence. It is usually obtained by interviewing and interrogation. Events which witnesses see, smell, and hear are described to the investigator.

Documentary Evidence

This type of evidence is in the form of writings, and includes official records. Documents differ from other real type evidence in that the contents speak for themselves when read by the investigator.

Physical Evidence

This includes objects that must be evaluated to determine their relevance to the investigation. Physical evidence is obtained through searches at the crime scene and through follow-up procedures such as search warrants.

Uses of Evidence

The above forms of evidence can be used to prove facts in dispute in one of two ways. As direct proof, evidence can be used to prove the facts without any inference or presumption. The sole determination the investigator must make is whether the evidence is true. The two most common types of direct proof are eyewitness testimony (a witness testifies about what he observes) and confession (the suspect admits what he did).

Circumstantial evidence is evidence that can be used to prove a fact in dispute by proving one fact which gives rise to an inference or presumption about the existence of another fact. Examples of circumstantial evidence include motive, the reason a crime was committed (e.g., revenge, hate, or a jilted lover), and opportunity, being in a position to commit the crime.

Other examples of circumstantial evidence include declarations and acts indicative of guilt, including actions on the part of an individual which raise an inference of guilt; preparation for the commission of a crime, i.e., acts prior to the crime which are necessary for its commission; possession of fruits or evidence of crime which raises a presumption that the suspect was connected with the crime; modus operandi (MO), a suspect's pattern or method of operation (because human beings are basically creatures of habit, it is assumed that a successful criminal will perform his act in essentially the same manner each time he commits it); associative evidence, the physical evidence which links a suspect to a crime scene; and criminal potentiality, the possession of the knowledge, skills, tools, or facilities that could be easily adapted to criminal use.

DEVELOPMENT OF A SET OF SUSPECTS

Elimination of Nonsuspects

At the start of a criminal investigation, the suspect of the crime could be anyone. As witnesses are interviewed, physical evidence is collected and analyzed, and other investigative leads are pursued, the number of potential suspects is reduced by eliminating nonsuspects until the focus is upon a single individual. This process is similar to a mathematical set theory.

METHODS OF INVESTIGATION

A criminal investigator is a person who collects facts to accomplish a threefold aim: to identify the guilty party, to locate the guilty party, and to provide evidence of his guilt. The tools of the investigator are referred to as the three I's, namely, information, interrogation, and instrumentation. By applying the three I's, the investigator gathers the facts that are necessary to establish the guilt or innocence of the accused in a criminal trial.

Many crimes are not solvable because there is insufficient evidence. The absence of eyewitnesses, identifiable motives, and physical clues will preclude a solution unless the criminal confesses. Often, the *corpus delicti*, or the fact that the crime was committed, cannot be established, and even a confession is of little value.

To the general public, the term "solving the crime" describes the process of discovering the identity of the suspect and apprehending him. These are only two of the objectives of an investigation, and accomplishing these alone would leave the investigator far short of his ultimate goal of presenting sufficient evidence in court to obtain a conviction.

Information

Information describes the knowledge obtained by the investigator from other people. There are basically two kinds of information. The first type is obtained from regular sources such as public-spirited citizens, company records, and the files of other agencies. The second type, which is of particular interest to the criminal investigator, is the knowledge gathered from cultivated sources such as paid informants, bartenders, cab drivers, former criminals, or friends. Of the three I's, information is the most important because it usually reveals who committed the crime.

Professional crime is usually motivated by economic gain. Larceny, robbery, and burglary share this motive. Assault and homicide are often incidental to crimes of greed or are the product of disputes over divisions of spoils or rights. The crime of greed, when perpetrated by the professional, is most frequently solved by information.

Interrogation

Interrogation is the skillful questioning of witnesses as well as suspects. The success of an interrogation depends on the intelligent selection of informative sources. The effectiveness of interrogation varies with the craft, logic, and psychological insight with which the investigator questions a person who is in possession of information relevant to the case. The term interview means the simple questioning of a person who has no reason to withhold information and is expected to cooperate with the investigator. The term interrogation means the questioning of a suspect or other person who may normally be expected to withhold information concerning the subject under investigation.

The novice investigator often overlooks the most obvious approach to the solution of a crime by asking the suspect if he committed the offense. The guilty person is in possession of most of the information necessary for a successful prosecution, and if he is questioned intelligently, he can usually be induced to talk. A confession, which includes details that could not be known by an innocent party, is a convincing form of proof. If the accused can be induced to talk, the chances of a successful prosecution are usually great.

In the absence of eyewitnesses or an admission by the accused, it is rare that the available circumstantial evidence is strong enough to support a conviction. The physical evidence may place the suspect at the scene or associate him with the weapon but will contribute little to proving malice, motive, intent, the criminality of the act, or matters relating to the state of mind of the suspect.

The investigator should look upon a suspect or a reluctant witness as a person who will provide the desired information if he is questioned with sufficient skill and patience. To acquire the necessary proficiency in interrogation usually takes several years.

Instrumentation

Instrumentation includes the application of instruments and methods of the physical sciences to the detection of crime. Physics offers aids such as microscopes, photography, and optical methods of analysis. Chemistry, biology, and pathology are particularly important in crimes of physical violence. The sciences that apply to crime detection are called criminalistics. Their usefulness is usually associated with physical evidence.

Instrumentation also includes all the technical methods by which the fugitive is traced and the investigation advanced. Fingerprint systems, modus operandi files, lie detectors, communication systems, surveillance equipment, searching apparatus, and other investigative tools are included in the category of instrumentation. Instrumentation is most effective in cases where physical evidence is abundant.

Phases of the Investigation

The objectives of the investigation are divided into three phases. The criminal is identified, he is then traced and located, and the facts proving his guilt are gathered for court presentation.

Identifying the Criminal

The criminal is identified in one or more of the following ways: confession, eyewitness testimony, or circumstantial evidence. Confession is an excellent means of identifying the criminal. However, it must be supported or corroborated by other evidence.

Eye Witnesses

The ideal identification is made by several objective persons who are familiar with the appearance of the accused and who personally witnessed the commission of the crime. When the witness and the accused are strangers, the validity of the identification depends on the ability of the witness to observe and remember the specifics of the accused's appearance. and can be affected by lapse of time between the criminal event and the identification.

Circumstantial Evidence

Identification may be established indirectly by proving facts or circumstances from which, either alone or in connection with additional facts, the identity of the perpetrator can be inferred. Evidence of this nature usually falls into one of the following classes: motive, opportunity, or associative evidence.

Tracing and Locating the Criminal

The question of the criminal's whereabouts is usually solved once he has been identified. Usually, the criminal is not hiding, he is simply unknown. The amateur usually commits a crime because of an exceptional opportunity. It is to his advantage to maintain his normal hang-outs and schedule because flight might betray his guilt. However, in many cases, it is necessary to trace a fugitive who is hiding. Tips, interviews, and information obtained through interrogation will be the most useful means of tracing the fugitive.

Proving Guilt

When the criminal has been identified and is in custody, the investigation is still not complete. It has entered the most difficult phase, that is, gathering the facts to prove the guilt of the accused beyond a reasonable doubt. The fact that the accused may have confessed is not sufficient.

The final test of a criminal investigation is the presentation of evidence in court. The defendant must be identified and associated with the crime scene; competent and credible witnesses must be available; the physical evidence must be appropriately identified, its chain of custody established, and its connection with the case shown; and all this must be presented in an orderly and logical fashion. The complete process of proof must establish the elements of the offense.

Corpus Delicti

Early in the criminal trial, the prosecution must prove the *corpus delicti,* the fact that a crime was committed. The *corpus delicti* is proved by showing that there exists a certain state of facts that form the basis of the criminal act charged, and by proving the existence of a criminal event which caused the state of facts to exist. The state of facts should be established by direct and positive proof, but circumstantial evidence will suffice.

Elements of the Offense

By adding certain facts to the *corpus delicti* concerning the accused, such as his identity, we have the elements of the offense and the necessary sufficient conditions that must be fulfilled before the guilt of the accused has been proven. The three elements of the offense include the form, the accused and the acts alleged, and the intent.

- Form — to acquire knowledge of the elements of criminal offenses, the investigator must study the penal law of the jurisdiction under which he is operating. The elements of an offense will consist of the fact that the accused did or admitted doing the acts as alleged. The circumstances are as specified.
- The accused and the acts alleged (the first general element) — the identity of the accused must be established and his connection with the acts clearly shown. A close causal connection must be established between the accused and the offense. It must be shown that his objective in acting could not have been accomplished without violating the law.
- Intent — the investigation must be designed to develop facts that give evidence of the frame of mind of the accused. Intent is an essential element. Some crimes include the additional element of malice, that is, the intent to do injury to another. This is the mental state of the accused when performing the act. Motive, or that which induces the criminal to act, must be distinguished from intent. Motive may be the desire, while intent is the accomplishment. Motive need not be shown, but intent must always be proved. To establish the motive of revenge, hate, or jealousy, the investigator should look into the history of the victim.

INFORMANTS

An informant is a person who gives information to the investigator. He may do this openly and even offer to be a witness, or he may inform surreptitiously and request to remain anonymous.

A confidential informant is a person who provides an investigator with confidential information concerning a past or projected crime and does not wish to be known as the source of information. The investigator must take special precautions to protect the identity of such an informant because his value as a source is lost on disclosure.

An informant may volunteer information for any number of reasons, such as vanity, civic-mindedness, fear, repentance, avoidance of punishment, gratitude or gain, competition, revenge, jealousy, and money or other material gain.

Protecting the Informant

The investigator should compromise neither himself nor his informant in pursuit of information. He should make no unethical promises or deals and should not undertake commitments which he cannot fulfill. The investigator should safeguard the identity of the informant, first, as a matter of ethical practice and, second, because of the danger of undermining the competence of his source. The identity of an informant should not be disclosed unless absolutely necessary and, then only to the proper authorities. To avoid discovery of the identity of the confidential informer, great care must be exercised when a meeting or communication is planned.

Treatment of the Informant

To aid the investigator, some general rules are provided. The informant should be treated fairly and with consideration regardless of character, education, or occupation.

The investigator should be fair in the fulfillment of all ethical promises which he has made. Any other policy results in distrust and loss of the informant. The informant should not be permitted to take charge of any phase of the investigation. The investigator should always be in control of the investigatiion.

Communicating with the Informant

In order to avoid revealing the status of the informant, the following points should be observed. Meetings should be held at a place other than the investigator's office. The proper name of the informant should not be used in any contacts. Designation by code may be used, and the investigator's organization should not be identified in any communication with the informant. Confidentiality on behalf of the investigator and the client is a requirement in many states.

Evaluating the Informant

The investigator should continually evaluate his informants and form an estimate of reliability. The information received should be tested for consistency by checking against information obtained from other persons. The motives and interests of the informer should be considered in the evaluation.

RULES OF EVIDENCE

The success or failure of a criminal prosecution usually depends upon the evidence presented to the court. Evidence is all the means by which an alleged fact, the truth of which is submitted to scrutiny, is established or disproved. The purpose of evidence is discovery of the truth of the charge. The laws of evidence are the rules governing its admissibility.

Classification

Evidence may be divided into three major classifications. *Direct evidence* is evidence which directly establishes the main fact. *Circumstantial evidence* is evidence which establishes a fact or circumstances from which another fact may be inferred regarding the issue. Where direct evidence is the immediate experience on the part of the witness, the essence of circumstantial evidence is inference. *Real evidence* is comprised of tangible objects introduced at trial to prove a fact. The evidence speaks for itself. It usually requires no explanation, merely identification.

Admissibility

In order to be admissible, evidence must be material and relevant. The rules of evidence are concerned with admissibility of facts and pertinent material, and not with their weight. The weight of the evidence is a question for the judge or jury to determine.

If the fact which the evidence tends to prove is part of an issue in the case, the evidence is material. Evidence which proves something that is not part of the issue is immaterial. To be material, the evidence must significantly affect an issue of the case. Evidence which tends to prove the truth of a fact at issue is called relevant.

Competency of a Witness

A competent witness is one who is eligible to testify. The mental and moral competency of a witness over 13 years of age is presumed. Mental competency refers to the ability to see, recall, and relate. Moral competency implies an understanding of the truth and consequences of a falsehood. A record of convictions of crimes is unrelated to competency but may affect credibility.

Impeachment of a Witness

Impeachment is the discrediting of a witness. A witness may be disqualified by showing lack of mental ability, insufficient maturity, previous convictions of crimes, or a reputation for untruthfulness.

Judicial Notice

Certain types of facts do not need to be proved by the formal presentation of evidence because the court is authorized to recognize their existence without such proof. This recognition is called judicial notice. The general rule prescribes that the court will not require proof of matters of general or common knowledge.

Burden of Proof

No person is required to prove his innocence. The burden of proof for a conviction rests solely with the prosecution. In criminal cases, the prosecution has the burden of proving the accused guilty beyond a reasonable doubt. However, the accused must prove his allegations when making claims regarding alibis, witnesses, self-defense, and insanity.

Presumption

A presumption is a justifiable inference of existence of one fact from the existence of some other fact founded upon their previous connection. Presumptions generally serve the purpose of shifting the burden to the other party to establish contradictory facts. Conclusive presumptions are considered final, unanswerable, and not to be overcome by contradictory evidence. Rebuttable presumptions can be overcome by proof of their falsity.

RULES OF EXCLUSION

Much of the body of the rules of evidence concerns the rules of exclusion. These are the conditions under which evidence will not be received. They are often extremely technical in nature. The rules of exclusion are primarily to control the presentation of evidence in a trial before a jury. The function of the rules is to limit the evidence a witness may present to those things of which he has a direct, sensory knowledge. The witness may relate what he saw, felt, touched, heard, and smelled.

All direct and circumstantial evidence, if material and relevant, is admissible except for opinion evidence, evidence concerning character and reputation, hearsay evidence, privileged communications, and secondary evidence.

Opinion Evidence

The general rule is that opinion evidence is not admissible in a trial. A witness may testify only to facts, not to their effect or result, or to his conclusions or opinions based on the facts. He can bring before the court only those facts which he has observed through the five senses.

Exceptions to the Opinion Rule

Several exceptions are attached to the opinion rule. The following exceptions are recognized.

- Certain simple judgments based immediately on sensory observation are a matter of common practice in the mind of the average man and may be given greater reliability than the word opinion ordinarily describes.
- The court recognizes that the opinion of certain specialists in regard to their specialties should be treated with greater consideration than mere opinion. The lay witness may express an opinion on matters of common observation. These opinions are permitted only concerning subjects of which the average man has considerable experience and knowledge.
- Expert testimony is given by a person skilled in some art, trade, or science to the extent that he possesses information that is not common knowledge. The testimony of an expert can be admitted to matters of a technical nature that require interpretation for the purpose of assisting the judge and jury in arriving at a correct conclusion. Expert testimony is not proof, but is evidence that can be accorded its own credibility and weight by each member of the court.

Evidence Concerning Character and Reputation

As a general rule, testimony concerning a person's character and reputation cannot be introduced for the purpose of raising an inference of guilt. The usual exceptions to this rule are when the defendant introduces evidence of his own good character and reputation to show the probability of innocence. When such testimony has been introduced, the door is open for the prosecutor to introduce evidence concerning those specific areas of character treated in the defendant's testimony. Also previous acts of crimes of the accused may be introduced as evidence if they tend to show that the defendant actually committed the crime for which he is being tried. Some examples are modus operandi, previous acts, identifying evidence, guilty knowledge, or intent.

Hearsay Evidence

Hearsay evidence comes not from the personal knowledge of the witness, but from repetition of what the witness has heard others say. Hearsay applies to oral statements as well as written matter.

Hearsay evidence is excluded because the author of the statement is not present and under oath, and there is no opportunity for cross-examination afforded to the defense.

Exceptions to the Hearsay Rule

There are numerous exceptions to the rule of exclusion of hearsay including confessions; conversations in the defendant's presence; dying declarations; spontaneous exclamations — utterance's concerning the circumstances of a startling event by an individual in a condition of excitement, shock, or surprise which lead to the inference that the exclamations were spontaneous and not the product of deliberation or design (such a statement is admissible when made by anyone who heard it); documentary evidence; and matters of pedigree (family tree).

Privileged Communications

Information obtained in the course of certain confidential relationships will ordinarily not be received into evidence. The court considers such information privileged information. State secrets, police secrets, and personal privileged communications (i.e., attorney–client, clergyman–penitent, and doctor–patient) are examples of privileged communications.

Entrapment

In obtaining evidence of a crime, the investigator must not permit his enthusiasm to involve him in a situation where he becomes the cause of the commission of a crime. The term entrapment is given to an act of a government agent inducing a person to commit a crime not previously contemplated by that person, for the purpose of instituting a criminal prosecution against himself.

PHYSICAL EVIDENCE

Physical evidence may be defined as articles and material found in connection with an investigation which aid in establishing the identity of the suspect and the circumstances under which the crime was committed, or which assist in the discovery of the facts.

Care of Evidence

A few simple rules can guide the investigator in the protection of evidence from the time of its initial discovery at the crime scene until its final appearance in court. A violation of these rules may lead to a partial loss of the value of the evidence and, in some instances, to loss of the case.

Physical evidence can serve several investigative purposes. *Corpus delicti* evidence consists of objects or substances that are an essential part of the body of the crime or tend to establish the fact that a crime has been committed. Associative evidence links the suspects to the crime scene or to the events. Identity evidence is associative evidence which directly establishes the identity of the suspects (i.e., fingerprints or blood).

Before an object can become evidence, it must be recognized by the investigator as having significance with relation to the offense. The ability to recognize and gather valuable physical evidence must be supplemented by knowledge of the correct procedure for caring for evidence from the time of its initial discovery until its ultimate appearance at the trial. In order to introduce physical evidence in a trial, three important factors must be considered: the articles must be properly identified, continuity for chain of custody must be proven, and ompetency must be proven, that is, that the evidence is material and relevant.

Procedure for Gathering Evidence

A systematic procedure for gathering evidence consists of the following steps: protection, collection, identification, preservation, transmission, and disposition.

Chain of Custody

The number of people who handle evidence between the time of commission of an offense and the ultimate disposition of the case should be kept to a minimum. Each transfer of evidence should have a receipt. It is the responsibility of each transferee to ensure that the evidence is accounted for during the time it is in his possession, that it is properly protected, and that there is a record of the names of the people from whom he received it and to whom he delivered it, together with the time and date of such receipt and delivery.

Protection

The protection of physical evidence serves two major purposes. First, certain types of evidence, such as fingerprints, are so fragile in nature that a slight act of carelessness is handling them can destroy their value as clues and remove the possibility of obtaining information from them which would further the investigation. Second, it is necessary that the evidence presented in court be in a condition similar to that in which it was left at the time of the offense. Hence, evidence should be protected from accidental or intentional change during the period of its ultimate disposition at the conclusion of the investigation.

The exercise of a reasonable degree of care will minimize the possibility of alteration from natural causes, negligence and accident, and intentional damage and theft. Where physical evidence is not obtained at the scene, but is obtained from some other source such as an informant or from the possessions of a suspect, the investigator should take the necessary measures to protect it from any extraneous contact. Some risk of damage is incurred in the process of transporting the evidence. Much of the physical evidence collected in a typical criminal case is not found at the scene. Evidence is often delivered to the investigator by a victim or is found in the course of a search of a suspect's possessions. The investigator should improvise methods of collecting evidence until he has the proper equipment. Articles which can be removed and conveniently packaged should be placed in clean containers such as envelopes, pill boxes, large cardboard boxes, and glass containers. Ordinarily, there are two phases of the packing of evidence. The first is the transportation of the evidence from the crime scene (or place where it was obtained) to the office. Second, if the evidence is to be submitted for laboratory examination, it must be appropriately prepared for shipping.

Adequate facilities for storaging evidence should be maintained by an investigative agency. Each instance of deposit and removal of evidence should be recorded by inked entries indicating date the evidence was received; file number of the case; title of case; person or place from whom or at which the evidence was received; person who received the evidence; a complete description of the items including size, color, serial number, or other identifying data; disposition including the name of the person to whom the evidence was delivered or an indication of any disposition other than delivery to a person; and identification by signature of the investigator in control of the evidence.

Preservation

In taking measures against deterioration of evidence, the factors of time and temperature should be given special consideration. Certain types of perishable evidence require special preservatives to maintain their evidentiary value.

Collection

Most of the errors committed in connection with evidence take place in the collection of samples. Insufficient quantity of a sample and failure to supply standards of comparisons and controls are the most common errors. Take an adequate sampling, use standard or known samples (in cases of foreign substances or materials with stained backgrounds, two different samples should be collected, one bearing the stain trace and the other free from stain), and maintain the integrity of the sample (an evidence sample should not come into contact with another sample or with any contaminating matter). The simplest division of the types of evidence is into the two categories portable and fixed.

Identification

Evidence should be properly marked and labeled for identification as it is collected. The importance of this procedure becomes apparent when considering the fact that the investigator may be called to the witness stand many months after the commission of the offense to identify an object in evidence which he collected at the time of the offense.

Marking solid objects of one cubic inch or greater should be done with the initials of the investigator who receives or finds the evidence. The identification should not be placed in an area where inventory traces exist. Whenever practical, articles of evidence should be enclosed in separate containers and sealed so that they cannot be opened without breaking the seal. The investigator's initials (or name) and the date of sealing should be marked on the seal with ink. After the article of evidence is marked and placed in a sealed container, a label should be attached bearing the following information: case number, date and time of finding the article, name and description of the article, location and time of discovery, signature of the investigator who made the discovery, and names of witnesses to the discovery.

ROLE OF THE POLICE

The police are government agents charged with maintaining order and protecting persons from unlawful acts. In most modern democratic nations, the police provide a variety of services to the public including law enforcement (detection of crime and apprehension of criminals; crime prevention (preventive patrol); and maintenance of order, resolution of disputes, among other tasks). In the United States, the police force is the largest and most visible component of the criminal justice system.

Role in Society

The role of police involves law enforcement, maintenance of order, and community service. The police are given a great deal of authority to enforce the law. They can arrest, search, detain, and use force — all actions that disrupt personal freedom — yet democracy requires the police to maintain order to make a free society possible. Thus, policemen must act within the confines of the Constitution and case law while enforcing the laws and satisfying a public that expects protection.

Selection and Training

In selecting police officers, police agencies use a number of criteria to pick the best qualified people. These include a written exam, a background investigation, an oral interview, and a medical exam. More recently, psychological testing has been used to eliminate undesirable candidates.

Virtually all departments have minimum requirements for age, height, weight, and visual acuity. Standards vary for each of these categories. Most departments require a high school diploma as a minimal level of education. The formal training of a police recruit primarily involves the technical aspects of police work and includes the details of criminal law procedures, internal departmental rules, and the care and use of firearms.

Operations

The range of police activities is quite broad. It involves patrol, detective work, traffic control, vice, crime prevention, and special tactical forces.

Patrol

Often called the backbone of police work, the patrol function has three basic components; to assist/answer calls for assistance, to maintain a police presence, and to probe suspicious circumstances.

Detectives

Primarily concerned with law enforcement activities after a crime has been reported, detectives are involved in an investigative function, relying on past criminal history files, laboratory technicians, and forensic scientists for help in apprehending a criminal.

Specialized Operations

These are units set up to deal with particular types of problems. The traffic control function includes accident investigation, traffic direction, and enforcement. Enforcement of vice laws (i.e., prostitution, gambling, or narcotics) is an area that involves undercover work and the use of informants. Juvenile divisions process youth arrests, prepare and present court cases in which juveniles are involved, and often divert juvenile offenders out of the system. The Special Weapons and Tactical units (SWAT) are trained in marksmanship and are equipped with weapons and specialized equipment useful in dealing with snipers, barricaded people, and hostage takers.

GOVERNMENT AGENCIES

The U.S. police establishment operates at several levels. A number of federal law enforcement units exist in different U.S. governmental agencies. The Federal Bureau of Investigation (FBI) is the largest. Other prominent federal units include the Drug Enforcement Agency (DEA), Immigration and Naturalization Service (INS), Secret Service, Internal Revenue Service (IRS), Customs Service, and Bureau of Alcohol, Tobacco, and Firearms (ATF). Along with the FBI, these make up the seven most important federal agencies.

All states except one (Hawaii) have state-level police units with sworn personnel engaging in law enforcement functions. These are classified as State Police (23 states) and State Highway Patrol (26 states). Highway patrols direct their efforts to highways, motor vehicles, and traffic safety functions. State police authority includes jurisdiction over many criminal activities as well as traffic services.

Virtually all of the nation's 3000 counties have their own police forces, most directed by an elected sheriff. Municipal departments constitute the largest number of police agencies in the country. Nearly three-fourths of all of the 650,000 full time police employees work for municipal agencies.

The London Metro Police Department, with its headquarters at Scotland Yard, is the largest agency in Great Britain. The Royal Canadian Mounted Police (RCMP), which is mandated to enforce Canadian federal laws, is the counterpart of the FBI in Canada. The U.S. is a member of the International Criminal Police Organization (INTERPOL), which exchanges information among its police members about criminals who operate in more than one country, whose crimes affect other countries, or who have fled from one country to another to escape prosecution.

NUTS AND BOLTS

In a criminal investigation such as homicide, there are several keys to a successful investigation. The following are offered as helpful guides.

1. Take the time to read and understand the statutes charged in the crime. You cannot defend someone if you do not understand the crimes they are accused of committing.
2. Create a time line; that is, a list of events in chronological order. Time lines have been shown to be successful in many major cases, such as the O.J. Simpson murder trial, and can be beneficial in any criminal case.
3. Interview the defendant. For the investigator to fully understand the case, he must interview the defendant. How else will he know who, what, when, and where events occurred?
4. Conduct background investigations on all the individuals involved in the investigation. You never know what may turn up about someone.
5. Find experts that can help your client. Your expert may be able to shed a different light on the examination of evidence that the prosecution expert overlooked.

CONDUCTING A CRIMINAL INVESTIGATION

An investigator should follow these steps when conducting a criminal investigation.

Interview the attorney and the client.
Obtain evidence. Check police reports, ambulance/medical/hospital records, court transcripts from all proceedings, complaints/indictments, the physical evidence, and check and review statements of prosecution witnesses for inconsistencies.
Visit and dissect crime scene and interview witnesses:
- Police, medical, or hospital personnel
- Factual witnesses
- Circumstantial witnesses
- Alibi witnesses
- Character witnesses
- Expert witnesses — for both sides if possible

Examine and analyze the evidence.

Understand the defense theory — what is the defense attorney attempting to establish or disprove?

COMPONENT METHOD™ OF CRIMINAL DEFENSE INVESTIGATION

The Component Method™ was developed by Brandon A. Perron, a board-certified criminal defense investigator, to provide public defender investigators and private investigators with a formula for conducting successful and comprehensive criminal defense assignments. In his book, *Uncovering Reasonable Doubt: the Component Method — a Comprehensive Guide for the Criminal Defense Investigator,* Perron writes that his method utilizes accepted and proven investigative procedures in an easy-to-follow format. Each component of the investigation process is designed to uncover leads and develop questions leading to the next component. The subsequent components support the investigator's efforts to track leads and answer questions developed in previous components. Utilization of the Component Method™ allows the criminal defense investigator to begin and end an investigation with the knowledge that an effective and professional investigation was completed.

The Component Method™ also performs well as a management tool. Senior investigators maintaining supervisory roles, as well as the responsibility for a significant caseload, are able to utilize the system to monitor the progress of subordinates. Historically, the problems associated with "passing the torch" of experience to entry-level criminal defense investigators have been significant. Adherence to a specific methodology allows the supervisor and field investigator to cultivate and pursue a team approach while still allowing for individual critical and creative thinking. The Component Method™ provides a general course of action while conducting comprehensive assignments. Utilizing this methodology provides an understanding between the supervisor and field investigator regarding expectations and the general course of inquiry.

The six components of criminal defense investigation defining the Component Method™ are investigative case review and analysis; the defendant interview; crime scene examination, diagrams, and photographs; victim/witness background investigations; witness interviews and statements; and the investigation report and testimony. The Component Method™ reinforces the investigator's role as the primary investigator in control of the course of the investigation. Utilization of resources such as forensic experts and specialists to support the primary investigator and his pursuit of the truth is also explored. In addition, the investigator's responsibility as a thinker and strategist is discussed on an intellectual as well as practical level. The Component Method™ maintains that the investigator must be an impartial and objective advocate of the truth. This requires discipline, integrity, and an unwavering sense of honor.

The Component Method™ is intended to be a guide to assist the criminal defense investigator in the course of his investigation. Utilizing the Component Method™ as a reference source for fundamental information, techniques, and skills will enable the criminal defense investigator to perform assigned tasks effectively and efficiently. The Component Method™ can be utilized as a preliminary or comprehensive plan. The individual components can be limited or expanded to conform to the specific needs of each case. Proper execution of the Component Method™ allows the criminal defense investigator to submit his final report with the confidence that a thorough investigation has been accomplished. The report of investigation documenting the criminal defense investigator's findings will allow defense counsel to develop a defense strategy based upon facts and not abstract theory or conjecture. Subsequently, defense counsel may request additional investigation based upon initial findings, investigative recommendations, or supplemental discovery.

Uncovering Reasonable Doubt: the Component Method is a complete and definitive resource that can be purchased from the Criminal Defense Investigation Training Council on their Web site at www.defenseinvestigator.com. Anyone interested in specializing in criminal defense investigation should become a member of the organization and undergo the recommended training.

DEATH INVESTIGATIONS CHECK LIST

THE INVESTIGATION:
The primary issues to be investigated are identification of the subject, and the circumstances surrounding the causing the death, providing the death itself has been established.

A point to be kept in mind is motive. If there is a beneficiary to an insurance policy, there is a financial motive for fraud.

SUBJECT IDENTIFICATION & BENEFICIARY IDENTIFICATION:
By the time the investigator is instructed the subject's body has been buried, cremated, or otherwise disposed of, and is not available to view or examine. Identification is therefore based on identifying details; primarily the full name and/or photographs.

The investigator througout the course of the investigation should attmept ot examine and copy all available documents containing full name, identity card number, passport details, date of birth, place of birth, previous name/s, marital status and spouse details, permanent address, previous address. I recommend throughout the investigation to have a camera with color film, and to always photograph any document containing a photograph of the subject.

During interviews, ask for a detailed description of the subject or a photograph, which is usually available from relatives and friends.

The beneficiary must also be identified based on documentation, and (Beneficiaries Relationship to the Deceased).

Beneficiaries Relationship to the Deceased - Prove based on document - if widow/widower, then photograph I.D. card which states husband/wife, or marriage certificate, or other document to prove relationship as stated in policy of insurance.

DOCUMENTATION:
Documentation is important in a death investigation, however, it should always confirm information obtained from other sources. This is important, as in many foreign countries original and certified copies can be purchased due to corruption. Originals are sought whenever possible. When not possible, certified (signed and/or stamped) copies, notarized by a public notary or certified by an attorney as "identical to original". Wherever possible, notarizations, certifications, and/or translations should be effected at the American Embassy.

Documents of any type should always be put into a plastic sleeve or envelope for protection. Never write on, mark, or alter documents or photgraphs in any manner.

Page 1

Figure 8.1 Death investigations checklist

On receiving any type of document and/or document certification always note the full name, position, department, and other relative details of the provider. If documents are nto received from the source, always go to the issuing authority to confirm the document's authenticity. When photographing, always make note of the subject, location, date, and time.

DOCUMENTS:

This is by no means a complete listing of documents. Depending on the country, circumstances surrounding the death, and other factors, some documents will not be available. For example, in Syria and most Arab countries, the profession of private investigation is illegal, and only police are permitted to investigate. It is therefore understood that an operative in Syria would not legally be in a position to obtain a police report.

- Death Certificate
- Hospital Records
- Medical Examiner Reports
- Police Reports
- Cemetery — Forms, Documents, Burial Register. In addition, photographs of the cemetery, burial site, and any inscriptions on the subject's tombstone.
- Funeral Home — Forms, Documents, Register, Other.
- Newspaper Articles and/or Obituaries
- Ambulance Forms, Reports, Bills, Payment Receipts

INTERVIEWS:

Interviews and statements are a primary source of information. Often a familiy member, friend, neighbor, or business associate will divulge information pertinent to the investigation not apparent in any documentation.

Topics which should be covered during all interviews would include the subject's identifying details, circumstances surrounding the death, cause of death, health, marital and family status, civil and criminal court status, and financial status.

Sources to interview should include:
- Individual/s who identified the body; when, where and how the body was identified, and who was present at the time.
- Physican who pronounced the death.
- Relatives
- Friends
- Neighbors
- Business Associates
- Previous husbands or wives
- Cemetery Care Taker/s
- Funeral Home Employee/s

Page 2

Figure 8.1 (continued) Death investigations checklist

APPENDIX 1

THE GRAND JURY

An institution of legal and historical stature, the grand jury existed in England for some 700 years and was inherited during the early colonial period as a feature of the American legal system. Its repressive potential is disguised by a structure that would appear to be the opposite of arbitrary government action. The grand jury is composed of ordinary citizens who must grant their approval before another citizen can be prosecuted for a serious crime. The Supreme Court maintains that protection against arbitrary prosecution is the main function of the grand jury.

Grand jurors return indictments for criminal offenses and presentments, which differ from indictments in that the grand jurors themselves can initiate the investigation and can offer any evidence they personally possess. Presentments signify noncriminal complaints usually against public officials, but criminal charges can only be brought under an indictment prepared by the prosecutor.

After 1776, the grand jury was included in many state constitutions, and the Fifth Amendment assured that any serious federal criminal charge would be screened by a grand jury. The federal constitution's provisions were adopted because many colonists were fearful of creating a powerful central government that could arbitrarily use the criminal process against its political enemies. The grand jury never fully developed into a consistent neutral institution, carefully sifting the evidence, and providing protection only for the innocent. It frequently reflects local or prevailing prejudices in its decision to indict or not to indict.

Grand juries at both state and federal levels operate best when dealing with routine matters. This is because a prosecutor has no interest in bringing weak cases before the grand jury. With strong cases, the jury's function will be to confirm a reasonable discretionary judgment.

The scope of state grand juries is much broader than that of the federal grand jury because the former are authorized to investigate any criminal matter that violates the common law including such offenses as murder, burglary, and robbery. Because the federal grand jury can indict only for federal offenses, it had a limited scope of operations until Congress recently passed more federal statutes.

It was generally thought that federal grand juries were empowered to investigate and indict only for statutory offenses. Today, they have much more latitude in conducting criminal investigations. Previously, they were not as accessible to pressure applied by lay citizens regarding the operation of the federal government. Today, the federal grand jury has become an instrument for prosecution by a centralized government administration.

The history of the grand jury shows that grand jurors will support indictments against the enemies of the government if the public from which they are drawn perceives the enemies the same way.

All kinds of evidence that cannot be used at trial are permitted into the grand jury (e.g., hearsay), but the absence of procedural protection is more extensive than that. The constitutional prohibition against double jeopardy bars the government from giving the defendant a second sentence for the same offense. This is not the case in the grand jury. None of the Miranda or other constitutional safeguards are afforded any grand jury witness, not even the prime suspect, should he be called as a witness. The witness has an obligation to testify before the grand jury to answer all questions except to those which he makes a specific timely objection on Fifth Amendment grounds or on the basis of some other well established privilege (i.e., attorney–client).

In this sense, the subpoena is similar to that issued to require a witness to testify at a criminal trial or similar to an arrest and the beginning of a police interrogation. The courts have also said that a witness or suspect must respond to questions to which he cannot invoke the Fifth Amendment because he may be a source of evidence on other offenders.

In addition to the limits on a witness Fifth Amendment rights, Fourth Amendment rights may also not be respected in the grand jury. A witness may be forced to produce evidence even though the prosecutor offers no proof that it is linked to criminal activity. The witness can also be the subject of an unlawful invasion of privacy in which the police have broken into his house without a warrant and still be made to answer questions on the basis of what the police may have seen or taken.

In general, a witness is not afforded the legal rights provided to a defendant because at that point he is not being charged with a crime. Even a witness whom the prosecutor seeks to indict does not have the protections that must be afforded to defendants in interrogation by the prosecutor or the police outside the grand jury.

Attorneys are barred from the grand jury room because the proceedings are nonadversarial and the witness is deemed to have the maximum protection that he needs because he can invoke his right not to give testimony that is incriminating. Other negative consequences result from the fact that contempt of grand jury proceedings is technically civil and not criminal. Thus, a witness does not have the right to a jury trial, because no criminal offense has been committed. Rather, the court is using "remedial" measures to deal with the obstruction of its process by the witness. Under civil contempt, the witness can secure his own release any time he chooses to testify. Because the imprisonment is not for a fixed and definite term, it is not a criminal sentence. Thus, a second refusal to testify becomes a new occasion for the application of the nonpunitive measure, and the witness has the ability to avoid imprisonment by testifying.

A defendant cannot object to evidence seized in violation of the constitutional rights of another person. A defendant can only object to evidence seized in violation of his own constitutional rights. However, the Supreme Court, by the slimmest margin (5 to 4), held that a witness could not be convicted of contempt when the government refused to deny that its line of questioning was based on illegal wiretapping (*U.S. vs. Gelbhart*, 408 U.S. 41).

Because the grand jury is designed for, and may even be limited to, investigations of criminal activity, it should primarily be an instrument used to look at past events in gathering evidence to prove a prior offense. It can also look at any current ongoing criminal schemes; it is not in theory or purpose supposed to be a data or intelligence gathering mechanism, especially if the government's only purpose is to monitor the activities of its lawful citizens.

Open and unlimited probing is possible because most rules of evidence that normally protect a defendant in a criminal trial, such as barring hearsay or irrelevant and prejudicial evidence, need not be observed in grand jury proceedings. The court's explanation for the lack of limitations on these probings is that the grand jury is engaged primarily in protecting the innocent, a notion belied by history.

Congress strengthened the statutory basis for potential harassment of witnesses by enacting portions of the Organized Crime Control Act (OCCA) of 1970 that regulates granting witnesses immunity from prosecution when giving grand jury testimony. The 1970 legislation established "use immunity," which provides much less protection to the individual. The prosecution is only barred from using the witness' testimony in later attempts to develop evidence to prove any offense the witness is charged with, but the witness may be prosecuted on offenses about which he can be compelled to testify. The Supreme Court has said that the use of immunity statutes does not violate the Constitution.

9

INSURANCE AND ARSON INVESTIGATION

INSURANCE

What is Insurance?

Insurance is a social service that combines the risks of individuals into a group using funds contributed by members of the group to pay for losses. The essence of the insurance concept is that it is a social device that involves the accumulation of funds. It also involves a group of risks that each member of the group transfers to the entire group.

Purpose of Insurance

The fundamental purpose of insurance is to reduce the uncertainty caused by potential loss. This is accomplished by spreading the economic burden of losses among members of the group. Insurance does not prevent the loss from happening, but it relieves victims of the financial burden created by the loss.

What Do Insurers Do?

Insurers estimate the possible size of a loss, estimate the probability of a loss, spread the risk by pooling, accumulate funds to pay for losses, retain only what they can bear, re-insure what they cannot bear, and refuse to assume risks for inadequate premiums.

How Insurance Works

Risk assumption — Insurance is created by an insurer who assumes financial risks transferred to it by its insured members. Most insurance contracts are expressed in terms of money, although some indemnify those insured by providing services (e.g., a life insurance contract obligates the insurer to pay a specified amount upon the death of the insured).

A *liability policy* not only requires the insurer to pay money on behalf of the insured, but also to provide legal and investigative services needed when the event insured against occurs.

Health insurance policies require medical and hospital services for the insured when he is sick or injured. Whether the insurer meets its obligation with money or services, the burden it assumes is financial.

Risk

Why is the insurer better able to assume a financial risk than the insured? The fundamental difference between the insurer and insured lies in predicting future events. You must predict what will happen to you as an individual, but the insurer makes predictions with regard to all insured clients as a part of large groups of risk. Therefore, the insurer can make more accurate predictions with regard to possible risks. The reason for this difference lies in the concept of pooling. By pooling its risks, the insurer is able to improve its predictions. This, in turn, results in smaller deviations from expectations. Pooling changes the nature of the risks and improves predictability.

An insurer assumes risks with the expectation of substituting average losses for actual losses, thereby reducing uncertainty for the insured. Because the funds that are used to pay for losses suffered by the insured are collected in advance, it is critical that the insurer be able to predict losses accurately. The premium fee for assuming risks is based on accurate predictions and the predictions, are based on probable estimates.

Probability

A person who says that there is a great or little chance that something will or will not happen is thinking in terms of probability. Probability is a measure of the chance of an occurrence. When there is no possibility of an occurrence, the probability is zero. When an occurrence is certain to take place, the probability is one. Probability may be expressed as a fraction or as a percentage. If there are two possible outcomes, each of which is probable, the probability is one out of two, or 50%. The numerator is the number of favorable or the unfavorable happenings, while the denominator is the number of all possibilities.

Deductive and Inductive Reasoning

Estimates of probability may be made through deductive or inductive reasoning or a combination of both methods. The deductive approach involves determining all factors that can influence the outcome and using logical reasoning to arrive at an estimate of the actual outcome. When the number of possible outcomes is known, the probability of any one is one minus the sum of the probability of all others.

Sometimes it is impossible to calculate every factor that will determine an outcome. In that case, the deductive process will be unreliable. When this happens, probability estimates of outcomes must be made through the inductive process. The inductive process involves observing what has actually happened in the past and assuming (predicting) that the same will happen in the future if the same conditions prevail.

The Law of Large Numbers

The law of large numbers states that the greater the number of trials, the more nearly the experience will approximate the underlying true probability. If we flip a coin for an indefinite length of time, the distribution of heads and tails will approach 50% as the number of trials increases. In other words, actual results tend to equal expected (probable) results as the number of independent events increase.

Insurance companies are affected by the law of large numbers in two ways. In order for accurate estimates of the probability of an occurrence to be made, insurance companies must consider very large numbers of cases. After an estimate of probability is made, it can be used as the basis for predicting future experience.

Investigators should be familiar with the term credibility, which indicates the degree of reliability that can be placed on the use of past experience to predict what will happen in the future.

Adverse Selection

Adverse selection is the tendency of people who have a greater probability of loss than the average to seek insurance. It can result in much greater losses for the insurer, and insurers try to prevent this by applicant screening.

Ideal Requirements for Insurability

The ideal risks for the insurance company would be as follows. The potential loss would be significant, but the probability would not be high, making insurance economically feasible. The probability of loss would be predictable. There would be a large number of similar exposure units.

Losses which occur would be fortuitous (a matter of chance). Losses would be definite in time and place. A catastrophe would not occur.

Re-insurance

Re-insurance is an agreement by which an insurance company transfers all or a portion of its risks under a contract to another insurance company. This protects the insurance company from all or part of the losses of its policyholders. In this process, the company transferring the risk is called the "ceding company" and the insurance company assuming the risk is the "re-insurer." When there is a claim on the policy, the re-insurer is liable to the ceding company, not the insured. The amount which the re-insurer is willing to assume is called its retention.

The main purpose of re-insurance is that the ceding company wants to protect itself against losses in individual cases beyond a specific sum. Re-insurance is significant to the buyer for three reasons. First, re-insurance spreads the risks and increases the financial stability of the insurers. Re-insurance reduces the costs of the buyer and seller by being able to place the policy through another company. It helps small insurance companies stay in business, thereby increasing competition in the industry. Without re-insurance, small companies would find it much more difficult to compete with large companies.

Insurance Contracts

The process of transferring a risk to an insurance company is commonly referred to as buying insurance. In effect, the insured buys a promise from the insurer. The written agreement between the two parties is called a policy or policy contract. The policy states in detail the legal rights and duties of the parties to the contract.

Basic Legal Prinicples

Indemnity

This means that the insurer agrees to pay for no more than the actual loss suffered by the insured. The purpose of the indemnity concept is to restore the insured to the same economic position that he had prior to the loss but not improve that position.

Insurable Interest

If the occurrence of risks such as fire or auto collision will cause loss to a person or firm that is the subject of a risk, an insurable interest exists.

Examples of insurable interests include ownership of property; the mortgage holder of property, building, or auto; a secured creditor; a tenant with a long term lease; and your own life or the life of another (based on relationship or other financial consideration).

Subrogation

This is a contract right that gives the insurance company claim against third parties as a result of a loss for which the insurer paid. The actual cash value of a loss equals replacement cost less depreciation. When the insurer is considering accepting a risk, it must have accurate information to make a good decision. The person who makes the decision about insurability is called an underwriter, and the decision-making process is known as underwriting.

Warranties

Absolutely true statements made by the insured to the insurer about the risk. Based on warranties, the insurance company may make a favorable decision to insure the risk. Once the warranties are put into a contract, they have to be strictly true, not approximately true. This places the burden of absolute accuracy on the insured.

Representations

Representations are statements made by the insured for the purpose of inducing the insurer to enter into the contract. If the insured misrepresents a material fact, the insurer can void the contract or refuse to pay a later claim.

Concealment

Concealment occurs when an applicant for insurance fails to reveal material facts about the risk which only he knows. The insurer cannot be held to the contract if the insured concealed important and material information.

Waiver

Waiver is the intentional giving up a known right. In order to waive a right, the person must first know and understand that he has the right and then give it up intentionally.

Estoppels

Estoppels prevent a person from alleging or denying a fact when he has previously admitted the contrary. For example, an insurance company cannot waive a right and then assert it later. Once an agent waives the right to refuse coverage to the applicant, that company is estopped from denying liability for losses that occur while the contract is in force.

Requirements of Insurance Contracts

The relationship between the insurer and the insured is spelled out in the insurance policy. The policy is a contract between two parties. A contract is an agreement enforceable by civil law. If an agreement is to be considered a valid and enforceable contract, it must have a legal purpose. There must be an offer and acceptance, which are essential to the creation of an agreement. An agreement is reached when one party makes an offer and the other party accepts.

Another requirement is consideration. The premium payment that the insured makes and the insurer's promise to pay losses are the consideration of the contract.

The final essential element for a contract is that the parties must be competent. Examples of incompetent parties would be insane or intoxicated persons or someone under legal age.

A contract is therefore an agreement between two or more competent parties, supported by a consideration and having for its purpose a legal objective.

Components of the Insurance Contract

A *statement* is a declaration that the insured makes to identify himself. Statements also give information about the risk and the premium.

A *binder* is a temporary contract to provide coverage until the policy is issued by the agent or company.

The *period of coverage* is period of time during which coverage applies.

A *named peril policy* provides protection against loss caused by the perils listed.

An *all-risk policy* provides protection against loss except loss caused by the excluded perils. The policy names the proximate cause, that is, the actual cause of the loss. It also names exclusions. In order to know what the policy covers, you must know what it does not cover. This includes the excluded perils, excluded property, and excluded losses. Generally, whether the policy is all-risk or named peril, the coverage it provides cannot be determined without first examining the exclusions.

Conditions describe the duties of the parties to the contract. Failure of one party to perform relieves the other party of their obligation.

Riders and *endorsements* are two terms with the same meaning. Riders are used with life and health policies, while endorsements are used with property and liability policies. These articles make a change in the contract to which they are attached. They may increase or decrease the coverage, change the premium, make a correction, or make any number of other changes.

Negligence

Every form of personal, business, or professional activity is exposed to loss because of liability claims based on negligence. If a negligent act or omission interferes with the rights of any individual, the party responsible for the negligence is liable for the damages to the injured party. To meet the legal consequences of all these exposures, liability insurance has become essential.

During recent years, great losses from fraudulent claims have resulted from alleged injuries. An invasion of the legal rights of others is the legal basis for liability claims. Legal rights impose responsibilities and obligations such as not invading privacy or property, or not creating an unreasonable risk or actual harm to others.

The invasion of such legal rights is a legal wrong. A wrong may be criminal (public) and may be an injury involving the public at large and punishable by the government. A wrong may also be civil (private) and may be based upon the concept of a tort. This is a wrong independent of contract (e.g., assault, fraud, liable, and slander). It may also be based on a contract and may involve legal wrongs when implied warranties are involved or contract obligations are breached.

The government takes action with respect to crimes, but civil injuries are remedied by court action instituted by the injured party. In a civil suit, the remedy is usually the award of monetary damages to the injured party. Liability insurance focuses on civil wrongs, and in particular, on torts. Of greater importance to the investigator are torts based on negligence (intentional acts or omissions).

Requirements for Negligence Liability

Negligence is the failure to exercise the proper degree of care required by circumstances. Requirements for negligence liability include a legal duty, a wrong, a proximate relationship between the wrong and the injury, an injury or damage, and foreseeability. Four forms of negligence are contributory negligence, comparative negligence, presumed negligence, and imputed negligence.

Comparative Negligence

Anyone who was so negligent in an act as to contribute to his own injuries or damage cannot recover losses from another party for these injuries. Comparative negligence modifies the common law doctrine of contributory negligence, because only a very slight degree of negligence on the part of the injured person would bar recovery. A majority of the states have now passed statutes which say that contributory negligence shall not bar recovery for damages. However, damages shall be reduced by the court in proportion to the amount of negligence attributed to the person injured.

Presumed Negligence

In order to establish a case, the claimant must show a failure to exercise reasonable care. This is known as presumed negligence. The burden of proof is on the claimant. In certain cases, presumed negligence may be assumed from the facts. The legal doctrine which applies, *res ipsa loquitur* (the thing speaks for itself), establishes a prima facie case of negligence. This doctrine operates when an accident causes an injury if the instrument would not normally cause injury without negligence, especially if inspection and use of the instrument is within exclusive control of the party to be held liable, or if the party to be held liable has superior knowledge of the cause of the accident and the injured party is unable to prove negligence. In the case of presumed negligence, there cannot be contributory negligence, and the accident must be of such a nature that injury would not ordinarily occur without negligence.

Imputed Negligence

Not only is a person responsible for his own acts, but he may be held liable for the acts of others (e.g., employers and supervisors, landlords, parents, and auto owners). This is called imputed negligence. Vicarious liability includes those liability situations when the responsible person is not present.

Insurance Adjusting

Loss Payment

The basic function of insurance adjusting is loss payment. There are five types of insurance adjusters. Agents settle small losses and help in many other losses depending on the type of insurance. Staff adjusters are full time salary employees of the insurer and are active in fields such as automobile losses. Independent adjusters represent various insurers on some losses. Adjustment bureaus regularly represent many insurers and are especially useful in fire, wind, and storm damages. Public adjusters are hired by the insured to settle difficult claims.

Liability Insurance Clauses

The adjustment of liability claims differs from the adjustment of direct damage claims in that the claimant is not the insured. A liability claim carries with it a basic element of conflict with respect to the claim because one person has caused someone else either property damages or personal injury. The extent of a claim for damage to property is measured by the amount of loss to the property owner. Most persons insure their homes, auto, or other property before insuring their life and health.

Types of Insurance

Individual Health Insurance

Health insurance applies to those forms of insurance that provide protection against the financial impact of illness or injury. Health insurance has as its purpose the payment of benefits for loss of income and expenses arising from illness and injury. Not only is loss of time from the productive enterprise a source of loss to the insured, but the cost of care and necessary medical attention adds to the amount of the loss.

Health insurance provides protection against loss of time or earning power, and added medical expense. Health insurance losses fall into two major categories: cost of medical care and loss of income.

An exception in a health insurance policy is a provision where coverage for a specified hazard is entirely eliminated.

Fire Insurance

The purpose of fire insurance is to indemnify a named insured in the event that certain described property is destroyed by the peril of fire. The basic parts of the standard fire policy are the declaration statement as to the parties, period, property, perils, and premiums of the contract. The insuring agreement (the heart of the contract), which includes exceptions and termination, property and location, personal nature, actual cash value, perils insured against (proximate losses caused by hostile fires and lightning), and assignments. The conditions and exclusions explain the control terms as to concealment or fraud, excluded property and peril suspension, added provisions and cancellations, and loss provisions (including mortgage, interest, the pro rata liability clause notice, and proof of loss, appraisal, repair, and subrogation rights).

Insurable Interest

The element of insurable interest makes a fire contract a contract of indemnity. When the nature of an interest or a liability in regard to property is such that the insured would suffer financially if a loss occurs, then insurable interest exists.

Perils Insured Against

The standard fire contract is a named perils or specified perils contract. It covers only the listed perils in the contract. The perils are "fire, lightning, and by removal from the premises articles endangered by the perils insured against in this policy." The courts have defined fire as "oxidation which is so rapid as to produce either a flame or a glow. Fire is always caused by combustion, but combustion does not always cause fire."

Excluded Perils

Excluded perils include hostile or war-like actions; insurrections, rebellion, revolution, civil war, or action by government authority in defense of such occurrences; theft; and neglect to prevent further damage by the insured.

Direct Loss

The insuring agreement specifies that to be covered under a policy, a loss must be a direct loss. This has been interpreted by the court to mean that fire must be the immediate or proximate cause of the loss as opposed to the remote cause.

Examples of losses included in the term direct or proximate are loss or damage caused by smoke or heat from a hostile fire, damage by water or other materials used to extinguish the fire, damage caused by the firefighters, and unavoidable exposure at or following the fire. The proximate cause is held to be the efficient cause, that is, the cause that sets intervening agencies into motion.

Assignment

The transfer of the legal right of interest in an insurance contract to another person is called assignment. Under the terms of the fire insurance contract, an assignment is valid only with the written consent of the insurer.

Misrepresentation

The entire policy shall be void if either before or after a loss, the insured willfully conceals or misrepresents any material facts or circumstances concerning the fire insurance, the property insured, or its interest, or in the case of any fraud by the insured. False statements, concealment of salvage, falsification of records, false testimony given under oath, and false written proofs of loss are also fraud and will void the policy. Certain types of property are excluded from coverage of the policy, such as accounts, bills, currency, deeds, evidence of death, money, or securities, unless specified in writing in the policy.

General Liability Insurance

There are two basic types of general liability insurance: bodily injury, sickness or disease, and property damage (the physical injury or destruction of tangible property).

The insured's duties in the event of occurrence, claim, or suit are a combination of the three requirements for notice of accident (in writing, as soon as possible, explaining the circumstances), assistance, and the cooperation of the insured (for settlement, in hearings and trials, etc).

The treatment of a patient by a medical practitioner (i.e., surgeon, physician, or dentist) with a lack of care or professional skill and with injurious results constitutes malpractice. Liability for personal injury in such instances is known as professional malpractice liability. Professional liability insurance has been extended into fields to cover losses where monetary damages (as opposed to bodily injury) are a consequence of the negligent professional services of the insured. Architects, accountants, attorneys, insurance brokers, real estate agents, stock brokers, consultants, private investigators, and many others can be held liable for their professional errors or mistakes.

Employer's Liability and Worker's Compensation

Worker's Compensation is a combination of social and private insurance. Worker's Compensation laws in all states require employers to provide certain benefits for occupational injuries and diseases. The statutory requirements in most states can be fulfilled by the employer purchasing Worker's Compensation insurance from a private insurer or by qualifying as a self-insurer.

Occupational disability because of work injuries is a peril of great importance to business and society. The solution to the financial burden of disability because of employment is a dual one: many of the state government's requirements for Worker's Compensation insurance are met by insurance contracts purchased from private insurers.

The theory behind Worker's Compensation legislation completely disregards the old idea of liability based on negligence. Rather, the theory is based upon the idea that the cost of occupational injuries and many diseases will be charged to the employer regardless of liability and then passed on to the consumer as part of the cost of doing business.

Worker's Compensation laws make the employer responsible for indemnity to the disabled employee without regard to the matter of fault or negligence. The amount of indemnity to apply in particular cases is predetermined by law, although it does not equal the full income the employee would have received. The laws relate payments to injuries and sickness; if these are fatal, death benefits are provided for the employee's dependents. Medical expenses, income, and rehabilitation benefits are included.

Based upon employee's rights, there are two types of Worker's Compensation laws: compulsory and elective. Almost all states (except three) are compulsory, which means that all employers to whom the laws apply are required to pay for work injuries or diseases as specified under the compensation statutes.

Compensation is provided for all injuries and many diseases arising out of and occurring in the course of employment. No benefits under compensation acts are allowed when it is proved that the injury was caused by the willful acts of the employee or by intoxication while on duty. Willful misconduct can be defined as any act or service performed by an employee who willfully disobeys all the safety rules of which he has full knowledge.

Occupational disability includes both injury and disease. Occupational diseases are defined as diseases peculiar to the occupation in which the employee is engaged and caused in excess of the ordinary hazards of employment. In the case of occupational disease, there must be a cause-and-effect relationship between the occupation and the disease as well as frequency and regularity of the occurrence of the disease in a particular occupation. The basic types of benefits include medical expenses, income benefits, death benefits, and rehabilitation benefits.

Financing of Benefits

The employer has the direct responsibility for paying benefits to qualified workers in accordance with Worker's Compensation laws. Insurance may be provided either through a state fund or by private insurers authorized by the particular state to conduct the business of Worker's Compensation. More than two million persons per year are hurt at work in the United States, according to the National Safety Council, which estimates annual compensation payments and production losses at $16 billion, including 240 million work days in time lost annually.

In the majority of states, the funding is regulated by the state but accomplished through nonstate insurance or self-insurance means. Regulation of the law is under the Division of Worker's Compensation of the Department of Labor and Employment Security. In the state of Florida, Statute 440.9 states that every employer shall be liable for and shall secure the payment to his employee of the compensation payable. Compensation shall be payable regardless of fault or cause for injury. The liability of an employer shall be exclusive and in place of all other liability of such employer to any third party and to the employee or legal representative thereof, and to anyone otherwise entitled to recover damages from such employer on account of injury or death.

Employer and Employees

The law defines an employer as one who must secure benefits for an employee at any level, including the state, political subdivision, public, and quasi public corporation. Employment includes private employment with three or more employees and all other jobs without regard to the number of employees. An employee is defined as a person engaged in any employment under any appointment or contract of hire including aliens and minors. The term employee does not include independent contractors, casual laborers, and volunteers.

Injuries Covered

Benefits are payable to any employee who suffers an injury. Injury is defined to be personal injury or death by accident arising out of and in the course of employment and such diseases or infection that result from such injury. Accident means any unexpected or unusual event or result that happens suddenly. It does not include mental or nervous injury owing to fright, excitement, disability, or death due to the accidental aggravation of a venereal disease or of a disease owing to the habitual use of alcohol or drugs. Occupational diseases are treated as injury by accident. An employee is not entitled to compensation if the injury is caused by the employee's intoxication or wrongful use of drugs, or willful intention to injure or kill one's self or another.

Benefits

Benefits may include payment of medical expenses, compensation for disability, and death benefits. The obligation of the employer is to furnish any required medical treatment, care, and attendance under a qualified physician, nurse, or hospital. There is no dollar limitation upon this obligation. Disability means incapacity because of the injury to earn, in the same or any other employment, the wages that the employee was receiving at the time of the injury. Compensation is for such wage loss or difference. The measure used to determine disability benefits is the average weekly wage of the employee at the time of the injury.

The Occupational Safety and Health Act (OSHA)

Job safety for employees became the top Worker's Compensation issue with the passage of OSHA in 1970. The federal law took considerable control of work safety regulations from the state and mandated that the state must put into effect rules at least as strict as the federal standards in order to maintain jurisdiction for work safety conditions of its employees. The penalties that can be imposed (fines of $10,000 or more) and investigative role of OSHA are extensive, including inspections by 1400 officers across the United States.

Automobile Insurance Coverage

Basic coverage for automobile insurance usually includes liability, medical payments, uninsured motorist coverage, and physical damage protection. Basic policy forms are standardized for insuring individuals and businesses. Automobiles are classified as private passenger, commercial, public, dealers, or miscellaneous.

Three viewpoints are relevant in determining the need for auto insurance. These include society, automobile motorists, and the injured victim of an auto accident. More than 87% of all traffic accidents are reported to involve improper driving. In fatal accidents, speeding is a factor in 33% and drinking drivers are a factor in about 50%. Approximately 50% of all states have compulsory laws requiring insurance. All owners of cars are required to produce an insurance policy before registration and plates will be issued. In essence, this makes financial responsibility mandatory in order to own and use a car.

The basic parts of the personal auto policy (PAP) illustrate the readable contract trend with personalizing and simplifying the format. This includes declarations and contains basic data about insurance, automobiles, types of coverage, and the insuring agreement and definitions. Following are the six major parts of basic insurance policy coverage.

> **Part A: Liability** — this is the most important coverage and includes bodily injury and property damage in a single limit of liability; defense and supplementary payments for defense investigation and bonds, covered persons insured, which are carefully defined, and policy limits and other insurance conditions which are explained.

Part B: Medical payments — to cover the cost of medical services for the named insured, relatives, and anyone else in the insured's car. This does not apply to pedestrians or occupants of buildings or other vehicles into which an insured vehicle may crash. This coverage is quite broad for all reasonable medical expenses including surgical, dental, ambulance, hospital, nursing, as well as funeral expenses.

Part C: Uninsured motorists — by definition, an uninsured automobile is one which is not covered by bodily injury, liability, policy, or bond at the time of the accident. It also includes other cars for which no insurance applies, such as stolen or improperly registered autos. The insurance applies whether or not the injury caused by the uninsured motorist results from an occupied automobile. Many unowned autos are operated by the named insured; therefore, only the named insured and relatives are covered.

Part D: Damage to your own auto — physical damage coverage for your own car; collision losses may be excluded if the collision peril is not shown in the declaration section as covered. Towing and labor costs may be included. The importance of physical damage insurance is related to the value of the car and to the need and ability of the owner to repair or replace the car if damaged.

- Collision coverage — reimburses you for damage to your car sustained by reason of a collision with another car or with any other object, moveable or fixed. Collision is one of the most common situations in which subrogation may apply. When you collect your damages from the insurer, they take your right and sue the responsible party to recover the payment made to you. Collision insurance is also a common illustration of the use of the deductible to avoid high cost and administrative expenses of frequent small collisions and losses. The normal collision deductible provides there shall be no liability on the part of the insurer unless the loss exceeds the named amount (usually $50, $100, $250, up to $1000).

- Comprehensive coverage — comprehensive physical damage is virtually an all-risk physical damage coverage. Protection is provided for direct and accidental loss or damage to your car and its normal equipment. Basically, it is used to pay for a loss caused by something other than collision to the insured auto. Among the perils covered are fire, theft, larceny, wind, storm, earthquake, flood, vandalism, etc.

Part E: Conditions in order to collect under the contract — these are the conditions that the insured must fulfill following an accident or loss. Failure to fulfill these conditions could result in the insurer not having to pay the loss. When an accident occurs, you must provide (written) notice to the insurer as soon as possible. You should give the insurer notice as to whether you were liable. You must comply with state requirements for reporting accidents. You should make a duplicate copy on any written reports and provide it to your insurer. You must provide assistance and coop-eration to the insurer in the settlement or adjustment of a suit.

Part F: General provisions — cancellation provisions require the insurer to give the policy holder 10 days notice in writing, with a proportional return of the unearned premium to the end of the policy.

Assigned Risk

In addition to the basic financial responsibility law or the compulsory auto liability insurance law, assigned risk plans have been developed to meet the problems of rejected risks. Provisions have been made by the state for taking care of higher risk drivers by distributing individual rejected risks among all insurers. Assigned risks are rotated among the different insurers in proportion to the business that each insurer writes in the state.

No-Fault Insurance Plans

The fundamental basis for a no-fault system is that it abolishes tort liability in car accidents, with drivers or owners accepting responsibility for some or all of the losses sustained by pedestrians or by occupants of their own vehicle in return for immunity from liability for those losses. The need for establishing fault before loss payments are made is eliminated by such plans. The insured motorist has the right to collect directly from his own insurer. Vehicle damage liability does not come under most no-fault (more correctly called "payment without fault") laws.

Uninsured Motorist

Uninsured motorist (UM) coverage is a form of insurance to pay compen-satory damages for bodily injuries under one's own policy for amounts which would otherwise have been recovered from the liability insurance of another — either an uninsured motorist or an under-insured motorist, one who carries liability limits that are lower than the insured's damage. Determination of damages may be decided through an agreement between the insured and the UM insurer, or by arbitration proceedings between the insured and the UM insurer. If the UM insurer refuses to arbitrate, then coverage will be determined by joint suit against the other party and the UM insurer.

The law permits the insurer to limit UM coverage in several ways. Ordinarily under some states' laws, the coverage provided for two or more vehicles may be added together to determine the limit of coverage available to an injured person in any one accident. This practice is called stacking. However, the company is permitted to issue an endorsement which provides that limits may not be stacked. In other words, two or more coverages may not be added together. If the insured agrees to this limitation and signs the endorsement, the company must issue the policy at a reduced premium.

The coverage available to a person injured while occupying a motor vehicle is the same as the coverage available to that motor vehicle.

An injured person is entitled to the highest limits of UM coverage that apply to any vehicle for which he is a named insured or family member of an insured if that injured person is occupying a motor vehicle that he does not own or is not owned by a member of his family who resides in the same household. This coverage is in excess of coverage on the vehicle the injured person is occupying. Coverage applies to the named insured and family members in their own vehicles, any other vehicle, and as pedestrians. Other persons are covered only while occupying the named insured's vehicle. Under UM coverage, the injury must be caused by a vehicle that does not have liability insurance or liability insurance with a limit that is lower than the insured's damages. Additionally, coverage applies if the other party's liability insurer is broke or if the other vehicle is a hit-and-run and cannot be identified. Limits of coverage are offered the same way as auto liability coverage.

Automobile Insurance Claims

If someone commits a tort, negligence, liability, fraud, etc. he can be held responsible for damages in a court of law. There are three types of damages in auto accidents.

1. Special damages are the out-of-pocket losses incurred by the insured party. They usually include such items as medical bills, lost wages, and property damage, as well as funeral expenses.
2. General damages refer to real losses which cannot be measured and where no bill or receipt or loss of money can be demonstrated. Concepts of pain and suffering and loss of use come under this heading. The accident victim is compensated for the pain and suffering that he experienced or will continue to experience from the accident. Loss of use attempts to compensate for the loss of a body part or function.

3. Punitive damages are designed to punish wrong-doers who intentionally engage in misconduct. Sometimes punitive damages are also awarded for gross negligence, which is negligence so horrible that it deserves punishment.

Plaintiffs usually hire attorneys on a contingency basis, which means they will pay the attorney a percentage of the amount of money the attorney collects on their behalf. There are costs such as paying court reporters for depositions and court filing fees. Clients are responsible for these costs regardless of who wins the law suit. Another expense is medical treatment and doctor testimony.

Liability Coverage: Driving outside the standard of care required of operators of automobiles is considered careless driving. Negligence requires more than mere speeding. In order for negligence to arise, there must be some form of actual harm or damages which directly result from bad driving. If your negligent driving causes death or injury to another, you must pay monetary damages that result from the accident.

Medical Payments: Two classes of people are entitled to receive benefits, the insured and family members of the insured in the same household, and any passenger injured in the covered auto.

Collision and Comprehensive: Collision protection is subject to a deductible. Vehicles that are damaged or stolen may be covered in one of two ways to be decided by the insurance company. The insurance company may pay the amount necessary to repair the vehicle or replace the property lost, or it may pay the cash value of the stolen or damaged property (i.e., totaling the car). Collision coverage is not dependent on fault. Your collision policy will pay benefits for vehicles you do not own.

Government Regulation of Insurance

Insurance has characteristics that set it apart from tangible goods industries and account for the special interest in government regulation. Insurance is a commodity that people pay for in advance whose benefits are reaped in the future, often by someone entirely different than the insured. Insurance is affected by a complex agreement that few lay people understand and by which the insurer could achieve a great and unfair advantage if inclined to do so.

Insurance costs are unknown at the time the premium is agreed to, and there exists a temptation for unregulated insurers to charge too little or too much. Charging too little results in removing the security that the insured thought was being purchased; charging too much results in unwarranted profits to the insurer. Insurance is regulated to control abuses in the industry. The insurer is the manager of the policyholder's funds.

The management of other people's money, particularly by one of the largest industries in the nation, requires regulation because of the temptation for the illegal use of these funds.

As in any business, abuses of power and violations of public trust occur in the insurance industry. These include failure by the insurer to live up to contract provisions, drawing up contracts that are misleading and appear to offer benefits they really do not cover, refusal to pay legitimate claims, improper investments of policyholder's funds, false advertising, and many others. Some state insurance departments maintain offices to handle customer complaints against insurers and their agents and to effect settlement of disputes without formal court action. Most insured clients do not find it practical to sue under insurance contracts unless the sums involved are relatively large. Abuses in insurance have been such that major investigations of the insurance industry have taken place, many of which resulted in reformed legislation that is currently reflected in the regulatory environment.

Insurance traditionally has been regulated by the individual states. Each state has an insurance department and an insurance commissioner who has several specific duties. The National Association of Insurance Commissioners proposed a bill which later became known as the McCarron–Ferguson Act. This act declared that it was the intent of Congress that state regulation of insurance should continue and the Federal Trade Commercial Act would apply to insurance, but only to the extent that the individual states do not regulate insurance.

Federal regulation of insurance is carried out by many different federal agencies. The Federal Insurance Administration (FIA), which administers several government insurance programs, was involved in an extensive federal investigation of Worker's Compensation and no-fault automobile insurance. The Federal Trade Commission (FTC) regulates insurance commission mergers, mail-order advertising, and other trade practices affecting competition. Regulations of the Securities and Exchange Commission (SEC) governed the insurance of variable annuities and some aspects of insurer accounting practices. The U.S. Department of Labor (DOL) influences coverage for coal miners with black lung disease. It also operates with OSHA, which affects risk management practices. The DOL together with the IRS administrates the Employee's Retirement Income Securities Act (ERISA), under which the operations of private pension plans, many of which are insured, are carefully regulated.

FIRE AND ARSON INVESTIGATION

Arson has been identified as the fastest growing type of crime in America today. National statistics show that when measured on a cost-per-incident basis, arson is the most expensive crime committed. Less than 20% of arson arrests result in convictions. Arson for profit is responsible for approximately one-half of all fire related property damage in America. Insurance fraud is the most common target for an arson-for-profit scheme. Insurance fraud has been referred to as "the modern way to refinance."

The primary role of the fire investigator, as with any criminal investigator, is to determine the truth. In seeking the truth, the investigator must complete a post-fire examination of the structure or vehicle that is the subject of a suspicious fire and determine the cause and origin of the fire. Interviews must be conducted, evidence collected, and comprehensive reports of all findings must be prepared. If, during the initial stages of inquiry, actions indicating criminal conduct or evidence of criminality are uncovered, the fire investigator must immediately shift to his secondary role to identify and move against those responsible.

Investigative Checklist

An investigative checklist is used to ensure that every pertinent fact about the case has been identified. It is also used to identify those cases to be assigned to case management. Finally, it may serve as a supervisory tool in evaluating an investigator's performance and in the assignment of additional cases based on case load. An investigative checklist should include the following types of data.

Identity of the assigned investigator
Victim identification
Suspect/defendant information
Detailed information relating to the incident including time, address, identity of the fire chief, first firefighter, and police officer at the scene, etc.
Classification of the offense (e.g., arson, occupied or abandoned, etc.), arson/homicide
Detailed information relating to the investigative procedures and steps taken (e.g., photos, sketches, canvas, etc.)
Identification of physical evidence and followup procedures (e.g., laboratory analysis results)
Identification relating to prosecution of the case (e.g., grand jury, assigned prosecutor)
Witness information

Types of data to be determined from related reports would include a chronological listing of incidents; date and time; classification, including whether residential or commercial, occupied or abandoned, forest or brush; point of origin (where fire started); type of accelerant used or suspected; classification of damage; and death or other injury.

Commercial Fires

It is important to start gathering information as soon as possible after the fire. The investigator should ask to see business records and tax returns and should check the answers to the following questions.

What is the relationship among owners of the business?

What are the names and addresses of the suppliers?

What is the dollar value of the business on a weekly basis?

What are the owner's gross earnings per week?

Does the owner have any financial interest in other businesses nearby?

Were the storeroom and shelves checked for merchandise that is the most expensive?

Were the suppliers asked if bills were overdue or if checks were bouncing?

How much money is owed to suppliers?

What is the name of the owner's insurance company and the extent of the coverage?

Has the owner applied to the Small Business Administration or any other agency for a loan?

Is the business protected by an alarm? What time of day is it turned on? Was it on or off at the time of the fire? Was it circumvented?

Was the sprinkler system working?

Are any flammable liquids kept on the premises? What type and why?

The elimination of all possible accidental causes of the fire is one of the most difficult duties of the fire investigator. Unless all of the relevant accidental causes can be eliminated, the fire must be declared accidental, the presence of direct evidence to the contrary not withstanding.

Vehicular Fires

The overwhelming majority of vehicular fires are intentionally set. The primary motive seems to be economic. For the most part, automobile arsonists are "selling" their cars to the insurance company.

Investigation of a vehicular fire requires a two-part approach. The first involves the completion of a post-fire automotive salvage examination to determine the cause and origin of the fire. The second, which hinges upon the determination made during the first, involves interviewing and/or interrogating the vehicle's owner. The purpose of the interview is to elicit statements that would implicate the vehicle's owner.

Suspicious Indicators

Any fire in which fire damage extends "bumper-to-bumper" should be considered highly suspicious. A fire that accidentally starts in one of the three interior compartments will tend to stay in that compartment. A person intending to burn his car may remove good tires and replace them with old or worthless tires before starting the fire.

The presence of either separate (distinct) or primary and secondary burn patterns on the vehicle's exterior is highly suggestive of intentional damage. If the ignition key is found in the debris, this fact alone may be enough to rebut a statement or claim that the vehicle had been stolen. Any time the driver of a vehicle sustains or is treated for burns associated with a vehicular fire that is under investigation, the investigator should attempt to obtain the doctor's or other official diagnosis regarding the patient, the degree, and the location of such burns.

Arson

Arson is traditionally defined as the willful and malicious burning of the dwelling of another. Today, statutes define arson as the willful burning or destruction by explosion of a structure of another, the personal property of another, or for the property of arson if done for the purpose of defrauding an insurer. The main task of the investigator is to determine whether a fire or explosion was intentionally (incendiary) set or accidental. The investigation and prosecution of incendiary acts is similar to investigation of other crimes.

Most fires are started by accident. If an accidental cause cannot be readily established, the investigator should assume that the fire was set on purpose. Unintentional destruction of property, while not punishable as a crime, may still be the object of legal liability in a civil suit. It is estimated that 150,000 fires are set intentionally each year. Property losses from incendiary fires account for more than 10% of all fire losses and also account for about $2 billion per year. Thus, annual dollar losses from arson are higher than losses from any other crime except larceny. In addition, approximately 1000 people die each year because of incendiary fires.

Crimes of arson have a very low solution rate, approximately 10%. Similarly, the percentage of conviction for those arrested is quite low. A large percentage of intentional burnings is the work of juveniles who generally are not processed through the normal criminal justice system.

Juveniles are usually not required to make restitution for the loss. No reliable data exists on recidivism (repeat rate) for arson.

Motives of Arson Offenders

As with other serious crimes, arson is committed for a reason. Determining the motive of the offender may help to narrow the suspect list. There are several basic motives for arson fires. The first motive is fraud. Because the cost of fire insurance is slight in comparison to the value of the property covered, a fire to collect from the insurer may be profitable to the owner. Fires to defraud insurers are sometimes used to dispose of buildings that are not easily marketable, to recover cash for obsolete machinery, or to liquidate business enterprises.

Fire may be the result of political activities. In the 1960s, this was a frequent motive for the massive burnings which accompanied inner city riots. The likelihood of political motive depends upon the social and political situation in the community in question.

Because an intense fire and the means to control it (water, chemicals, etc.) often alter or destroy property, arson maybe used to cover up the commission of another crime. Similiar to any destructive act, an incendiary fire may be a means of gaining revenge (spite) against an enemy. Anger, jealousy, and ill will toward another may be sufficient motivation for the destruction of property by arson.

On occasion, an arsonist may set a fire in order to attract attention to himself. Often, this takes the form of setting a fire and then saving lives or property by reporting the blaze in hope of recognition (vanity) for such actions. Pyromania may also be a motive, and finally, a large percentage of incendiary fires are set by vandals and juveniles seeking a thrill. Many small fires are started for this reason.

Procedures for Investigating Arson

Incendiary fires can pose many problems for the investigator. The following steps should be observed when conducting an arson investigation. During the fire, observe the scene to the extent possible. The arson investigator should respond to all major fires at commercial establishments, because observations during the fire are often as valuable as a later search of the property. The investigator should be alert to the following characteristics.

Location, Extent, and Direction of Flames

Focusing on the specific area of the fire and direction of spread helps pinpoint the point of origin of the fire. Due to variations in construction materials and wind direction, fires rarely burn equally in all directions. The existence of two or more separate blazes may indicate an intentional fire.

Color and Height of Flames

Observing the appearance of flames at the fire will aid in determining the intensity of the fire and the presence of accelerants. Flame color is a function of temperature which, in turn, depends upon the nature of the fuel. Flame color will range from red to yellow to blue to white, depending on the temperature. The caloric value of certain substances causes them to emit a distinctive color when burned.

Color of the Smoke

Fire produces a vapor which contains minute particles of the fuel being burned. The color of this vapor, commonly called smoke, can indicate the nature of the burning fuel. Thick black smoke indicates a heavy carbon fuel such as gasoline, oil, tar, or paint. These substances are popular accelerants for arsonists. Gray or white smoke is evidence of burning dry wood. Gray smoke with blowing ash is evidence of loosely packed organic matter such as straw or waste paper. Yellow or brown smoke is evidence of nitrate compounds, such as farm fertilizer.

Odors at the Scene

Odors at the scene may also provide evidentiary clues. Kerosene and gasoline have distinctive odors. The investigator should also be familiar with the odor given off by other popular accelerants such as as lacquer and paint thinner.

Weather Conditions

Weather conditions at the site should be noted by the investigator. Warm, humid days are more conducive to spontaneous combustion and the likelihood of an accidental fire than hot days. The local weather bureau can provide information concerning relative humidity at the time of the fire. Wind direction and intensity should also be noted.

Witnesses

The investigator should identify and, if time permits, interview any witnesses at the fire scene. He should be alert to anyone who appears out of place at the scene because of dress, mannerisms, or the time of day.

Photographs of Fire

If practical, the investigator should take color photographs of the fire scene. Such pictures report flame color, wind direction, smoke color, and other visual details. Attempts should be made to record the fire's pattern and progress with photos. Photographs of onlookers should be made, especially if pyromania appears to be a possible motive. If the arson investigator arrives at the scene after the fire has been extinguished, he may contact local newspapers or television stations to determine whether they photographed the scene.

Photographs of Scene

After the fire is exetinguished, the charred remnants of the fire should be photographed. Because most remains from the fire have a dark color, greater exposure time and aperture openings are generally required to obtain high contrast quality photos.

Search of Scene

A search of a fire scene should be conducted by the fire investigator. The investigator should dress for safety and comfort in clothing that will resist smut and water. Boots, raincoat, gloves, and safety helmet are mandatory. The search should be conducted after the fire is extinguished but before any clean-up efforts begin. The investigator should be alert to the possibility that fire personnel may have accidentally moved or destroyed evidence while fighting the fire.

Normally a fire area is treated as a zone, so the search begins at the exterior and moves toward the interior. During the exterior search, the investigator should be especially alert to evidence of outside activity indicating an incendiary fire such as footprints or empty gas containers. During the interior search, the point of origin of the fire should be the focus. Any pertinent evidence such as soot, ashes, charred paper, and matches should be collected. The presence of vapors from possible accelerants may be detected by using a sniffer (an instrument for detecting hydrocarbon gases that is commercially available). Vapors and chemically saturated lumber should be collected at the scene.

Point of Origin of the Fire

The key to determining whether a fire was intentionally set requires identifying its point of origin. The point of origin is most likely to yield evidence on the cause of the fire. The presence of an igniter, an unnatural kindling agent, or a delay fuse is strong evidence of an incendiary fire.

All fires must be started in some manner. If nonaccidental igniters such as matches, candles, or cigarette lighters are found, arson is likely. Because a high temperature must be reached before most substances will burn, a strong sustained flame is often necessary to cause standard building materials to ignite. An arsonist may use kindling or accelerant to start the fire. The presence of unnatural kindling agents would indicate arson.

The point of origin of a fire may be found in several ways. The firefighters should be interviewed because they may have observed the point of ignition while fighting the fire. Observation based on recognized principles of combustion may elicit clues. A fire burns in a triangular pattern away from its source in the direction of prevailing air currents. The point of origin is generally on the windward tip of this triangle.

Fire burns upwards rapidly, but downwards slowly. Thus, the lowest level of destruction will be near the source of the fire. Where a roof or floors have collapsed, the investigator must separate fallen debris from stationary burned objects in order to determine the point of origin. The point of origin tends to be the place at which maximum destruction and charring has occurred. This general principle may vary under special circumstances.

Once the crime scene has been searched, the investigator should complete his investigation as follows.

Interview of Owner

A comprehensive interview of the owner and/or occupants of the structure involved should be conducted. In particular, the investigator should try to determine where the owner was at the time of the fire, the size of the loss, whether the victim had any enemies, whether the victim had received threats to his life or property, and whether the victim had experienced vandalism to his property in the past.

Insurer

The investigator should find out the name of the owner's insurance carrier. The insurance company should be contacted to determine the scope and value of the owner's coverage and any limitations on payment. Arson may be likely if the building is over-insured, if the insurance coverage in the owner's policy is greater than the market value of the building and its contents, or if the investigator discovers the existence of co-insurance (two or more policies covering the same risk). Normally, the owner can lawfully collect on only one policy.

The Property Insurance Loss Register (PILR) is a cross-check of policy holders and claimants maintained by the insurance industry to detect fraudulent schemes such as collection on the same property from several companies, phony ownerships, false claims, and people who suffer fire losses more than once.

Cause of Fire

The physical cause of the fire should be determined by the investigator. This is a necessary element in proving arson because an incendiary act is required. The cause of the fire may be obvious once the investigator examines the point of origin. The cause may be established by examining possible accidental causes and either accepting or eliminating them as the cause of the fire. If an accidental source is not apparent but no evidence of an intentional fire is located, one must assume the fire is of unknown origin until the cause can be established by proof outside the scene.

Motive for Setting the Fire

Establishing a motive may aid in developing a suspect list. Evidence of elaborate preparations (i.e., gasoline soaked walls, delayed ignition) indicate fraud as a motive. Minor preparations may indicate spite or revenge as a motive. Use of combustible materials normally at the scene (i.e., rags, newspapers) would indicate vandalism. The presence of pornographic material at the scene strongly suggests pyromania.

APPENDIX 1

LIABILITY CLAIMS INVESTIGATION

Liability is a present or potential duty, debt, obligation or responsibility to pay or do something, which may arise out of a contract, tort, statute or otherwise. The rules for investigating liability involving questions of negligence are basically:

1. What is the duty owed?
2. Was there a breach of that duty?
3. Was that the proximate cause of the resulting damage?
4. Was the other party guilty of any contributing negligence?

Duty Owed

Duty is that which a person is obliged to do or refrain from doing, a responsibility which arises from the unique relationship between particular parties, or what one should do, based on the probability or foreseeability of injury to a party. Statutes affect "duty owed," and the claims adjuster should be aware of the laws that affect duty. A very important law is the statute of limitations. Duty owed is also limited or affected by exculpatory notices, contracts and sub-contracts, leases and subleases, declarations of condominiums, indemnity agreements, certificates of insurance, rental forms, warranties, guarantees, covenants, deeds, bills of lading, etc.

Proximate Cause

The proximate cause is something which produces a result, and without which a result could not have occurred; it is any original event, which in natural unbroken sequence produces a particular foreseeable result, without which the result would not have occurred. The question to resolve is whether the alleged breach of duty is the proximate cause of the resulting damage. The adjuster must be prepared to show who (if not the insured) or what was the proximate cause of the loss.

Contributory Negligence

As mentioned earlier, contributory negligence is the failure to exercise care by a plaintiff, which contributed to the plaintiff's injury. Even though a defendant may have been negligent, in the majority of jurisdictions, contributory negligence will bar a recovery by the plaintiff.

Any claim, when properly investigated, can result in decreased exposure for the primary culprit. Implied reasonable assumption of risk is a defense when the injured party had knowledge of the risk or danger. Establishing the status of the party will help in this process, for example, determining whether the claimant was an invitee or a trespasser).

No-Fault Law

The no-fault law intended to eliminate contributory negligence. A loophole in the law called "tort threshold" made it necessary to incur at least one thousand dollars of legal expenses before a tort claim could be made.

10

DOMESTIC INVESTIGATIONS

Domestic investigations are the least favorite and most dangerous of all investigations conducted by private investigators. They are the basis of most of the stereotyping of investigators found in the media, movies, and television: the private investigator jumps out of the bushes to photograph the cheating spouse. That stereotype does not portray private investigators in the most favorable light. Does that mean that domestic investigations are not worthwhile? Absolutely not! They are very necessary and a major source of income for many investigators.

Some investigators will not do domestic investigations that have the purpose of "catching" the cheating spouse. In some states, such as Florida, divorces are no-fault — there does not have to be an allegation of wrongdoing to obtain the dissolution of the marriage. Therefore, it is not necessary to determine if one of the parties is unfaithful. However, it is human nature for the parties to want to know if their spouse is committing adultery.

There are many other types of domestic investigations including determination of custody, locating children abducted by their noncustodial parent, and asset investigations of the parties involved. In the custody issue investigation, the role of the investigator is to document the fitness of one or both of the parties to obtain primary custody. The location of abducted children usually revolves around the location of the missing parent. The asset investigation is designed to uncover all assets, hidden and obvious, of one or both of the parties. All of these investigations result in evidence being presented on behalf of one of the marital parties to support his/her position.

Like most of the investigations that have been described in this book, domestic investigations are, in essence, legal investigations designed to produce testimony at some point in time that will be used in court by one or both parties. See Figure 10.1 for a sample data report. The investigator may be called upon to refute or confirm claims on a financial statement, or present testimony and evidence regarding the suitability of a parent seeking custody of a child.

One area that sometimes requires investigation in domestic matters is the duration of residence. Most states have a residency requirement, usually six months, before a party may file for divorce. Therefore, among the issues that the investigator must clarify is whether both parties have resided in the state for the required time period. This may be accomplished this by determining ownership of property within the state, date that a driver's license was issued in the state, date that the party registered to vote, whether there has been extensive travel outside the state by either party, and any other proof that can be identified by the investigator.

State law usually requires some ratio for the distribution of assets, called the equitable distribution of assets. In some states, the requirement is that assets be "equitably distributed" between the parties. However, in order to equitably distribute the assets, both sides need to determine what assets to be divided. This is where the investigator can help one party determine the existence of the marital assets of the other party. This becomes most significant in the case of a nonworking wife in a marriage with a "wheeler dealer" husband who may attempt to hide assets. In particular, the court takes into consideration any intentional dissipation, waste, depletion, or destruction of marital assets that has taken place after the filing of the Petition for Dissolution (divorce). Things the investigator may be looking for include spending sprees (clothes buying, cruises, etc.), unexplained major expenditures, consistent expenditures for things such as controlled substances, excessive alcohol consumption, and gambling, as well as unexplained missing or stolen assets.

In some states, the court must decide whether alimony is appropriate and, if so, what the appropriate award should be. Factors that the court considers include the standard of living established during the marriage; duration of the marriage; ages and physical and emotional condition of each party; financial resources of each party; contributions of each party to the marriage including but not limited to services rendered as a homemaker, child care, education, and career building of the other party; and all sources of income available to either party. In many cases, the role of the investigator would include investigation of the physical and emotional condition of each party (i.e., is the party who is claiming emotional and physical damage able to conduct normal activities such as tennis, jogging, night life, etc.?), discovering the financial resources of each party and standard of living of each party while the divorce is pending, and any proof of marital infidelity, especially where it has resulted in substantial expenditures (such as jewelry, trips, cars, living accommodations, flowers, etc.).

The issues that the court must consider in determining the best interests of the children are, which parent is more likely to allow the children frequent and continuing contact with the nonresident parent; the love, affection, and emotional ties existing between the parent and the children; the capacity and disposition of the parents to provide the children with food, clothing, medical care, and other remedial care as needed; the length of time the child has lived in a stable, satisfactory environment; and the desirability of maintaining this continuity. Other issues include permanence, as a family unit, of the existing or custodial home, the moral fitness of a parent, the mental and physical health of the parents, and the home, school, and community records of the children. The reasonable preference of the children, if they are of sufficient age and intelligence in the opinion of the court, the willingness and ability of each parent to facilitate and encourage a close and continuing parent/child relationship between the children and the other parent, and any other factor considered by the court to be relevant would also be included in determining the best interest of the children.

Obviously, the role of the investigator in providing evidence related to any of the aforementioned issues could determine the outcome in a custody case. The investigator may be required to conduct surveillance of the child and parent together, determine the moral fitness, and/or mental and physical stability of the parent, investigate school records, and check any other records that may exist with respect to the children.

In conclusion, not only do the issues described previously need to be investigated by a qualified individual, there is a recent development within the area of domestic or family law. In the new age of the private investigator, people are not conducting background checks of their dates. According to a recent article in *The New York Times*, "…many single women in this age of risky romance are hiring private detectives to check the backgrounds of their suitors."

It is the choice of each investigator working in the field to decide whether domestic investigations are appropriate for his/her agency. Based upon my personal experience, they are very lucrative, however, they can be heart-wrenching. One is dealing with heightened emotions on both sides and, therefore, there may be danger not only to the investigator but to any of the parties involved.

MATRIMONIAL PRELIMINARY DATA REPORT

FILE#_____DATE:_____TYPE OF CASE:_____

CLIENT: _____TEL #:_____

ADDRESS:_____

BUSINESS ADDRESS_____TEL
#:_____
OTHER PERSON TO CALL:_____TEL
#:_____
VEHICLE DESCRIPTION:_____

SUBJECT:_____MAIDEN
NAME:_____AGE:_____DOB:_____
                                                          DISTING. FEAT.
HT:_____WT:_____RACE:_____HAIR:_____EYES:_____BUILD:_____GLASSES:_____FACIAL HAIR:_____

RELATIONSHIP TO CLIENT:_____YEARS
MARRIED:_____
OF CHILDREN:_____ NAME(S)/AGE/SEX:_____

HOME ADDRESS:_____TEL
#:_____LISTED/UNLISTED:_____
DIRECTIONS:_____

VEHICLE DESCRIPTION:_____CAR TEL
#:_____
OCCUPATION & ADDRESS:_____TEL #:_____

SS#_____CREDIT CARDS:_____

PARENTS NM/ADD:_____FRIEND(S):_____

ADDITIONAL INFORMATION: _____
_____

OTHER PARTY INFORMATION: _____AGE:_____DOB:_____
                                                          DISTING. FEAT.
HT:____WT:____RACE:____HAIR:_____EYES:_____BUILD:_____GLASSES:____FACIAL HAIR:_____

MARITAL STATUS:_____NAME OF SPOUSE:_____#/NM
/CHILDREN:_____
HOME ADDRESS:_____TEL
#:_____LISTED/UNLISTED:_____
DIRECTIONS:_____

VEHICLE DESCRIPTION:_____CAR TEL
#:_____
OCCUPATION & ADDRESS:_____TEL #:_____

ADDITIONAL INFORMATION:_____

REFERRED BY:_____RECD BY:_____ATTORNEY/TELE:_____

FINANCIAL ARRANGMENTS:_____RETAINER CONTRACT:_____

Figure 10.1 Sample data report.

11

DUE DILIGENCE AND BACKGROUND INVESTIGATIONS

Employee theft cost American business $60 billion.

Over 20% of lawsuits for premises liability result in awards of over $1 million.

Approximately 75% of people who perpetuate white collar crime in a given company did so at a prior company.

These are three very good reasons for corporate America to conduct background investigations prior to acquiring new companies or businesses, hiring new employees or executives, or investing time and money in a new venture. It is a good idea to know who you are doing business with before you become involved. See Figure 11.1 for a sample background checklist. These are some of the reasons that investigators who specialize in background investigations can be very busy. Let us look at some of the different types of investigations that can be conducted.

DUE DILIGENCE INVESTIGATIONS

A growing number of court decisions have held that an employer *can be held liable* for the criminal actions and negligent behavior of an employee. In particular, the failure of an employer to thoroughly investigate employees background can result in a judgment against the company.

Checking the asset quality of a prospective business partner or senior level employee before a deal is consummated or an individual is hired may prevent future losses or lawsuits for businesses and financial institutions. Checking the asset quality of an individual involves research to determine if there are any "skeletons" or problems in their background that could financially impact the company following the acquisition.

A due diligence investigation is, by nature, a search for negatives. In contrast to investigations conducted in the context of litigation, due diligence inquiries are usually conducted in a friendly, cooperative atmosphere of an anticipated business deal. This does not mean that the investigative agency should not do a thorough search for the facts. Regardless of whether the deal succeeds or fails, the investigation will be scrutinized to determine appropriateness and fairness.

In addition to pursuing leads suggested by public records research, an investigator should seek information from the company's competitors, labor unions, and other potentially knowledgeable groups, after weighing the obvious risks involved. Former high-level employees of companies are often premium sources of adverse information about the company that is would not otherwise be disclosed.

When hired to conduct a due diligence investigation, the recommended steps to be taken are to first establish ground rules and strategies. Cost (budget) and time frame (deadlines) are two factors that must be considered with or without the subject's (target's) knowledge. Obtain a signed release. Next, interview key executives and other important personnel within the company. The investigator should search public records, including local newspapers and business publications, secondary magazines and industry newsletters, and federal, state, and local courthouses for civil suits, liens, judgments, divorces, criminal cases, UCC filings, bankruptcies, property tax assessments, land records, mortgages, and so on. The investigator should also check courts where federal agencies file suits such as U.S. district courts, tax courts, bankruptcy, and so on. He may check filings by companies and individuals at relevant federal agencies (SEC, FTC, FCC, etc.) as well as public materials generated by those agencies; that is, complaints or consent decrees, incorporation and other filings with the secretary of state including articles of incorporation, amendments, and annual reports; motor vehicle and driving records; the Better Business Bureau, consumer protection agencies, and the state attorney general's offices for complaints or other indications of investigations; state and local licensing agencies; and other related state and/or federal agencies with regulatory oversight responsibility (i.e., the state comptroller's office).

To complete the profile, check the target business. The investigator needs to identify significant business, partnership, or ownership interests of parties involved, verify business and banking references, and identify and interview anyone who has left senior management within the last five years and include reason for departure and current whereabouts. Identify the principals and ascertain if they have been arrested or convicted of crimes, are the target of any criminal investigation, the target of an SEC (or other regulatory agency) litigation, signatory, or consent decree, or any other type of administrative investigation. Check for personal or corporate bankruptcy; determine whether or not the individual was a plaintiff or defendant in any civil litigation, including suits alleging fraud or misrepresentations, and if the individual was the subject of any suits brought by creditors or any government agency.

Follow up the investigations and write a final report. Include the interview of the sources. The investigator selectively interviews persons who have been identified as having adverse information about the target. It is important to determine the motives of these people for providing the information. Re-interview key personnel to clarify problems or discrepancies that have arisen during the course of the investigation. It is important to carefully report interim results to the client and stress that only preliminary conclusions are to be drawn. Credibility of sources providing critical information must be carefully assessed. The interim report should contain a recommendation as to what extent each item of information should be relied upon.

The final report of the investigation should include a review of all investigative steps taken, the overall results, and an assessment of the credibility of the information gathered. If further investigation is needed, it should be described in detail with a plan for implementation.

BUSINESS BACKGROUND INVESTIGATION

Before entering into any business deal or partnership arrangement or hiring a senior executive, it is strongly recommended that a thorough background investigation be conducted. This may well prevent future losses and lawsuits. In fact, the success of the business may depend on this investigation.

Any history of personal litigation, including small and large suits; management track record; personal and business credit problems; criminal history including convictions, association with organized crime offenders, drug traffickers, and white collar criminals; and material misrepresentation, conflict of interest, or character defects all need to be investigated.

APPLICANT BACKGROUND INVESTIGATION

The chief reason for a background or screening investigation is to establish that the applicant has truthfully related all relevant information. Prospective employers have the option of rejecting applicants for employment at their own discretion except for reasons dealing with ethnic or racial origins, religious preferences, age or sex, or further requirements of the National Labor Relations Act. Similar state laws say that there shall be no discrimination based on workers' rights to collective bargaining. The employer is otherwise unregulated with respect to reasons for rejecting employment applications. Many kinds of personal behavior and activities might be considered unsuitable for a prospective employee. See Figure 11.2 for a sample background investigation form.

The employer has an obligation to be prudent and reasonable in the selection of an employee. The company has no information about the applicant until he applies, and then it has only what the applicant provides. To make a decision about potential employment on the basis of such information alone would be foolish. No testing will confirm statements about past history or any other information unless the employer goes beyond the applicant's own statements. A variety of relationships arise with employment that can threaten the employer's assets. Short of self-inflicted injuries, the developing trend in compensation law is to permit awards for any and all injuries sustained at, in the course of, going to, or leaving the business. An applicant's history with respect to unsafe practices and prior injuries is important.

Employers with health insurance programs beyond Worker's Compensation coverage are in even greater jeopardy from malingerers who may have already demonstrated by past record taking maximum advantage of such programs. Hiring people with active histories of alcohol and/or drug addiction can be the start of a widespread and continuing problem.

Suitability of employment should be evaluated. It would be a disservice to a person convicted of a larceny, who served a prison term, to assign him to a position involving responsibility for access to cash, not necessarily because the employee might steal again, but because if a loss should occur after his hiring, he would be a natural suspect.

Criteria for Employment

Major attention should be given to a company's initial establishment of standards under which suitability for employment will be judged. The final determination of those criteria should be a function of management, because the criteria will reflect basic business policy. Such criteria are important because they deal with aspects of personal suitability, integrity, sobriety, truthfulness, financial responsibility, and so on.

The purpose of a background investigation is to determine whether an applicant has been complete and truthful in his answers and whether his past history shows the presence of any relevant unfavorable information. The purpose of the employer making the final hiring decision is to be sure there is no information concerning the applicant's technical qualifications or past history that would deem him unsuitable.

Application Form

The application form is the most important document that an applicant will submit. It should be designed to draw the maximum amount of lawful, relevant information from the applicant and to prevent omission or misstatements. Included on the application form should be the following:

- Name
- Residence
- Education
- Employment
- Licenses and special qualifications
- Military service
- Personal/business references
- Criminal convictions

With respect to criminal information, there is a trend toward narrowing the scope of such questions. A significant decision was made by the U.S. District Court in California in the case of *Gregory v. Litton Systems Incorporated* (316 F.S. 401, 1970). This case held that a policy of rejecting employment applicants because of multiple arrests was a violation of Title 7 of the Federal Civil Rights Act of 1964, because it had the foreseeable effect of denying applicants an equal opportunity for employment. The court held that the question was discriminatory.

Pre-employment investigations can be a prudent precaution, provided that such investigations comply with the law, are not the basis for improper discriminatory practices, and serve their primary purpose of providing confidence in a prospective employer's decision about an applicant.

Authorizations and Agreements

In addition to questions related to specific employment requirements, it is useful to have the applicant, when he signs the application form, execute an authorization and release regarding the investigation of his statements. The applicant should be advised about the nature of the relationship created by his submission of the application and the effect of providing false or misleading information. This caution should appear close to the authorized release and near the applicant's signature. See Figure 11.3 for a sample disclosure and release authorization.

The most carefully designed employment application will fail its purpose if the applicant is permitted to not complete it adequately. Prior to being accepted, the completed application form should be reviewed with the applicant by a staff member. Each field should be completed. If review of the application reveals any questionable items, prompt follow-through can save hours of investigative labor and much cost.

Scope of Investigations

Three considerations will affect the extent to which investigations are carried out: cost, available time, and investigative resources.

The cost of the background investigation should be regarded in the same way as any other cost in recruitment and hiring. It should be held to a minimum, consistent with objectives, but not allowed to lessen the need for investigation. The absolute cost in dollars will depend upon how much investigation is conducted and by whom. Cost ranges extend from $25 for an abbreviated report by a credit agency to $1000 or more for a comprehensive report by a private investigator. Arriving at the appropriate amount of investigation and related cost is the task of the employer or personnel manager. Knowledge of resources available and how to utilize them comes from experience and training in the field of investigation.

Content of Investigations

Education

For positions that do not require a specific educational background, no investigation of education is necessary. When specific education is required for a position or is a basis upon which wage rate is determined, education should be verified.

For each school checked, the following items are significant: inclusive dates of attendance; the program or course in which the applicant was enrolled; the degree, diploma, or certificate awarded; student's conduct; reason for withdrawal or termination if prior to graduation or completion; and applicant's class standing and grade point average.

Prior Employment

Most unfavorable information about applicants will come from sources connected with prior employment. A sufficient period of time should be investigated to allow for developing information. For an entry-level employee, a suggested minimum is the preceding five years or last two employers, whichever is longer. For technical or supervisory employees, the period should be extended to 10 years or the last three employers, whichever is longer. For management and executive personnel, the entire business career should be investigated or a minimum of 15 years.

Information to be obtained from each place of former employment includes dates of employment, type of work performed, previous employment noted on application (applicant may have omitted positions from the application for reasons unknown), reason for termination, evaluations by former supervisors, eligibility for rehire, interviews with previous supervisors and co-workers, attendance records (whether the person was usually on time or chronically late), work habits (amount of supervision required, responsibility, honesty, and reliability). Was the employee considered an asset to the company?

The investigator is interested not only in verifying the exact dates of employment, but also in determining whether there were any periods of unexplained unemployment. Anything over 30 days may be looked upon with suspicion. Where was the applicant during this time? Did the applicant include reasons for periods of unemployment?

Residence

In conducting an investigation with neighbors, be certain to impress upon them that the purpose of the interview is for employment screening. Factors that the interviewer should focus on are how long neighbors have known the applicant; do they know the applicant's family; do they hesitate in answering any specific questions; are their recommendations sincere, lukewarm or enthusiastic; do they appreciate the nature of the investigation which you are undertaking; and do they offer assistance in answering questions or do they appear cautious in responding?

If neighbors do not know the applicant well enough to answer specific questions, can they furnish names of anyone who might know the applicant better? In the event that a neighbor furnishes derogatory information regarding the applicant, such statements must be verified through other neighbors or discounted as unverified. A particular neighbor may not get along with the applicant and, thus, provide negative information. At least three neighbors should be interviewed to complete this phase of the investigation. Derogatory information will require a more intensive search and interviews.

References

Personal and business references listed by an applicant interviewed thoroughly. Business references can be asked about the applicant's character and reputation. Would they recommend the person for the position to be filled? References are also good sources of information for any family problems that may have been uncovered in some other phase of the investigation. Social references are individuals who may be closer in age and better able to provide information relative to the applicant's reputation and peer relationships. Furthermore, they will know whether the applicant has a history of drug or alcohol abuse.

Credit History

Without signed releases, most companies will not cooperate in making these available. Credit bureau information is useful with respect to the history of trade account delinquencies, suits or judgments, and personal or business bankruptcies. Care must be exercised, because these records are often partial or preliminary, and can be used as leads for further checks.

Medical History

Signed releases by the applicant are essential for examination of medical records. The investigator needs to determine any physical problems that could be chronic and preclude hiring. It is presumed that information obtained from these records and from any physical examination can determine the applicant's fitness for employment.

Criminal History

It is important to determine if the applicant has any criminal history and if any arrests in the past five years have resulted in convictions.

Legal Constraints

The Privacy Act of 1974 controls the gathering and dissemination of personal information by certain federal agencies. Some states have or are enacting similar legislation. This act ensures the individual's right to obtain information written about him or her. The individual can then contest the accuracy of the information. The Privacy Act requires the hiring agency that has gathered the information to notify the applicant, on request, of the uses it has made of the information, and the applicant may refuse to disclose his social security number unless it is required by federal statutes.

The Family Education Rights and Privacy Act of 1974, also known as the Buckley Amendments, guarantees parents' access to school records of their children, and places restrictions on dissemination of this information to third parties.

In addition to various state laws dealing with credit reporting agencies, Congress passed a comprehensive measure in July, 1999 revising the Fair Credit Reporting Act, and enacted the Right to Financial Privacy Act.

Pre-Employment Screening

Approximately 30% of employees from retail, restaurant, manufacturing, and health care industries admit to theft.

Approximately 60% of salaries reported on resumes are inflated; 5% of personal references are non-existent, and 14% of educational references are bogus.

Job candidate deception mjust be considered in hiring an employee. Studies have shown that application and resume fraud are at an all-time high — 30% of all resumes are fraudulent. Employers cannot afford the luxury of hiring the wrong employees. Lost money from training and paying unsuitable employees makes a dramatic difference in the year-end profit and loss statement.

The instability of operation by high turnover rates, internal theft, losses owing to worker-related litigation (i.e., sexual harassment, Worker's Compensation cases, etc.) all impact on the stability of a business and the bottom line profit/loss statement.

Screening Problems

A thorough review of the resume and interview of the candidate *are not sufficient* in today's marketplace. A more exhaustive investigation is required of the finalists for positions in order to determine the most appropriate and best qualified candidate for each position.

Due diligence and background investigations are an integral part of investigations including legal, domestic, and fraud investigations. The well trained investigator have a comprehensive understanding of all the components of conducting thorough background investigations.

BACKGROUND INVESTIGATION CHECK LIST

FILE#: _____ DATE: _____ FEE INFO:

CLIENT:_____ TEL #: _____

ADDRESS: _____ FAX:_____

SUBJECT: _____

ADDRESS: _____ TEL #: _____

COUNTY: _____ MARITAL STATUS: _____ SPOUSE:

DOB:_____ SS#: _____ DL#: _____

POSITION DESIRED: _____

_____/_____   CONFIRM ADDRESS/ DATA ON APPLICATION
DATE   INT

_____/_____   CONFIRM EDUCATION/ APPLICATION

_____/_____   CONFIRM EMPLOYMENT/ APPLICATION

_____/_____   PERSONAL REFERENCES/ APPLICATION

_____/_____   PROFILE   _____/_____   DMV RESEARCH

_____/_____   CRIMINAL   _____/_____   _____

_____/_____   CIVIL   _____/_____   _____

_____/_____   WORKERS COMP   _____/_____   _____

_____/_____   PHYSICAL SURVEILLANCE/ PERSONAL VISIT

Figure 11.1 Background investigation checklist.

MCMAHON & ASSOCIATES

Pre – Employment Screening / Background Check Authorization

1. I _____ as a precursor to employment by, or business involvement with _____ give my permission for _____ and their assigns (hereafter referred to as "employer") to research any and all information pertaining to those parts of my personal, financial, employment, and legal history having a direct bearing on our business relationship and/or my ability to carry out all requirements of said relationship. Furthermore I agree to hold harmless "employer", their assigns, and any and all information sources from liability stemming from the discovery of truthful information causing termination of said relationship.

2. I understand that all information gathered will be kept in the strictest confidence.

I understand the course of this background check will include (but is not limited to):

> **A.** Criminal History. **B.** Civil Litigation History **C.** Verification of work history, education and/or information provided on resume/application. **D.** Credit History, Credit Report. **E.** Driving record, DMV record. **F.** Military Service

3. Applicant Information:

First:_____Middle:_____ Last:_____

Address:_____Apt:_____

City:_____ State:_____ Zip:_____ - _____

Length of time at this address:_____   List previous address below:

Address:_____Apt:_____

City:_____ State:_____ Zip:_____ - _____

Phone: (_____)_____-_____ E-Mail:_____

Sex:_____ DOB:___/___/___ SSN:_____-___-_____ Marital Status:_____

Place of birth: Country:_____State:___ City:_____ County:_____

4.

Applicant's Printed Name:_____

Applicant's Signature:_____ Date:_____

Witness/Notary:_____ Date: _____

Notary Seal:

Figure 11.2 Sample background investigation form.

DISCLOSURE AND RELEASE

In connection with my application for employment (including contract for services) with you, I understand that consumer reports, which may contain public record information, may be requested from (YOUR COMPANY NAME HERE), Chicago, Illinois. These reports may include the following types of information: names and dates of previous employers, reason for termination of employment, work experience, credit history, accidents, etc. I further understand that such reports may contain public record information concerning my driving record, workers compensation claims, credit, bankruptcy proceedings, criminal records, etc., from federal, state and other agencies which maintain such records.

I AUTHORIZE, WITHOUT RESERVATION, ANY PARTY OR AGENCY CONTACTED BY (YOUR COMPANY NAME HERE) TO FURNISH THE ABOVE-MENTIONED INFORMATION.

I have the right to make a request to (YOUR COMPANY NAME HERE) upon proper identification, to request the nature and substance of all information in its files on me at the time of my request, including the sources of information; and the recipients of any reports on me which (YOUR COMPANY NAME HERE) has previously furnished within the two-year period preceding my request. I hereby consent to your obtaining the above information from (YOUR COMPANY NAME HERE) and I agree that such information which (YOUR COMPANY NAME HERE) has or obtains, and my employment history with you if I am hired, will be supplied by (YOUR COMPANY NAME HERE) to other companies which utilize (YOUR COMPANY NAME HERE)

I hereby authorize procurement of consumer report(s). If hired (or contracted), this authorization shall remain on file and shall serve as ongoing authorization for you to procure consumer reports at any time during my employment (or contract) period.

_____   _____
PRINT NAME   SOCIAL SECURITY NO.

_____   _____
APPLICANT'S SIGNATURE   DATE

F/DISCLOSURE & RELEASE VTS

Figure 11.3 Sample disclosure and release form.

12

LOCATES AND SKIP TRACING

THE BASICS OF SKIP TRACING

What is Skip Tracing

Skip tracing is the art of locating someone. A skip is a person who, for whatever reason, chooses to leave a given area. Most skips eventually leave either paper trails, verbal trails, or both.

There are many reasons for a person to skip, such as marriage, divorce, and revenge; escaping debt; boredom and frustration; amnesia; rebellion and/or adventure; and running from the law.

Skips can be divided into four main groups:

1. Unintentional skip — the person is not intentionally hiding but is secretive about his location.
2. Intentional skip — the person intentionally conceals his location to avoid creditors or others.
3. Marital skips — one party is overwhelmed by the pressures and stress of a divorce.
4. Criminal skip — the person is hiding to avoid apprehension by law enforcement.

Relevant Federal and State Statutes

The Fair Credit Reporting Act (FCRA), a federal statute, governs the investigation of information on debtors as well as the rules for the collection of debt. The FCRA was revised in July 1999. For complete information, refer to Chapter 4 of *The Professional Collections Agency*.

In some states, for example, Florida Statute 119 (Public Records Law) "it is the policy of this state that records shall at all times be open for a personal inspection by any person."

Some of the exemptions to this statute are criminal records (open cases), informant information, and intelligence information. All other records are open for review. According to the Sunshine Law in Florida, public officials must maintain records of official meetings and make these records available for inspection to the public.

Beginning the Process

The first step in locating a skip is to review all information currently available on the skip from in-house records. Second, profile sheets should be prepared and a search undertaken for any information that is not complete through public records searches, database searches, government records, and Internet sites. That will be discussed in a later section of this book.

A skip trace should start with the basics — telephone directory information, criss-cross directories, and directory assistance for new listings. A skip tracer should keep a flow chart to keep track of information, searches, and leads. This will prevent him from becoming sidetracked. He should also keep an activity log so that if the records are subpoenaed or used in court, his documentation will be unchallenged. Finally, when all public and database sources have been exhausted, interviews with family, friends, employers, and enemies (i.e., ex-wives) should be conducted for leads to the current whereabouts of skips.

Researching Public Records

This is often the beginning to any investigation. Use telephone books, records, and listings; cross-reference books; do neighborhood and employment investigations; check postal records and public records, including search of microfiche; voter registration; birth, death, and marriage records; real property records; fictitious business files; municipal, county, state, and federal civil court records; state and federal criminal records; corporate and partnership filings; DMV records; church, medical, and dental records; credit history records; union records; state licensing boards and law enforcement agencies; and check the trash (dumpster diving).

Interviews

After searching public records, if you still are unable to find the person, you must seek other sources of information. It is now time to polish your interpersonal skills and call or visit anyone who may have information about the whereabouts of the person you are trying to locate. Start with the people you have identified: ex-wives, ex-employers, former friends, etc. Ask if they have any knowledge about the person, or who else might have contact with the person. Follow all leads and interview as many people as necessary to get the information you need.

SKIP TRACING RESOURCES

Public Records

A driver's license (DL) often contains all the identifying information required to find someone. The most important pieces of information are social security number (SSN) and date of birth (DOB). If the SSN is not shown on the DL, at least you will have the DOB to distinguish people with the same or similar names. This is the single most useful resource of the skip tracer.

If you cannot find the subject via his driver's license, a search of motor vehicle registrations is suggested. With the large number of seasonal visitors and tourists in a state such as Florida, for example, sometimes people do not obtain driver's licenses, preferring to maintain the license of their home state. However, the person may keep a car registered in a seasonal home. From that registration, you will obtain the DOB if it is not a lease car, and you may obtain the SSN.

Depending on the type of case you are working on, and whether you have legal process (i.e., judgments, liens, etc.) or a signed release, you can obtain a credit report or, alternatively a header report. The Fair Credit Reporting Act is very specific as to who is entitled to obtain credit reports. Penalties are severe for violations; criminal and civil penalties may be imposed. Exclusions to the act include court orders, that is, judgments or process (604(1)), or use of information in connection with a credit transaction or "collection of an account" — that is, judgments (604(3)(A) #5). In the absence of a credit report, you can obtain credit header reports (address information only) from certain database providers.

Many people are found by simply looking them up in the phone book. You can use a reverse directory, by phone number — name and address provided or a cross directory, by address — name and phone number provided. You can even go back and use the city directories if you have old addresses for the subject.

One of the most useful searches on the local level is searching traffic offenses. Search of these records in the local courthouse may reveal a traffic infraction. Search of the court docket will provide the subject's home address. Search of the state and federal civil records will provide names and addresses of all plaintiffs, defendants, and witnesses in lawsuits. On the criminal side, records will provide names and addresses of defendants in criminal cases, as well as witnesses called to testify.

The Division of Corporations at the Department of State, provides the names of all officers and registered agents of all corporations doing business in the state. Out of state corporations doing business are required to register in some states. The address provided might only be the corporate address, but, by law, the officers are responsive to process served on the registered agents.

Searching occupational records in the county offices and City Hall will reveal the names and address of business owners.

Database Resources

Autotrack—the Investigator's Edge, Choice Point, Inc., is the largest database service in Florida and possibly the entire United States. It is used everyday by investigators all over the country. This Florida-based company started as a small company in 1992, offering investigators driver's license and motor vehicle information from the state of Florida. Now they have more than 4 billion current and historical records on individuals and businesses from every state. Initially, this was a subscription service and you paid by the minute. They recently started offering information through the Internet at Autotrackxp.com, where you pay for the search or for a comprehensive report. It is the most widely used database by the investigative industry.

Information America is a very large database that provides access to over 800 million records (infoam.com). They have both "person locator" and "skip tracer" database information resources. It is also a subscription service database.

CDB Infotek is a database company that provides access to over two billion records of federal, state, and county governments, as well as telephone directories and Dun and Bradstreet reports.

The KnowX.com database is a subsidiary of Information America. They specialize in low price information on the Internet. Their "Ultimate People Finder" searches telephone directories, real property databases, and death records. They have access to millions of records.

Virtual Databases claims access to 278 million records and over 170 million missing person files. They sell CD-ROMS including SkipBase America, Mover's Database, and Protracker Profile Series, in addition to their online services at www.virtual-database.com.

IRSC is another subscription database company that recently was taken over by Choice Point, Inc. They provide document retrieval searches from a menu of options.

Merlin is a database company that offers CD-ROMS for sale with lists of names taken from public records, that is, voter registration lists, property records, and so on. They also offer online services at merlindata.com.

IQ Data Online is another database that provides access to billions of records. They also offer document retrieval services.

Locateme.com is an online database search company that accesses approximately 422 million records. They also specialize in adoption searches.

Government Records

Government records that may be used to locate people include drivers' licenses, motor vehicle registrations and the U.S. Postal Service. Previously, investigators could obtain change of address information under FOIA requests. Since that pratice has been discontinued, an address correction notice can be done by sending a letter marked "Do Not Forward. Address Correction Requested," you can obtain the new address from the Post Office.

Civil and criminal records can be reviewed at the County Clerk's Office. By checking the Department of Health, Office of Vital Statistics, obtain birth and death records can be obtained under certain circumstances.

The Department of State, Division of Corporations may have records on corporations, officers and registered agents, partnerships, and fictitious names for businesses. The Board of Elections, Voter's Registration has the names and addresses of all registered voters in the county. The Property Records Office maintains the names and mailing addresses of all property owners.

The Freedom of Information Act (FOIA) will reveal the present duty assignment of military personnel, as well as information on discharged personnel. You may contact the U.S. Locator Service 10, at P.O. Box 2577, St. Louis, MO 63114; telephone (314) 423-0860, or send e-mail to uslocator@earthlink.net. See Figure 12.1.

Under certain circumstances, addresses can be obtained from the Social Security Administration or provided to other government agencies (i.e., deadbeat dads, etc.). You may also obtain information from the U.S. Passport Office. Civil, criminal, and bankruptcy information is available from the courts.

In the County Recorder's Office, official index, deeds, liens, and judgments are available for review. From the Bureau of Alcohol, Tobacco, and Firearms, you may obtain the names and addresses of all owners and operators of establishments where alcohol or tobacco are sold. The Federal Aviation Administration will provide the names and addresses of all pilots or owners of aircraft.

Internet Sites

The following are a list of Internet Web sites that will assist in locating skips and other missing persons.

http://www.411locate.com/
http://www.555-1212.com/
http://www.bigfoot.com/
http://www.anywho.com
http://www.anywho.com/telg.html
http://www.infospace.com/
http://www.intersurf.com/~lizcabom/links.html
http://www.ftc.gov/os/statutes/fcra.htm
http://www.pimall.com/digdirt/moore.htm
http://www.virtuallibrarian.com/it/
http://199.72.15.157/findet.htm
http://www.crimetime.com/online.htm
http://www.iqdata.com
http://www.well.com/user/fap/foia.htm
http://www.looking4u.com/
http://www.whowhere.com
http://www.tracersinfo.com
http://www.infousa.com/
http://www.dbisna.com/
http://www.cyberspydetective.com/
http://www.interagencyla.com/
http://www.nara.gov/regional/stlouis.html
http://www.militaryusa.com/
http://www.ancestry.com/ssdi/advanced.htm
http://www.iaf.net/
http://www.onestopinfo.com/

Bypassing Barriers:
Sharing Information on Military Personnel

The Bottom Line (simple approach to getting it all):

Send one written request to the facility's credentials office:
**Request the privileging/risk management information you need
**If they refuse, get written explanation
**May need to work through higher headquarters
**Use exception to Title 10 to force release (see notes on privacy act)

Send second written request to the facility's legal office:
**Request copies of all "command directed formal and informal investigations of allegations of misconduct against (person's name)"
**Include personnel's waiver of Privacy Act, if you have one
**If legal office refuses, ask for written explanation of denial

[Using a subpoena makes requests more powerful; If denied information, your recourse is to go to a federal judge with the agency's written explanation of denial and get the judge to force them to release info]

Terms to Know:

DOD or DoD—Department of Defense

MTF—Medical Treatment Facility—Marines do not have Medical
—only Air Force, Army and Navy

JAG—Judge Advocate General—the legal office or officer(s)
CJA—Center Judge Advocate—lead attorney for a specialized center
SJA—Staff Judge Advocate—attorney for a major command/installation

FOIA—Freedom of Information Act

"Protected under Title 10"—refers to confidentiality of medical quality assurance
records—under Title 10, US Code, Section 1102

Article 15—non-judicial punishment used by military commanders
--May be used in lieu of court martial for some offenses
--Serious for an officer to have one (usually a career killer)
--Virtually automatic for DUI, illegal drug use
--Used for shoplifting, breach of ethics, false statements
--Max punishment for officer; not more than one-half of one month's pay for 2 months, 30
days house arrest, 60 days restriction, and reprimand
--known as "Captain's Mast" in the Navy

Figure 12.1 Information on military personnel.

Court Martial— used for a wide range of violations of military law
  --Enforces the Uniform Code of Military Justice (UCMJ)
  --Includes typical criminal actions, but also others (conduct unbecoming)
  --Used for larceny, child abuse/pornography, spouse abuse w/injury and typical major crimes (murder, etc.)
  --Used if command is seeking officer's dismissal from service (Extremely Serious—result is like "Branded")
  --This is a federal conviction; however, since some of the "crimes" in the military (such as Article 133) do not fit in the scheme of civilian laws, they may not appear in an NCIC report

Conduct Unbecoming an Officer (Article 133 of UCMJ)—unique to military law
  --Used for broad range of breaches of discipline
  --Inappropriate conduct that brings disrepute to the military
  --Includes offenses not covered in civilian law, for example
        --Cursing at a neighbor
        --Associating with people involved with drugs
        --Male dancing at a club as female impersonator
  [--Selling items to a subordinate (such as multilevel marketing)—Art 92]

OMPF—Official Military Personnel File (provided on microfiche)—has complete service record
  --Any service member (present or past) may get a copy
  --Obtained from service personnel command
  --Contains efficiency reports, disciplinary actions, but not privileged info
  --Efficiency reports are highly inflated; if not glowing, look for a problem.* OERs tend to be inflated
  --If average or below average report—read the verbiage carefully
  --However, with new Army reports (>1998), center of mass is OK
  --With a waiver of Privacy Act, agency may obtain a copy

DD 214—Documents release from active military service (everyone on active duty gets a green card and anyone not on active duty any more has one)
  --Includes courts-martial convictions, awards, time of service
  --Copy given to every service member when leaving military
  --Used as proof of past military service for government agencies

15-6 Investigation (Army) – (might not be used by Navy) —command directed administrative investigation; statements made or sworn statement in a 15-6)
  --Other military services have similar informal investigation systems
  --Can be done by individual or tribunal (done by a senior officer who has knowledge of the incident)

Need to know who denial authority is – appeal to them – get denial in writing

---

*If OER says anything negative, it is a huge event.

Figure 12.1 (continued) Information on military personnel.

Excuses for not releasing information

"That's Quality Assurance information and is protected under Title 10" (National Defense Authorization Act for Fiscal Year 1987—Public Law no. 99-661, Section 1102, Title 10, US Code)

--provides that records created by or for DOD in a medical or dental QA program are confidential and precludes release, EXCEPT **disclosure** of records or testimony **is allowed** to government boards, agencies, or professional health care societies/organizations **if needed to perform licensing, credentialing, or monitoring of the professional standards of any present or former member of the DOD (Title 10, Section 1102, para (c)(1)(C).**

--Local MTF may say they cannot release information, however, it may (and should) be released by their higher headquarters such as MEDCOM (US Army Medical Command), BUMED—HLTHCARE SUPPO (US Navy Bureau of Medicine and Surgery—Healthcare Support Office), or AFMOA (US Air Force Medical Operations Agency). Expect this for any adverse information. If local level is non-responsive, push them that they must give you written denial of release from their denial authority (if still balking, suggest that <u>denial authority</u> review the law—remind them of the exception).

"That's protected under the Privacy Act" (5 USC Section 552A)

--If they are claiming they are protecting the personnel's privacy, get a waiver of the Privacy Act from the personnel. Have the personnel sign a statement saying "I hereby waive my rights under the Privacy Act of 1974 to allow the XYZ medical board access to any records concerning my medical privileges/practice during the period of (date) to (date)". Alternatively, apply for the information under as above under QA Information or via the FOIA (below).

--Privacy Act should not be used as an excuse for non-release of QA information to a government licensing agency.

--If they claim they are protecting patient privacy, request they simply blacken out the patient's name and identifying number, but leave all other info.

"We can't release that under the Freedom of Information Act (FOIA) because it is medical/personal information" (5 USC Section 552)

--Although medical/personal information is generally thought of as protected from release, the regulation actually only excludes information where disclosure would clearly be an invasion of privacy. The agency that receives the request for release of information should do a balancing act between the invasion of privacy and the public's interest in disclosure. If you suggest that it is in the best interest of the public to release the information, it may help. The local MTF is typically NOT the denial authority—they have to send the FOIA request to a higher level for denial.

--Requesting information via FOIA is the common man's subpoena—anyone may request information under FOIA; however, the government may turn down the request for a variety of reasons outlined in the act.

Figure 12.1 (continued) Information on military personnel.

Send request to MTF Credentials office – They typically release routine favorable information, but will refer the request to higher headquarters if there is adverse information. This is a good route to request "QA" information (credentials, risk management). Generally, a written request for release of the privileging or risk management information should get you what you need, though it may be slow because of needing to go through higher headquarters. [May choose to sight the exception to Title 10 (see next page)]

Send FOIA Request to the MTF JAG —You may NOT request QA information via a FOIA request. Need to be done as separate requests.

Note: Privacy Act waiver by personnel should help you get what you want; however, see next page.

Note: Subpoena for "command directed formal and information investigations of allegations of misconduct against (person's name)" will help you get non-QA documents that may have useful information for your investigation. If you do not ask for this information separately, you may not get it—it may not be in the credentials file if credentials office is unaware or didn't use it to take action. (Judge signature = most powerful; if only agency subpoena, may not get the information—since military is federal, might not readily respond to state agency) Non-QA documents that might be useful could include EO investigations, criminal investigations, 15-6 investigations, and other administrative inquiries. (These are places to look for information that you might not usually encounter in a credentials file) If subpoena is denied, contact the JAG office for a <u>written</u> explanation

In some states, you can get an inexpensive and rapid background check by requiring the individual to get a permit for a handgun—if issued a permit, the individual has no felonies or misdemeanors involving domestic relations (Lautenberg Act, 1976)

Figure 12.1 (continued) Information on military personnel.

Contact/Reference information:

Credentials/Privileging information:
US Army MEDCOM (Medical Command)—210-221-6195
US Navy HLTHCARE SUPPO—904-542-7200 (might try ext. 8111)
US Air Force MOA (Medical Operations Agency): 202-767-4077

DOD:
Information and links: http://defenselink.mil
Publications: http://www.defenselink.mil/pubs/
Directives, instructions, and memos:
http://web7.whs.osd.mil/corres.htm
DD 214 information:
http://members.aol.com/usregistry/warlib25.htm
DD 214 codes: http://members.aol.com/usregistry/warlib45.htm

Army:
http://www.armymedicine.army.mil
Copies of regs: http://www.usapa.army.mil/
Personnel: http://www-perscom.army.mil/
AR 40-68 Quality Assurance Administration
AR 40-48 Non-physician Healthcare Providers
AR 40-66 Medical Records Administration

Navy:
Info and publications:
http://navymedicine.med.navy.mil/
BUMED Instruction 6320.66B Credentials Review and Privileging Program
BUMED Instruction 6320.67 Adverse Privileging Actions, Peer Review Panel
Procedures, and Health Care Provider Reporting

Air Force:
Copies of publications: http://afpubs.hq.af.mil/ (electronic publications)
Personnel info: http://www.afpc.randolph.af.mil/
AFI 44-119 Medical Service Clinical Quality Management

Miscellaneous:
CFRs: http://www.access.gpo.gov/nara/cfr/cfr-retrieve.html
        (Code of Federal Regulations)
Military Law info: http://www.freeyellow.com/members5/uppmlj/main.html
Administrators In Medicine: http://www.docboard.org/

Figure 12.1 (continued) Information on military personnel.

Sue Abreu MD - Colonel
>   Military Personnel/Communications

St. Louis is the depository for information in the military
>   -will take awhile to get information from this depository
>   -ORB—officer record brief – is kept at local level

PA's are not required to be licensed
NP's are not required to be licensed—but have to be licensed as RN and meet qualifications
of NP.

Fiugre 12.1 (continued) Information on military personnel.

13

SURVEILLANCE

DEFINITIONS

Be burnt — to have your subject know that he is being followed and who is following him.

Be hot — to have your subject suspect that he is being followed.

Be made — to be detected or suspected of being a surveillant by the subject.

Bugging — eavesdropping by electronic means such as a hidden microphone or radio transmitter.

Bumper beeper — a battery operated device that emits radio signals, which permit it to be tracked by a directional finder–receiver. Also called a beacon, transponder, or electronic tracking device.

Burn the surveillance — when the surveillant's behavior causes the subject to know he is under surveillance.

Close or tight surveillance — the subject is kept under constant surveillance. The aim is not to lose the subject even at the risk of being made.

Convoy — a countermeasure to detect a surveillance.

Loose surveillance — a cautious surveillance because the loss of the subject is preferable to possible discovery.

Moving surveillance — the surveillant moves about in order to follow the subject.

Open surveillance — a surveillance with little or no attempt at concealment.

Pen register — a device that records all numbers dialed on a telephone

Shadow — to follow secretly.

Stake-out — also called a plant or fixed surveillance; the surveillant usually remains in one fixed position or location.

Subject — the party under surveillance.

Surveillance — the secretive, continuous, and sometimes periodic watching of persons, vehicles, places, or objects to obtain information concerning the activities and identities of individuals. Observation of people to determine information relevant to an investigation without the subject being aware of the observation. Watching and/or following a person.

Surveillant — the person conducting the surveillance.

Tail — to follow and keep under surveillance.

Tailgating — a form of open surveillance in which the subject's vehicle is closely followed.

Technical surveillance — surveillance involving the use of scientific devices to enhance hearing or seeing the subject's activities.

THE SURVEILLANCE

General Rules

The three general rules to follow are obey the law, your life is more important than the assignment, and never tell anyone who you are.

It is better to lose your subject than to burn the case. Never forget that if a subject is lost, he can be found again later. However, once he is aware that he is being followed, your case is finished. Many subjects become hot, but with careful tail work, you can still keep contact without burning the case.

Dress in ordinary clothes that will match your environment. If you must change your appearance, do it by taking off or putting on a hat, a pair of glasses, or a coat. Never dress in conspicuous clothes, but always dress conservatively. If you are using a car, carry a change of street clothing and some work clothes. At night, dress in dark clothing. In this way, you will blend into a dark background.

Pre-Surveillance

Certain activities should be carried out by the investigator before a surveillance. The two most important are:

1. Obtaining nformation pertaining to the subject including a physical description (photo, if possible), the subject's name and current home address (this is useful for locating the subject if contact is lost during the course of surveillance), details of any vehicles that the subject might use, and any mannerisms or other characteristics that might be helpful for identification or other purposes.

2. Peforming relevant reconnaissance, taking in the target area, including traffic conditions, transportation that could be used by the subject, and determination of suitable sites for surveillance.

Foot Surveillance

Never, under any circumstances, lose sight of your subject. If you are following him in very heavy sidewalk traffic, stay about eight to nine feet behind him. If the streets are not crowded, remain further back and, if possible, on the other side of the street. Change position frequently behind the subject so that you are not always directly in back of him. Try to use other pedestrians as cover.

If your subject turns around, do not panic. He is probably looking for an address or something else. Never jump into a doorway or behind a tree or make any other sudden or obvious movement. If he stops and turns around, pretend to tie your shoe, look into a store window, buy a paper, or do anything else that would not look out of place. Do not be afraid to talk to people on the street if the subject glances your way. Most individuals are friendly and this would make the subject think that you live in the area and not tailing him. If you are too close, pass your subject and then pause at a window and slowly look back. Never look your subject directly in the eyes. If you do, he will probably remember you the next time he sees you because you have made an impression.

One man alone can do a successful foot surveillance, but a better foot surveillance can be accomplished with two or more. Never signal to the other investigator by obvious gestures such as waving or shouting.

On a close tail, do not hesitate to follow your subject into an elevator. If he gives a floor number, you can give the floor below or above it. Then run up or down the stairway and cautiously open the door to his floor. You will probably see what room he enters. Then proceed to the main floor and watch the most likely exit.

If the subject enters a restaurant and you have been instructed to enter also, sit to one side or behind him. Ask for the check when your food arrives and carry change so you can pay the bill in the exact amount if your subject leaves in a hurry. Leave a few minutes before he does, if possible, so that you will not be delayed when you pay the cashier.

At all times, carry a sufficient reserve of money for any emergency. You never know when a subject will take a bus, plane, or train to another city. It is also advisable to carry credit cards.

Automobile Surveillance

Never take any unnecessary chances. Do not instruct others to do so. A bad accident may mean a jail sentence, cancellation of insurance, loss of a driver's license, plus a life of misery if anyone was seriously hurt or killed. No reputable agency should expect this of employees nor should anyone work for an agency that expects such performances. Each person pays his own traffic tickets, insurance, and repair bills.

Use a medium-priced late model car in a neutral color — light blue, tan, white, or black. Avoid two-tone paint jobs. Never have a car painted in loud colors or drive a car with a noisy muffler or excessive chrome trim. Do not put decals, stickers, or other identifying marks on the car body or windows.

At all times, keep your motor, tires, and brakes in excellent working order. A stick shift is better for tailing, mainly because it will save gasoline expense. Make certain your headlights are properly adjusted so they will not be noticed at night.

In any type of surveillance, three important factors to be remembered are *patience*, *practice*, and *relax*. Reading books and articles on surveillance will not make you an expert. It takes many years of practice to acquire a feel for following people. A great deal of patience is required to wait hours for a subject to appear. Never become discouraged or leave the stake-out position. The minute you leave will be the time the subject decides to take off. Keep in mind that there is no easy way to watch a subject. You can do a better job when you are relaxed than when you are tense and nervous.

Before starting a new surveillance, have your car thoroughly checked. A full tank of gas is essential. You never know where the subject will go. If your gas tank is full, chances are he will need gas before you do.

If, for any reason, you feel that you might have been detected, or if you will be on a case for a long time, try to change cars. If only one car is employed, try to use two people in it. In this manner, one can drive while the other watches the subject. Also, one person can follow the subject on foot while the other parks the car.

In car tailing as in foot surveillance, do not remain directly behind the subject. Change lanes frequently, but never change at the same time the subject does. Attempt to keep a car or two between you and the subject (called a cover car). If the subject makes a turn before you can get into the turn lane, go to the next street and turn in the same direction as he does. This is called paralleling. Also parallel if your subject is driving on narrow residential streets. If you are on the same street, try to stay at least a block or two behind the subject, depending on traffic.

Be very careful when turning corners, because the subject may have parked immediately around the corner. In such a case, do not panic and stop in the middle of the street nor make any other overt actions. Pass the subject and come back around. The same applies to pulling behind the subject at a red light. Few drivers (unless they are hot) watch their rear view mirrors. Also, even hot drivers are usually only hot when they leave their homes for a rendezvous and/or when they approach the rendezvous spot.

If a subject goes slowly then fast, circles a block, looks in the rear view mirror, or makes a U-turn, it does not mean he is hot. Let him prove it. If he continues such tactics, then drop the surveillance unless you have enough cars to handle the situation.

Familiarize yourself with the city in which you are working. Knowing the area makes it easier to pick up your subject if you should lose him. In addition, acquire as much information as you can about your subject so that you can figure out where he might have gone if you lose him.

When using several tail cars, be sure to alternate cars in a pre-arranged method. Plan every possible eventuality in advance. The blinking of brake lights may be used for signals. However, the best way to communicate is to use two-way radios or cell phones.

If you use your own car, you should have field glasses (binoculars), city and county maps, camera, camcorder, and a change of clothing. It is also a good idea to keep some old clothes in the car. Common sense and good planning will tell you what is essential in all cases.

Stake-Outs

Often, obtaining a fixed observation post proves impractical, so the perfect answer is a stake-out truck. Stake-out trucks are usually old panel trucks or vans. However, a milk-type or walk-in delivery truck is recommended. This will allow you to stand up and stretch. Trucks suitable for this purpose can usually be purchased for very little money, if they are six to nine years old or older. It is not essential that the truck be new because trucks are usually only driven to the scene and left there until the stake-out is over. Trucks are seldom used for tailing, although if a truck is in good running order, it could be used occasionally as a second vehicle.

All locks on the truck must be in working order. A heavy curtain should be placed across the front of the truck, separating the driver's compartment from the rear of the truck. The curtain should be light-proof so that no light may be admitted to the back of the compartment. The rear windows should have hinged light-proof doors over them. The same type of window should be installed on both sides of the truck. One-way glass should be used for the windows. Mirrors of this type could be used, although many people are aware of those and you might be spotted.

When observing, use only one window at a time and keep all other window doors firmly closed. Keep a piece of tinted or shaded celluloid over the window you are using and stand back at least a foot. If the rear compartment is light-free, you will never be detected inside the truck.

Ordinarily, it is recommended to panel the inside of the truck and insert insulation behind the paneling. The truck will then remain cooler in the summer and warmer in the winter. A light-colored truck will reflect the sun's rays and be noticeable, whereas a dark color will absorb them and be less conspicuous. A carpet on the floor is mandatory, not only for insulation, but also to absorb noise and foot movement and render the truck more comfortable.

At night, it is essential to be close to the subject. It is advisable to sit low in the seat or in one of the corners of the back seat, where you will not be silhouetted by passing cars. Your windshield will often reflect light, so park in a good spot, then get out and walk a short distance to determine if you can see into your own car. Also ensure that street lights are behind your car rather than in front of it.

Before starting a stake-out, it is advisable to let the local police know you are in the vicinity (not the exact spot), how long you will be there, your license number, and the car's description. This may save your stake-out from being ruined when some nosy neighbor calls the police. If neighbors approach your car, tell them your tag number and to call the police to verify that they know you are there. As with any type of assignment, keep your credentials and business cards on your person at all times.

Tactics

A major problem that may develop is how to weigh the possible loss of contact with a subject against the risk of being detected or exposed. A quick, believable response is called for when a subject takes some action to determine if he is under surveillance. It is easier to drop a surveillance before being confronted than to respond to a confrontation by convincing the subject that he is mistaken.

If your subject comes directly to you and asks if you are following him, *never* admit it. Tell him you do not know what he is talking about, and walk away. Do not follow him again. Always make your subject prove to you that he is hot. Just because he looks or walks in your direction does not mean that you have been spotted. Make certain before you give up.

Hot subjects will seek to discover a tail by reversing their course of direction, watching mirror and window reflections of individuals following them, dropping a slip of paper to see if it is picked up (pick it up only if you can do so without detection), and by driving or walking around a corner and then stopping suddenly. If the subject pauses, keep on going. Do not stop and turn around until it is safe to do so without being detected. A subject also may use another person as a lookout to spot a tail. He may drive into a theatre, restaurant, or hotel parking lot. If several investigators are assigned, one should enter and the others watch the main exits. A subject also may drive into a residential area where a tail can easily be detected because of a lack of concealment.

SURVEILLANCE EQUIPMENT

Numerous items are required to conduct surveillances. Most surveillances require the basics, which are a flashlight, binoculars, pen and paper or a tape recorder to take notes of the investigator's activities, a camera, and a camcorder.

Video and Film

Video is an electronic medium. The light passing through the lens falls on to a light-sensitive component known as a charged-coupled device (CCD). A small electrical current is created, its strength varying with the intensity of the light. This current travels to the recording elements of the camcorder, which, in turn, create a small magnetic field which is recorded on the magnetic coating of the videotape. To view the image, the process is reversed. The magnetic field on the tape creates an electrical current which is used to generate the image on the television screen. One principle needs to be remembered — the process goes from light to electric current to magnetic tape.

Video Advantages

The great advantage of videotape over film is that you are dealing with an instant process, and the image you see in the electronic viewfinder is the one you will record, except that the viewfinder image is usually in black and white. Another advantage is that video cameras will record in very low levels of light, and many of the difficulties of lighting experienced with conventional film do not apply to video.

Camcorders

The development of home video making has followed three main stages. First there was the video camera and separate portable video cassette recorder. Then the camcorder appeared, in which the video recorder functions were incorporated into the body of the camera, making a single piece of equipment. The third phase has been miniaturization of the camcorder, so that some are now not much bigger or heavier than the conventional 35 mm camera. These developments have led to a number of video formats, each with their own advantages and drawbacks. As a general rule, miniaturization makes a camcorder more affordable and less obtrusive. The disadvantage is that the lighter the camera, the more difficult it is to hold it steady. While larger camcorders are usually designed to rest on the shoulder, smaller ones must be held unsupported in front of the eye.

Major Camcorder Elements

The three basic systems are the optical elements, the electronic functions (which control the video signal), and the recorder motor and controls. Power can be supplied either by a rechargeable battery or in most cases, a car battery. Familiarity with equipment, to the point of being able to operate it as second nature, is the foundation of good camera work. At first sight, there appear to be a number of controls on most camcorders. Usually they are placed in two groups: those that control the video signal and the light entering the camera, and those that operate the recorder functions.

Zoom Lens

Virtually, all camcorders have a zoom lens with zoom ratios ranging from 6:1 to 1000:1. The angle of view at the wide-angled end of the zoom range is approximately the same as that of a 35 mm camera with standard lens. Many camcorders also provide powered zoom, as is the case with all the automatic functions offered. The zoom is an excellent tool for framing — getting the subject exactly the size you want and then keeping it there. See Figures 13.1 to 13.3 for a cover sheet, photograph log, and sample display sheet.

Microphones

The built-in microphone is located above or to the side of the lens. The sound quality recorded will vary considerably, ranging from poor to good quality hi-fi sound. The sound being recorded can be monitored using headphones. Never record during surveillance. It is illegal to record conversations in most states without both parties' consent.

Formats

There are several different formats from which to choose. Each uses a different type of cassette and, with one exception, tapes and equipment made for one format are incompatible with those made for the others. VHS is the most popular format among home VCR users. Tapes are widely available in a range from 30 minutes to 6 hours. The main disadvantage of VHS cassettes is that they are large (they use 1/2 inch wide tape) and make for a bulky camcorder. A VHS-C camcorder accepts cassettes containing 1/2 inch tape which are far more compact. These tapes run from 20 to 90 minutes and can be played on a regular VHS

VCR using a special adapter. The third format is Video-8 or 8 mm which run from 2 to 6 hours. This also provides compact cassettes (using 8 mm tapes, which are only slightly larger than audio cassettes) and lightweight camcorders.

White Balance

The white balance and the daylight and tungsten filters on a video camera are used to ensure correct color. The daylight filter is engaged when shooting outdoors, and the tungsten filter is engaged when shooting under artificial light. These filters are necessary because in daylight, colors from the blue end of the spectrum tend to dominate, while artificial light has a reddish cast. The daylight filter removes the bluish cast, while the tungsten filter reduces the reds in artificial light.

Holding the Camcorder

Steadiness when holding the camera by hand is an important technique to master. Video cameras and camcorders weigh little more than a 35 mm camera. Their light weight makes them difficult to hold steady. The problem is greater with cameras that offer no shoulder support and must be held in front of the eye. A steady grip is important and comes with practice and concentration.

First, adopt a comfortable stance with legs slightly apart and elbows tucked into your sides to give firm support to the camera. The right hand does the steadying, leaving the left free to adjust the lens. If you must move to follow the action, turn from the waist at half speed, making your movements steady and deliberate, not jerky. Minimize your movements as much as possible. Adopt a camera position which allows full coverage of the action you wish to record. The more the action develops in view of the camera and the less obtrusive your movements, the more natural the result.

Another good technique when taking hand-held shots is to look for extra support such as a wall, doorway, or the back of a chair. For low angle work, kneel and rest your right elbow on your knee, or lie prone with the camera resting on a pile of books.

There will always be a degree of unsteadiness to hand-held shots, but this will be far less apparent using the wide angle end of the lens, particularly when close to the subject. No matter how skilled you become at hand holding the camera, you will never achieve the absolute steadiness that comes with using a tripod.

Technical Surveillance

Technical surveillance involves the use of electronic and visual enhancement devices to view or overhear subjects in the conduct of their daily affairs.

Bugs, Pen Registers, and Beepers

Ways to obtain investigative information in addition to wiretapping include bugs to eavesdrop on private conversations, pen registers to record all numbers dialed, and beepers attached to a person, an automobile, or anything being transported, to track the movement of a person or a piece of merchandise. The Fourth Amendment's impact on these devices ranges from a total ban to outright approval.

Unless there is a physical invasion of a constitutionally protected area, it would appear that electronic eavesdropping is permissible under the Fourth Amendment. However, the *Katz v. United States* decision of 1967 alters this view. In this case, the suspect, placing a call from a public phone, had his conversation recorded by government investigators who had attached a listening device to the outside of the telephone booth. The court held that the right to claim Fourth Amendment protection was not dependent upon the property right in the invaded place, but on a reasonable expectation of freedom from government intrusion. *Katz* is important because it provides the court's view on legitimate electronic surveillance.

In *Smith v. the State of Maryland,* the court ruled that individuals have no expectation of privacy in dialing phone numbers. The installation and use of a pen register, therefore, was not a search, and no warrant was required.

Monitoring Movement of Vehicles and Items of Commerce

The beeper is a device that tracks the movement of contraband, vehicles, or persons usually suspected of or engaging in crime. The beeper must be hidden in advance on the subject to be tracked to follow and trace to its ultimate destination. In 1982, the Supreme Court in *United States v. Knotts*, 460 U.S. 276 ruled that monitoring the beeper signals did not invade any legitimate expectation of privacy, thus there was neither a search nor a seizure under the Fourth Amendment. The beeper surveillance amounted principally to following an automobile on public streets and highways. The court approved the use of a beeper to monitor the movement of vehicles only on public roads. It refused to allow the government to monitor beepers on private property.

Electronic Communications Privacy Act of 1968

The investigative practices permitted by the New York Telephone Company were limited by federal legislation enacted in 1968. The law regulates the use of beepers and pen registers. The statute requires police to obtain a prior court order for any evidence obtained to be admissible in court. It also provides for criminal and civil penalties.

Visual Enhancement Devices

Other technical devices used to observe a subject, vehicle, or other object without detection can be quite simple (binoculars, camera, or telescope), while others are more intricate (infra-red snooper scope) and/or expensive (helicopter or airplane). There have been constitutional challenges to their use, although none have been challenged successfully.

Lower courts have ruled in some cases that visually enhanced observations may be viewed as searches under the Fourth Amendment. The issues of importance are:

- the nature of the area
- the kind of precautions taken by the subject to ensure privacy.
- whether an enhancement device is used to avoid detection of the surveillant after having first made observations with the unaided eye
- whether the investigator must do something unusual to make the observation, such as climb a fence to be high enough to view the activity or use a telescope
- the distance between the investigator and the behavior or activity of the subject under observation
- the level of sophistication of the viewing device

Practical Considerations

Surveillance should seldom be the task of one person. Vehicles equipped with direct communications systems are generally essential. Less expensive equipment such as CBs, high quality binoculars, and infra-red optical devices may assist in locating suspects without detection and to make a determination as to their activities.

Procedures for Interception of Wire or Oral Communications

Title III, Section 2518 of the Omnibus Crime Bill describes how to obtain an order from a judge authorizing interception of a wire or oral communication. In federal cases, the order must be approved by the Attorney General (or his designate); state cases require the approval of the principle prosecuting officer of the state or its political subdivisions. The applications must be in writing and sworn or affirmed, then submitted to the appropriate federal or state judge for approval.

The order may not remain in effect longer than is necessary to achieve its objectives, and no longer than 30 days. It must be executed promptly, minimizing any interference with communications not subject to interception. There is no limitation on the number of extensions that may be granted, but each must provide the required information and show probable cause. In executing the order, the investigator must avoid all unnecessary intrusions upon innocent communications, thereby respecting the right of privacy.

Photograph Log Cover Sheet

*****PHOTOS TAKEN*****

By _____   Case # _____

Date _____

Location _____

Incident_____

_____

_____

_____

_____

_____

Figure 13.1 Photograph log cover sheet.

Type of Film: _____

Photo #	Description	Shutter/f Stop	Time	Lighting	Weather

Figure 13.2 Photograph log.

PHOTOGRAPHS

Case Title:
Attorney:
Date/Loss:
VTS File:
FILM : 35mm LENS: 50mm
ISO : 100ASA FLASH :
Photo No : 0001
Date taken:
Location:
Photographer:

DESCRIPTION:

Figure 13.3 Sample display sheet.

14

SERVICE OF PROCESS

By definition, process means a formal document, authorized by law, directed to a person named in the document and commanding him to do or refrain from doing some act. Process is a form of writ, and is sometimes called a Writ of Process. The purpose of process and its service is to notify the defendant that he is being sued, tell him the nature of the litigation, give him an opportunity to defend himself, and confer jurisdiction of the court over the defendant's person.

In some states, Florida, for example, state law authorizes service by the sheriff in the county. It authorizes the sheriff to appoint process servers. The appointee is called an elisor. If the sheriff is unable to serve process for any reason, the court may appoint any competent person who has no interest in the action to make service.

TYPES OF SERVICE

Service of process is classified as personal, substituted, or constructive. Personal service is the physical delivery of a copy of the process and initial pleading to the person to be served by a person authorized by law to serve process. Substituted service is a similar delivery to someone other than the defendant who is authorized by law or contract to be served for the defendant. Constructive service is made by publication of notice of the litigation in a qualified newspaper or posting notice in the places required by law with the mailing of a copy of the notice and the initial pleading to the defendant if his whereabouts are known.

In some types of constructive service, only the publication is required. Both personal and substituted service give the court personal jurisdiction over the defendant so a judgment can be entered. Constructive service gives jurisdiction over some things that the court can act on to give relief to the parties seeking it. After the process has been properly served, the court can adjudicate the matter.

Service of process can be waived in two ways. Either the defendant can voluntarily serve responsive pleadings, motions, or papers prior to being served, or he may authorize his attorney to accept the initial pleading without service of process.

The method of service of process is a procedural matter. Service of original, cross-claim, and third party process is made by delivering a copy of the process and initial pleading to the person to be served. This method applies to all personal service, whether the person served is a defendant, officer, agent, or representative of an organization. Service of process on Sunday is prohibited unless a court order authorizing service is obtained.

PROOF OF SERVICE

The court cannot proceed in the action until proof of valid service has been made. The proof must specify the papers served, the person who was served, the date, time, address or place, and the manner of service, and must set forth facts showing that the service was made by an authorized person in an authorized manner. Proof of service shall contain a description of the person served, which shall include sex, color of skin, hair color, approximate age, height, weight, and any other identifying features. See Figures 14.1 and 14.2 for sample forms used by process servers to verify service of a process.

PITFALLS TO AVOID

The following pitfalls should be avoided.

Do not make service on Sunday.
Do not state anything about a certificate or affidavit of service that is not true.
Do not conceal process in any way or for any reason.
Do not conceal a summons in an envelope when delivering it.
Do not use trickery or deceit to effect service. Process servers should be resourceful, but must not misrepresent the process.
Do not give legal advice to anyone you may serve.
Do not take back the process after making service.
Do not use unreasonable force in effecting service.

```
                          CASE ACTIVITY RECORD
Civil Process: _____    Law Firm: _____
                              Attorney: _____
                              Address:  _____
                                        _____
                              Phone #:  _____
Same Day: _____    Expedited: _____    Date Received: _____

VS. _____

DOCUMENTS TO BE SERVED:

INDIVIDUALS/ADDRESSES FOR SERVICE:

ATTEMPTED:
SERVICE ON   ! DATE ! TIME ! LOCATION ! COMMENTS ! TIME ! EXP. ! MILEAGE
```

SERVICE ON	DATE	TIME	LOCATION	COMMENTS	TIME	EXP.	MILEAGE

```
SERVICE EFFECTED ON:              Date
   At:                            Time
   Cohabitant  Name/Relationship
   Accepted by:                   Title
   Direct      Substitute      Drop Service
===========================================================================
MISCELLANEOUS EXPENSES:
   Filing Fee  Freedom of Information  Documents/Copies  !_____!_____
   Other:                                                !_____!_____
===========================================================================
SERVERS COMMENTS:_____
_____
_____
_____
_____
```

Figure 14.1 Return of Service Affidavit.

R.J. McMahon & Assoc.
2150 NW 33 Terrace
Coconut Creek, FL 33066

DATE
RECEIVED

CASE NO
COURT
HRG DATE

TYPE OR WRIT

VS.

RETURN OF SERVICE
AFFIDAVIT

TO _____

RECEIVED THIS WRIT ON _____
AND ON _____ at _____ M., I SERVED IT ON THE WITHIN
NAMED _____ IN _____
COUNTY, FLORIDA

_____ INDIVIDUAL SERVICE: By serving upon the within named (Defendant/Witness) a true copy of this writ with the date and hours of service endorsed thereon by me and a copy of the Plaintiff's complaint, petition or initial pleading.

_____ SUBSTITUTE SERVICE: By serving a true copy of this writ with the date and hour of service endorsed thereon by me and a copy of Plaintiff's Initial pleading as furnished by the Plaintiff, at the within named (Defendant's Witness) usual place of abode with any person residing the age of 15 years or older to wit: _____
_____ or to _____ spouse of defendant, at _____
_____, or to _____ manager of defendant business _____
_____ and informing such person of their contents pursuant to: ❑ F.S. 48.031 _____
❑ F.S. 48.031 (2)(a)   ❑ F.S. 48.031 (2)(b).

_____ CORPORATE SERVICE: By serving a true copy of this writ and a copy of Plaintiff's initial pleading to _____
_____ as _____ of said
corporation in the absence of any superior officer as defined in F.S. 48.081, or by serving _____
_____ as an employee of defendant corporation in compliance with F.S. 48.081 (3) or by serving
_____ as a registered agent in compliance with F.S. 48.091.

_____ PARTNERSHIP SERVICE: By serving _____ , partner, or to _____
_____ a designated employee or person in charge of partnership.

_____ POSTED: ____ COMMERCIAL, ____ RESIDENTIAL, 1st Attempt _____ ___ PM 2nd Attempt _____ ___ PM

_____ NO SERVICE: For the reason that after diligent search and inquiry failed to find said _____
_____ in _____ County, Florida
COMMENTS: _____
_____
_____

I acknowledge I am certified/appointed in good standing in the judicial circuit wherein this process was served and have no interest in the above action.

The foregoing instrument was acknowledged before me this _____
day of _____ , 19 ____ by _____ , who is
Personally known to me or who has produced _____ (type
of ID) as identification and who _____ take an oath.
                           did or did not

_____   BY: _____
NOTARY PUBLIC   Certified/Appointment No.

Figure 14.2 Field Sheet Return of Service.

15

TESTIFYING IN COURT

Proper presentation of the investigator's testimony can be the deciding factor in a case. The first step in impressing the jurors is the initial appearance presented by the investigator. How he dresses and carries himself sets the tone for his testimony on the stand. The investigator should dress in fashionable, well fitting, conservative clothes. While in the witness chair, the investigator should exhibit an aura of professionalism. Testimony should be easily audible, concise, and crisp.

As a witness, the investigator should do pretrial preparation. He should familiarize himself with all material pertaining to the case. The investigator should meet with the attorney representing his client and review the material covering all questions that will be asked. The investigator should review with the attorney for his client any material that is likely to be covered by the opposing attorneys. He should concentrate on how to correctly answer any difficult questions that may arise. The investigator must learn what areas the attorney wants to avoid discussing. While waiting to testify and after testifying, he should avoid conversations with any other witnesses or members of the jury.

THE TRIAL

During the trial, the investigator should be well dressed, well groomed, and without excessive jewelry, makeup, or provocative clothing. While in the witness chair, the investigator should be calm, confident, and should sit upright with his feet planted on the floor and his arms resting on both chair arms. Testimony should be presented in a well organized, logical, and orderly fashion. All questions should be answered completely and as simply as possible. Information should never be volunteered. If he does not hear or understand the question, he should ask that it be repeated. The investigator, as any witness, should speak loudly, clearly, slowly, and use proper grammar without resorting to slang or jargon (i.e., the subject, suspect, "perp," etc.). Proper names and titles, i.e., Mr. (the defendant's name) or Dr. (witness), and so on should be used.

When on the witness stand, he should be serious yet relaxed in order to show that he is in command of the situation. He must always be truthful and as accurate and precise as possible. A witness should think carefully before answering. On cross-examination, he should allow time before answering to allow the attorney to object to the question if he so wishes. The investigator should look at the attorney asking the questions before answering (to avoid the appearance of being coached).

If he does not understand the question, he must seek clarification. He should try to avoid a yes or no answer that requires additional clarification. He should ask the judge to allow him to answer the question more completely. He should not play games or try to outsmart the opposing attorney.

The investigator should be professional in both demeanor and testimony. Remember, jurors view investigators as unbiased witnesses with valuable information. They should continue to feel that way after his testimony.

CROSS-EXAMINATION

During the cross-examination, the investigator should maintain composure. He should not be impatient or lose his temper. If he does, the attorney will have shown the jury that his testimony is biased. Some tactics an attorney may employ include rapid-fire questions and not allowing time to answer each question; a condescending manner; a benevolent or over-sympathetic manner or a friendly manner; and courteous, polite questions to lull the witness into a false sense of security. The attorney also may badger the witness. Other tactics used by an attorney include suggestive and leading questions to lead or confuse the witness; asking yes or no questions framed to produce a desired answer which is not necessarily the complete answer; reversing the witnesses testimony in framing additional questions; repetitive questions designed to elicit conflicting answers; conflicting answers designed to show inconsistencies in the investigation; and staring after the witness has answered, provoking the witness to add more information than the answer called for.

16

ETHICS

The values that guide our behaviors are called ethics. Many ethical guidelines of the past have become the laws and regulations of today. Businesses stress their ethical considerations in their promotional material or mission statements, but what do they really mean? They all state that they have a commitment to business ethics, but how should a client interpret a business' professional code of ethics and what should that code state? Ethical behavior goes beyond knowing what is right and what is wrong. It is simply doing what is right. The purpose of ethical business practices is to provide, in conjunction with laws, a structure that will promote and protect the greatest interests of the profession and the public from illegal or unethical performance. Making ethical choices in business ensures legal behavior and promotes a strong public image.

The uniqueness of the private investigation industry; that is, as legal investigators, must be recognized. The conduct of professional investigators must be ethical at all times. A private investigator must observe and adhere to the principles of honesty, goodwill, accuracy, discretion, and integrity. He must be faithful, diligent, and honorable in carrying out assignments, and in the discharge of his professional responsibilities. Intelligence gathering is not without controversy. It may be legal, but is it ethical? Because highly diverse values exist, managing ethics in the workplace is a difficult task.

Today's corporate intelligence operatives tread a fine line between honest inquiry and deception. Calling other companies' sales departments to acquire information about rates, lead times, and product availability is legal, but misrepresenting oneself is unethical. At trade shows, it is ethical that you wear an accurate nametag like everyone else. Where companies draw the line in their intelligence gathering is hard to document and are reluctant to discuss it.

Some agencies have little real world private sector investigative experience and lack even basic knowledge of applicable legalities and ethics. Many are uninsured. Other agencies may rely on one experienced supervisor to direct and correct the activities of a high-turnover staff of low-paid, inexperienced investigators who are sent into the field with little or no training. *Do not leave yourself open to these mistakes. You are judged by how you conduct your business, and how you are judged will affect your income.* Assuming the principles of professional conduct with legal and ethical standards of practice is necessary for success in today's competitive business environment.

The purpose of promoting an ethical business practice is to establish and promote clearly defined standards required by all investigators. These standards will assist in protecting the profession, the clients, and the public at large. Maintaining integrity and trust should be a continuing endeavor by professionals in accordance with the highest moral principles.

Outlined next are the major areas of concern to an investigator who conducts business with honesty, legality, integrity, and a code of ethics. Practice of these tenets will avoid conduct detrimental to the profession and to an agency's or individual's reputation. Additionally, individuals and agencies should adhere to all applicable standards and practices common to the general business community.

CONFIDENTIALITY AND PRIVACY

The purpose of confidentiality is to safeguard privileged communication and information that is obtained in the course of business. Disclosure of information is restricted to what is necessary, relevant, and verifiable with respect to the client's right to privacy. An investigator must not disclose, relate, or betray in any fashion the trust placed in him by the client, employer, or associate. In accepting instructions from clients, an investigator guarantees confidentiality and his protection and promotion of the interests of his clients.

When a third party is involved, the key when considering personal or confidential information is to make certain that the client is notified. To further a truthful and legitimate manner of operation, the rights of your clients must be respected. Refraining from divulging confidential information to newspapers, publications, or other media will protect your clients and prevent interference in the administration of justice or a fair trial in the courts.

A client's confidence must also be preserved beyond the term of employment. The disclosure or use of confidences for the private advantage of the investigator or his employees, or to the disadvantage of the client without knowledge or consent (even though there may be other available sources of information), would be a breach of confidentiality. Professional files, reports, and records should be maintained under conditions of security, with provisions made for their destruction when appropriate.

TRUTH

The obligation of commitment to the client's interest is primary but does not eliminate the obligation to determine the facts and render honest, unbiased reports. Investigators are dedicated to the search for truth and the furtherance of employers' or clients' interests. The search for that truth enables the establishment of ideals of fairness and justice for the benefit of the client in every case. The intention of every investigator should be to treat honestly, justly, and courteously all with whom they come in contact.

KEEP INFORMED

Investigators have an obligation to maintain technical competency at such a level that the client receives the highest quality of services that the investigators' discipline is capable of offering. It is important to keep informed on developments and changes in matters of law, proposed legislation, public policies, forensic or technical advances, and techniques that affect the profession. Local, state, and federal levels of information must be current to be able to offer an informed opinion and advise clients properly in an area of expertise and the feasibility of proposed assignments.

PROMOTE EDUCATION AND ADVOCACY

Industry programs must be promoted and supported. The educational intent should be designed to raise standards, improve efficiency, increase effectiveness, and enhance the private investigation industry. Direct and determined efforts should be made toward the support, advancement, and furtherance of high personal and professional conduct. An endeavor to provide the opportunity, training and education for the professional development and advancement of investigators will raise the standards of performance and the perception of the industry.

BUSINESS CONDUCT

Do not be party to any practices that are damaging to the good of the public or the profession. Do not engage in illegal or unethical practices as defined under the statutes and legal precedents in your respective jurisdiction. Never maliciously injure or defame the professional reputation or practice of colleagues, clients, or employers. When appropriate, explain to the public the role of your profession in the promotion of the administration of justice.

Guard against employing those techniques, or utilizing such equipment or devices, that may threaten the life, limb, or safety of another. Carry professional liability insurance for your own protection and the protection of affected third parties.

Labor diligently and unceasingly to elevate the standards of practice and do not tolerate unscrupulous invasion of business contracts by anyone who intrudes knowingly and willfully for his or her own private advantage or financial gain to the detriment and/or injury of another investigator.

AVOID CONFLICTS OF INTEREST

Refrain from accepting an assignment or employment if the mission will create a personal or professional conflict of interest. Extend the effectiveness of the profession by cooperating with other investigators and related professions, provided that this exchange does not violate the interests of their clients and/or employers. Respect the integrity of people with whom you work. When there is a conflict of interest, the nature and direction of loyalty and responsibilities must be clarified and all parties must be kept informed of that commitment. Private investigators should not enter into fee arrangements that would be likely to create conflicts of interest or influence testimony in any matter.

FAIR REPRESENTATION TO CLIENTS

Do not misrepresent or embellish your services to clients. The client should receive a factual report or summary of the services provided. Respect the best interest of your clients by maintaining a high standard of performance and reporting to your clients the full facts ascertained as a result of the work and effort expended, whether advantageous or detrimental to the interest of the client; nothing should be withheld from the client. Do not knowingly misrepresent yourself, your duties, or your credentials.

TREATMENT OF COMPETITORS

Never publicly criticize the business practice of a competitor or volunteer an opinion of a competitor's practice unless your opinion is sought. When asked to comment on cases being actively managed by another investigative organization, you should make every reasonable effort to conduct an in-person evaluation before rendering a conclusion, and give the other member an opportunity to respond. When an investigator deems it appropriate to respond, such opinion should be rendered with strict professional integrity and courtesy. Do not directly or indirectly injure the professional reputation, prospects, or practice of another investigator. Any discussion, comments, or criticism directed toward a fellow investigator or organization should be positive and/or constructive. Promote and protect the interest of fellow investigators.

However, when you have knowledge that another investigator has acted in an unethical, illegal, unprofessional, or unfair manner, present the information to the proper authority so that disciplinary action can be taken. Actively assist any regulatory agency charged with monitoring the profession.

Do not compete illegally or unfairly with other investigators in the solicitation of work. Do not seek any unfair trade advantage as deemed improper and/or illegal by state or federal laws or regulations. A private investigator working for one agency is forbidden to contact the client of another agency directly, unless instructed in writing to do so.

LEGAL ISSUES

Perform services within the boundaries of the law and do not permit or demand of any employee or fellow member any violation of the law or any manner of fraud. Do not knowingly violate any right or privilege of any individual which may be guaranteed or provided for by the U.S. Constitution or the laws of the state and federal governments. Cooperate with all recognized and responsible law enforcement and governmental agencies in matters within the realm of their jurisdiction. Investigators should not engage in illegal or unethical claim practices as defined under the statutes and legal precedents in their respective jurisdiction. Do not suggest, condone, or participate, in any fashion or degree, for any purpose whatsoever, in entrapment. Perform professional duties and business operations in accordance with the laws, and be familiar with what the laws are.

RENDER ONLY SERVICES THAT MATCH YOUR QUALIFICATIONS

Render only those services that you are competent and qualified to perform. Do not undertake to provide specialized professional services concerning something that is outside your field of competence unless you engage the assistance of someone who is competent in such service. Do not engage in the unauthorized practice of law. Do not promise or offer services or results that you cannot deliver or have reason to believe you cannot provide.

REPORTING

Make all your reporting based on truth and fact, and only express honest opinions. The services and submission of reports should be provided in a timely fashion and should respond to the purpose of the investigation and include recommendations, if appropriate. All reports should reflect objective, independent opinion based on factual determinations within the provider's area of expertise and discipline. Reports of service and findings should be distributed to appropriate parties and be in compliance with all applicable legal regulations.

COMPENSATION

Do not accept commissions or allowances, directly or indirectly, from independent contractors or other parties dealing with your client, employer, or associate in connection with work for which you are responsible. Do not solicit clientele for an attorney. Uphold, and never abuse, the principle of appropriate and adequate compensation for those who engage in investigative work.

A private investigator professional is responsible for all proper fees and expenses incurred by another agency for work undertaken under written instruction. Pay invoices in accordance with normal payment practices. Deal fairly and equitably with your client or employer, and clearly explain your duties and the basis for your charges in each undertaking. The investigator should advise the client of the fee structure in advance of rendering services and should furnish, upon request, detailed accurate time records. Avoid all controversies concerning compensation by using some form of written agreement or letter that states terms or fees as agreed upon by both parties. At all times, remember that the business of private investigation is a profession, and all financial dealings with clients should be handled on that basis. The private investigator should accept no compensation, commission, rebate, or other advantage from others without the knowledge and consent of his or her client.

ADVERTISING

When marketing services or products, advertising should be factually accurate and should avoid exaggerated claims as to costs or results. Refrain from using unprofessional media for advertising. Personal communications or interviews that fail to qualify you in a professional capacity can be detrimental. Do not misrepresent or exaggerate available services to clients. Do not advertise your work, skill, or merit in an unprofessional manner or in dramatic, misleading fashion, and avoid all conduct or practice likely to discredit or do injury to the dignity and honor of your profession. Competitive advertising should be factually accurate.

CLIENT RELATIONS

Do not accept instructions from any client where the proposed inquiries are judged not to be viable. Refuse to participate in practices that are conflicting with standards established by regulatory bodies regarding the delivery of services to clients. At the time of initial referral, identify to the client what services are available. All instructions both to and from clients should be acknowledged. Counsel clients against any illegal or unethical courses of action. Provide an efficient procedure for dealing with any client complaints, and comply with any decision determined by an arbitrator or court.

TESTIMONY

Investigators have the responsibility, when requested, for providing objective testimony. Investigative professionals provide services within the legal system and are called upon to testify to facts of which they have knowledge or to render a professional opinion on questions or factors affecting the outcome of a case. The testimony of an investigator should be limited to the specific fields of expertise of that individual as demonstrated by training, education, and experience. The extent of proficiency needed to testify is determined by the legal jurisdiction in which the professional is testifying.

EQUAL RIGHTS

Do not deny equal professional services to any person for reasons of race, color, religion, sex, handicap, sexual preference, or national origin, nor be party to any plan or agreement to discriminate against a person on the basis of the preceeding characteristics. Do not allow personal feelings or prejudices to interfere with factual and truthful disclosures.

17

FINDING A NICHE

Contrary to what you may want to believe, the entire planet is not your market. Only one part of the world is your customer, and another part is your competitor! In addition, it is expensive to try to market to the entire world. The difference between success and failure in the private investigative agency business is based on more than just being an exceptional investigator. Marketing techniques, management skills, and the ability to find your niche are the secrets to developing a lucrative private investigative practice.

The most common error made by amateurs in any field of business is thinking that by increasing their offerings, becoming a jack-of-all-trades and master of none, they will acquire additional business. Specializing and narrowing one's focus as much as possible will increase the probability of getting more business. When presented with a choice, consumers will go to a business that specializes in a unique area for which they have a need. Specialization is also an essential element of the marketing process. It is remarkably effective in creating "top-of-mind" consciousness among a target market.

The private investigator fits into an intriguing niche in our culture, filling the gap between crimes committed, serving the investigative needs of the legal industry, the public, and numerous government agencies short on personnel or resources for investigation. Law enforcement typically spends much of its time on crimes against people (rapes, murders, and robberies). They do not always have the time for civil issues or crimes against property such as burglary, theft, and larceny. This has created a void that private investigators are filling. Further defining that void into a niche or specialization will not only benefit an agency but also society as a whole.

Fifty years ago private investigators created a niche for themselves based on people's needs. The idea was, "If the police and Uncle Sam cannot help me, maybe Sam Spade can." The work was laborious and challenging, and sometimes perilous. For years, the private investigator's primary focus was matrimonial, fraud, and insurance investigations. In the 1970s things changed. Computer databases made it simple to find people and, in some states, no-fault divorce laws made pursuing most infidelity cases unnecessary. The role of the detective in today's world was changing. Today, investigators work for an increasing number of corporate clients, and the stakes are high. Methods of detection range from the simple to the sublime, from undercover intuition to undercover with a body wire. There are even more opportunities for specialization in today's market.

A niche or target market is a group of potential customers who share common characteristics, making them especially receptive to your service. Think of your niche as an area of business that is uniquely yours. Simply stated, your niche market is a targeted group of individuals who need or want what you have to offer. A niche does not rule out any prospects, but it gives a specific foundation and a place to concentrate your efforts. A niche can, change over time as an individual's range of experience grows or as market trends and needs dictate. You might find yourself with more than one niche as your business develops. By breaking out of the ordinary offerings in private investigative work and adding your own areas of expertise, you will increase the size of your agency.

As companies, Web sites, e-mail, and the media inundate us with information, and with limited time to shop around for the best product from the best company at the best price, we will more than likely go the store that pops into the mind first, and we do so only when the need presents itself. For example, we can purchase a toaster from a department store, a home furnishings store, an appliance store, a grocery store, a drugstore, and even a bank. If there were a store selling only toasters, we would probably go there first. Your job is to find your niche and to narrow it down as much as possible.

Success is hard to come by in a wide-ranging category like private investigation. You are competing with thousands of others, making it difficult for potential clients to locate you. Over one million people are privately employed in positions such as security officer, private investigator, security manager, and computer security. That is a huge choice for businesses or individuals in need of service. A prospective client will know exactly what he needs to accomplish or what information he needs gathered. Having your own niche allows you to have an individual identity, to stand out from the droves of investigators going after the same business. If there is an offer available from an agency that specializes in filling a person's specific need, that one projects gets the job, not the agency that does it all.

Specialization projects an impression of authority and exclusivity. When dealing with a specialist, people assume that he has superior expertise and knowledge about the discipline and, thus, offers a better service, because catering to a unique market, implies that the specialist will have a better understanding of the situation, needs, and concerns. This perceived impression is a major influence on people's business choices.

Identifying a target market makes it easy to plan effective marketing activity and develop a winning sales message. When you know the specific concerns of your market, you can tailor your message to focus on solutions to those concerns. Different sales messages can be created for different target markets. Defining your niche market will allow you to do vital things you cannot do without a niche. You will be able to maximize your ad budget by targeting only those in your niche market. You will know exactly where to advertise. You can design a marketing campaign to convey precisely how and why you can help solve the specific problems. Moreover, you will have the opportunity to develop additional new services that inherently appeal to your niche market, while establishing yourself as a leader in your industry.

You must not only become expert in the usual and customary desired services of an investigation firm, you must also place an emphasis on your forté. There is a specific group with an intense need or desire for the benefits you offer. Find that niche market and commit your efforts to getting business from it.

HOW TO FIND YOUR NICHE

Answer the following questions and apply the information in finding your target market and creating the sales material. Genuine opportunities require preparation, establishing objectives, and organizing priorities. You will make apparent the tremendous benefits you can present to this market and why these benefits are important. Just by structuring your advertising and sales material around this benefit, you will appreciate the proceeds from successfully targeting that niche market.

Who Are You?

What are your skills? Doing what you naturally do best is an easy way to find your niche. What is your passion? You must feel good about how you will spend most of your waking hours. Your positive attitude will motivate you. Where would you fit in and where would you not fit in? Where people have to or are prohibited from doing, certain things or are required to dress a certain way, do you agree? Are those people on the same wavelength as you? With whom and for whom do you want to spend time working? Working and being with intelligent people who share your passions and understand your sense of humor will have a strong effect on your attitude and success.

Who Is Your Competition?

Small business owners need to be concerned about competition from both small and large businesses. Identify your competitors, gather information on them, find out how they operate, and then apply the information to develop your unique niche in the market. Be aware of what your competition does — both positive and negative. Competing businesses push each other to be better. Look for ways to find your competitive niche. Find ways to capitalize on the strengths of your own business. Be a follower or improver of your competitors' service.

Though it is atypical for a small company to be a market leader, by considering its own resources versus those of its competitors, a small company can be innovative by concentrating on market segments that have the lowest probability of attracting larger competitors. Some of these segments may be too small for a larger company to specialize in, or some segments may just not receive the local or regional exposure from larger companies. Smaller companies possess unique strengths that must be applied to enhance their niche market offerings.

Is There an Untapped Market?

Find profits in one of the least-known commercial ventures, something innovative and new. Be a groundbreaking leader. Can you offer services in a niche that has not been filled before? If you can fill a void in the marketplace and build a business around it, you cannot go wrong.

What Are You Offering?

Start by listing all of the benefits, not the features, offered by your service. You must know the difference between benefits and features to market anything successfully. A feature is what something is, while a benefit is what it does. For example, a large agency may employ 20 investigators, which is a feature. The fact that the investigators are on call 24 hours a day, is a benefit. Understanding this difference is important. People never buy something to get a feature. They always buy something to get the benefit produced by the feature.

Who Are Your Prospects?

Can you list some of the characteristics of prospects whose current situation would be dramatically improved by your benefits? You should begin to see a definable group emerging as a niche or target market. Determine if the target group you have identified is a market you can reach and develop profitably. If it is, you will be able to answer yes to all of the following questions. Can you identify prospects with enough contact information to communicate with them? Can you deliver your sales message to these prospects in an acceptable and positive way? Do your potential prospects have a strong need or a strong desire for your services? Do your prospects have the financial ability to pay for what you are offering? Is the group of prospects large enough to produce the volume of business you need? Can you identify the biggest problem and offer a solution to it?

DOUBLE CHECK YOUR CHOICES!

Ask yourself, is your emerging niche something you know how to do? Can you do it well? It is something you like to do and would not mind doing day after day? It is something with a broad enough appeal to sell on a steady basis? Can it be sold at a price that will cover all of your expenses and overhead plus return a healthy profit? Do not waste your time on this market if you have answered no to any of these questions. It is not a niche market for you.

Do you have or can you raise enough funds to get the business started and keep it running until it becomes a profitable venture? You want to be the leader in your unique area of expertise. By doing so, free publicity will come to you fairly easily, since the media loves anything out of the ordinary. In a frenzied and cutthroat marketplace, specializing causes people and companies, along with specialized publications and cable, to seek you out. You arouse interest by offering a unique and expert public service and thereby generate indirect advertising.

Identifying the right niche market is crucial to your success. When you define your niche, you can focus your time, energy, and money on reaching only people who will most likely become your clients. Specialization is the wave of the future, and the greater the competition becomes, the greater the need for more specialists. As more and more ventures get started (and more and more Web sites populate cyberspace), the less time, energy, and money potential clients will have to spend in making choices about with whom they will do business. This can make the difference between frustrating disappointments and a prosperous venture that shines above the competition.

18

OPERATING A PRIVATE
INVESTIGATIVE AGENCY

CHOOSING A NAME

The first decision to be made is the name of the agency. Do you want to create a catchy sounding name, a name that will describe what your business does, or do you want to keep it simple? Pick a name that you are comfortable with and that will help you market your agency.

FORM OF OPERATION

There are four forms of operation to choose from: sole proprietorship, partnership, corporation, and an "S" corporation. Each has its advantages and disadvantages.

Sole Proprietorship

This is a business owned by one person. The advantage is that one person has complete control of the business. It is the easiest form of business to start. It can be set up and run any way the proprietor wants. The major disadvantage is that the liabilities and obligations of the business belong to the sole proprietor alone. The sole proprietor has personal liability for all business debts. If the business fails, it can bring financial ruin to personal finances.

Partnership

A partnership is an association of two or more persons for the purpose of business for profit. The advantages of forming a partnership are that more money, more knowledge, and more talents are available to get the business going. Also, liabilities are spread out among all the partners. The disadvantages are that all profits are shared, all partners have a voice in managing the business, each partner is personally liable for the actions of the other partners, and a change in the relationship between the partners can, like a marriage, have a devastating effect on the business.

Corporation

A corporation is an artificial person. It is a method of organizing a business where the business has a separate legal existence from its owner(s). The major advantage of creating this distinct entity is that it protects the owners from personal liability. Debtors can only obtain the assets of the corporation and cannot go after the owners' personal assets. The disadvantage is possible double taxation. First, as the owner/employer, you must pay taxes. Second, any profits the corporation makes are taxable.

"S" Corporation

The subchapter "S" corporation is given special income tax treatment by the Internal Revenue Code. While the owners of the business enjoy the same protection from liability as a corporation, the "S" corporation does not pay tax. Only profits passed through to the owners are subject to income tax, which makes the "S" corporation the preferable form of business where the corporation has less than 75 shareholders.

LOCATION

The first rule is to keep your overhead down. When you first start your business, you will want to keep basic monthly expenses to a minimum. You may consider operating the agency from your home and using a mailing address until you get your business established. Many economical business identity programs will provide you with a mailing address and, occasionally, an office to meet clients when the need arises. This will provide your agency with an address other than your home.

A great deal of thought should be given to determining what type of location is best suited to the proposed operation. A site in a central shopping district will provide very high traffic, but requires very high rents, and all other operating costs are high. Competition may be considerable, and most businesses are well established. Shopping centers provide modern interiors and exteriors with a medium amount of traffic. Rents are medium to high. Neighborhood shopping centers may also be chosen. Only light traffic can be expected, but rents are generally lower and overall operating expenses will be lower. The other stores will be small. Strip malls usually have very low rental rates, so the total operating cost will be much lower and there will be abundant parking space.

The requirements for different types of businesses may vary considerably, but some common areas to consider when choosing a location regardless of the kind of business you are setting up are accessibility to transportation, availability of manpower, proximity to clients, local ordinances and regulations, quality of local services (police, fire, etc.), water supply, power, and other utilities, space for future expansion, and tax structure.

PRICING

The price concept is closely affiliated with products and/or services and service management. Price involves the buying and selling process is affected by the law of supply and demand. Price is a useful tool in promotion and can help or hinder sales. Price can affect your bottom line figure for better or worse. Price can be an extremely valuable tool when used as a competitive weapon.

To the consumer, the price of a service represents the seller's interpretation, expressed in monetary terms, of the products usefulness — its ability to satisfy a consumer's wants and needs. Consumers may regard the price of an item as fair (consistent with his or her perception of its worth in dollars and cents) or higher or lower than fair. If the price is considered too high, customers resist purchasing the item; if the price is considered low, then it becomes a bargain (although a low price can also cause consumers to doubt the quality of the product). In pricing your services, take into consideration competitor's prices, local economic conditions, level of demand, desired profit return, other market factors, and the price/quality relationship.

Determine the best pricing strategy to employ relative to your competition. Logically, there are three ways to go. You may set your prices on the level with your competitors. You may deliberately price above the competition (if seeking a quality image for your firm) and use pricing to distinguish your product. You may also undercut you competitors to secure a foothold in a new market create a discount image, or obtain a heavier volume.

BOOKKEEPING

Bookkeeping is an orderly method of recording financial information. Financial statements are formalized reports summarizing financial data previously recorded. There are two basic reports. A balance sheet lists the agency's assets. Assets minus liabilities equal the agency's net worth.

The agency's worth may also be determined by compiling a total of assets plus liabilities for net worth as of a specific date. The second basic financial report is a statement of income and expenses (profit and loss statement). Gross profit is the difference between sales and the cost of sales. Net pretax is the profit that is, the difference between gross profit and expenses.

As you are running your business, you will rely on the monthly statement of profit and loss to determine if you made or lost money during the month. Consecutive months operating at a loss could mean the start of a "cash flow crunch." The business may appear to be running smoothly when suddenly receivables are high and cash outlay is great because you are busy working new cases. This means that you may not have enough cash to pay your present expenses until your past due receivables arrive. You may need a line of credit or a loan from the bank to carry you through. See Figure 18.1 for a sample client financial contract.

Purpose of Financial Statements

You cannot effectively plan for the future unless you have a sense of past history and know where you are at the present. If you do not control your business, it will control you. Proper use of your financial reports are the basis for control.

You should keep the following basic records. An income of receipts record should contain your total sales, listed by department, and should include all income received in cash, by check, or paid by credit card as well as the clients' names. Any other or sundry income such as commissions, rebates (cash discounts, etc.), or interest earned, should be included in the records. All payouts should be recorded, including cash payouts or cash disbursements such as postage, trucking, tips, etc. All merchandise pickups and capital expenditures including furniture, equipment, and machinery should be recorded, as should all payroll records. Be sure to keep actual records of hours for each person.

Record all payments made by check including expense items, merchandise, capital investments including furniture, equipment, and machinery, payroll (check register should show gross pay and itemized deductions such as taxes, etc.), and paid taxes including federal, state, county, and city taxes.

Records are not only for dealing with tax collectors. They are also a tool that can lead you to success. The best kept records are of no value if you do not use them to manage your business. See Figures 18.8 and 18.9 for two additional record-keeping forms.

Business Problems

Insurance coverage — that is too high can be expensive, while undervalued insurance coverage can be devastating in case of loss. In the case of tax problems, you are required to prove any statements made on tax forms. You are guilty until proven innocent by the IRS. Other common problems include excessive expenses, such as payroll, advertising, overhead, etc., a low volume of new cases, high advertising cost versus case volume, low net profit versus high costs, financial over-reaching or expansion, and bad debts.

Additional problem areas may include poor debts collection, high interest costs, and difficulty in borrowing. Banks will require a detailed profit and loss statement, a balance sheet and sometimes a cash flow chart. Make business comparisons to see how your business is operating as compared to other businesses of a similar type.

Keep an updated list of furniture and equipment already owned as well as that purchased as you go along. These items can be depreciated and represent a tax savings. Keep accounts payable current to avoid the loss of cash discount. Keep accounts receivable current to avoid collection expenses. Funds should be placed in a separate account to pay any taxes owed. If possible, a perpetual inventory of equipment, supplies, and other such items should be kept.

The good news is that there is a wide variety of software programs available to keep track of all your financial record-keeping. Programs such as Quicken and Quickbook Pro will solve your financial record-keeping needs.

TIPS FOR OPERATING YOUR AGENCY

Getting Business

Insurance companies, attorneys, and businesses that you know and use are the best sources of new business. Get involved in networking groups, chambers of commerce, bar associations, rotary, and so on. Go to breakfast meetings, luncheons, and dinners, and tell people about your business and what you do.

Marketing Tips

The more specifically you can target your efforts at publicity, the better your chance of success. Each magazine, newspaper, TV, and radio station represents a wide variety of targets. If you simply send a press release to a magazine editor, it could get lost before it arrives at the appropriate department. Mailing your release to the appropriate editor or section of the magazine or newspaper will most likely produce more favorable results. Do not make cold calls.

Ideally, your web site should pop up every time a prospective customer uses a search engine to locate your type of service. To make your web site as visible as possible to every search engine, consider all the specific words and phrases that people might use to search for it, and then make sure those words (key words) appear somewhere in your site's text.

Forms

See Figures 18.2 through 18.8 for examples of some forms that you may want to use in your business.

KEYS TO SUCCESS

1. Find your niche.
2. Be a professional in everything you do.
3. Join a professional association.
4. Treat your clients and employees with respect.
5. Provide a quality product for a fair price.
6. Get a mentor — someone you know and trust.

There are a lot of private investigative agencies. However, there are not many *good quality private investigative agencies* in existence. The key to success is quality personalized services in your specialized area of expertise.

Dear:

Thank you for employing _____ (hereinafter referred to as_____) to provide you with professional investigative services. We will do our best to provide you with efficient, economical and effective service. In order to confirm the terms of engaging_____ concerning the above referenced matter we forward this letter, which sets forth those terms, for your signature.

SCOPE OF EMPLOYMENT:

 You have requested that _____Investigations conduct an investigation of :

We will undertake all aspects of attempting to investigate said matters and will do so at our sole discretion, by way of any lawful and ethical means deemed appropriate, and necessary, in accordance with state and federal law, and accepted industry practices. You will indemnify and hold harmless_____, its agents, employees, and sub-contractors from, and against, any and all liability, loss or damage, including reasonable attorneys fees, that_____ may sustain as a result of any claims, demands, costs or judgments which may be brought against_____ as a result of the investigation that you have requested.

You will be kept apprised of the progress of the investigation via telephone and/or written reports. All reports, documents, tapes, photographs, video tapes and other exhibits prepared and presented as part of this investigation are deemed to be confidential, and are for the use of the client only. Any legal counsel, retained by you, is authorized to have access to said materials, at your discretion. The investigative materials may not be copied or released to the media or any other individual or entity without the express written permission of the client, and _____.

COMPENSATION/FEES:

This office will represent you at an hourly rate of _____ per hour. Depositions, statements and appearances in court, or any administrative hearing or meeting, by _____, its agents and employees shall be billed at the stated hourly rate.

EXPENSES:
In addition to the above hourly rate, you are responsible for payment of all out of pocket expenses which are necessary to conduct the investigation. A mileage expense for travel associated with this investigation, will be charged at the rate of $.___ per mile.

Figure 18.1 Sample client financial contract.

Other out of pocket expense may include, but shall not be limited to: copies, overnight or priority postage, long distance and cellular telephone calls, database research fees, public records research fees, video tape, photographs and overnight accommodations.

Out of pocket expenses that shall be borne by _____shall include gasoline, local telephone calls, tolls, and meals (unless on an overnight stay).

RETAINER:

You will be responsible for a retainer balance in the amount of $_____ in order for work to commence on your case. The remainder of any unused portion of a retainer will be sent to you with the final report.

BILLING:

You will receive periodic billing statements listing services performed and time and expenses incurred in your case. The present retainer will be applied to the initial billing. Payment of invoices which are normally prepared weekly, are due in full upon receipt. Any unpaid balance, outstanding over thirty days, may be assessed an interest charge of 2% per month.

We reserve the right and in all likelihood will cease work on any case where bills have not been paid in strict accordance with the above. In the event of any default of payment of the sums here under, and if this agreement is placed in the hands of an attorney, collection agency, or the small claims court, you will be responsible for all costs of collection, including but not limited to attorneys fees, court costs, sheriffs' costs and time necessarily spent by_____ in the collection of said moneys at the above mentioned hourly rate and expenses.

If the foregoing terms are acceptable to you, please indicate by signing below and return this letter to our office, with the retainer. You should keep the enclosed duplicate original for your own records.

BINDING EFFECT:

This agreement shall be binding and inure to the benefit of the respective successors, heirs, executors, administrators and assigns of_____, and you, the client.

    Very Truly Yours

I have reviewed the foregoing and agree and accept all of its terms and conditions.

Signature: Date:

Figure 18.1 (continued) Sample client financial contract.

The Nature of Investigations   As an aid to help our clients better understand the nature of the Private Detective industry, the processes by which we work, and the regulations by which we are governed, we have prepared this informational sheet so you may have more realistic expectations regarding the work **MCMAHON & ASSOCIATES** will conduct on your behalf.

1. We have no more authority than does a private citizen. We are not police officers. The training, testing, background checks, and certification process we go through in order to obtain our licenses is meant to set us apart as individuals who are committed to unbiased professionalism. As such, we are bound to rigid codes of conduct dictated by the State of Florida.

2. We are not magicians. Ours is an industry revolving around detail gathered through available information, the understanding of this detail, and the working knowledge of how to follow the trails we uncover. This detailed information is generated through diligence and knowing where to look. Just as librarians are not geniuses, they simply are trained on where and how to find the information.

3. Sometimes the information generated is contrary to what the client hopes to find. We cannot guarantee results. We can only guarantee that the necessary information, documentation, etc. will be searched for diligently, legally, expediently, and as economically as possible.

4. If surveillance is necessary we feel obligated to inform you of the "real life caveats." Surveillance, especially moving surveillance, is a hit and miss science. We can perform these observations under agreed upon time and location parameters but cannot promise activity on behalf of the subject. Similarly, moving surveillance carries with it inherent obstacles such as the unpredictable nature of traffic. There is no guarantee that contact with the subject can be maintained as we cannot predict traffic flow, traffic conditions, weather, or other unforeseen problems. As in number one above, we have no more authority than an ordinary citizen. This includes traffic laws.

5. **MCMAHON & ASSOCIATES** can, however, make a promise that most of the other agencies can't. That is, that we will do everything in our power to reach the goal of obtaining the information you need in a timely and economical fashion and conduct ourselves in a professional and discreet manner while representing you in your case.

INVESTIGATOR:_____, Signature:_____ Date:___/___/___

Figure 18.2 Sample information disclosure.

MCMAHON & ASSOCIATES
Activity Checklist - PI

Case#: _____ Client:: _____ Re: _____

		Case Start			
Date	IN	Activity	Date	IN	Activity
		Initial contact with client			
		Contract signed			
		All necessary releases signed			
		Info listed in case roster			
		Agent			

Case Final Disposition

Case: o Closed o Terminated o Suspended on: ___ / ___ / ___ Re:

Synopsis of final result:

Reopened on: ___ / ___ / ___ Re:

Court date of: ___ / ___ / ___ Court: _____ Judge: _____

Subject / Suspect	Notes:

Other disposition of main subject:

		Disposition of Evidence	
Date	IN	Activity	Note
		Police reports	
		Forensics reports	
		Witness Interview Tapes and Transcripts	
		Surveillance Reports and Materials	
		Number of audio cassettes:	
		Number of video cassettes:	
		Still photos: Total # rolls:	
		Courthouse or other legal doc. Copies:	
		Misc. items from trash run:	

		Billing and Accounting			
Date	IN	Activity	Date	IN	Activity
		Retainer of: $_____ collected w/contract			
		Case conclusion balance of:$_____			30 day notice sent
		Retainer refund or first bill of: $_____			60 day notice sent
		Payment of:$_____ rec'd			90 day notice sent
		Payment of:$_____ rec'd			Collection activity initiated
		Payment of:$_____ rec'd			

		Final Communication
Date	IN	Activity
		Final synopsis/report mailed to: o Client o Client's attorney o Other:
		Thank you notes sent to all applicable people (client, attorney, LEOs, stellar witnesses, etc.)
		All computer files copied to floppy and stored in evidence envelope inside The Case File itself.
		Case entered into master log and/or database o Case details entered into spreadsheet

Figure 18.3 Sample activity checklist.

MCMAHON & ASSOCIATES

OUTGOING CORRESPONDENCE / DOCUMENTATION

	Sent to:	Re:	Date Sent	Deliv ID#	)	Author	Comp File Nm		Copies				File
1													
2													
3													
4													
5													
6													
7													
8													
9													
10													
11													
12													
13													
14													
15													
16													
17													
18													
19													

"Copies" Column above: C = Client, J = "Judge" (Court), O = Opposing Counsel, I = "In house"

INCOMING CORRESPONDENCE

	Source	Re:	Author	Date Rec'd	Date Sent	Sent Via	RSVP	File
1								
2								
3								
4								
5								
6								
7								
8								
9								
10								
11								
12								
13								
14								
15								
16								
17								
18								
19								

MASTER CORRESPONDENCE LOG; INCOMING AND OUTGOING MAIL

Figure 18.4 Sample correspondence log.

MCMAHON & ASSOCIATES

Journal Entry Starter Page. Place plain notebook paper behind this page and use this sheet as a model for entering lengthy notes. These entries should directly correspond with day-date-time entries on "Daily Activity Log" located on top of these notes. No length limit here.

Date	Time	Notes

Date	Time	Notes

Journal Entry Starter Page

Figure 18.5 Sample journal entry starter page.

MCMAHON & ASSOCIATES
Investigator Assignment Log Sheet

Client or Case # _____

	Agent	Start Date	End Date	Hours	Tot Exp	Mil	Assignment, Results, Notes
1.							
2.							
3.							
4.							
5.							
6.							
7.							
8.							
9.							
10							
11							
12							
13							
14							
15							
16							
17							
18							
19							
20							
21							
22							
23							
24							
25							
26							
27							
28							
29							
30							

Figure 18.6 Sample daily activity log.

MCMAHON & ASSOCIATES
CASE "TO DO" LIST
"P" is Priority, "?" column is for your personal code symbols; "4" is to mark item completed

P	Due by:	2	3	Item	Assigned to:
P	**Due by:**	**?**	**3**	**Item**	**Assigned to:**

"P" is Priority, "?" column is for your personal code symbols; "4" is to mark item completed
CASE "TO DO" LIST

Figure 18.7 Sample case "to do" list.

MCMAHON & ASSOCIATES
Case Final Disposition Checklist - PI

Case#: _____ Re: _____

	Date	Int	Process
1			**Case**: o Closed o Terminated o Suspended:
2			**Re:**
3			Final synopsis mailed to o Client o Client's attorney o Other:
4			
5			Pertinent documentation sent to client. **Via:** **Doc.#:**
6			Pertinent documentation sent to attorney. **Via:** **Doc.#:**
7			Financial status report sent. o Balance due us: o Refund due Client:
8			**Billing details:**
9			First Bill:
10			Second Bill:
11			Third Bill:
12			**Paid in full via:** Cash $: Check #: MO.#:
13			Visa,MC, Amex, Discover Card #: Exp: __ / __ / __
14			Thirty day notice sent.
15			Sixty day notice sent.
16			**Notes:**
17			
18			
19			
20			
21			
22			
23			
24			
25			
26			
27			
28			
29			
30			
31			
32			
33			
34			**Double check "Evidence Tracking Sheet" for these items:**
35			Number of audio cassettes: Copy sent? Y N
36			Number of video cassettes: Copy sent? Y N
37			Still photos: Total # rolls: Total useable unique prints: Copy sent? Y N
38			Courthouse or other legal doc. Copies: Copy sent? Y N
39			Misc. items from trash run: Copy sent? Y N
40			Cross-checked for all info: o Daily Activity Chart, o To-Do list o "Report To Client" o Contract
41			Additional follow-up. **Re:**
42			
43			o **Thank you notes sent to all applicable people** (client, attorney, LEOs, stellar witnesses, etc.)
44			o **All evidence from Evidence Tracking Sheet accounted for**
45			o **Case entered into master log and/or database** o **Case details entered into spreadsheet**

Figure 18.8 Sample final disposition checklist.

19

PROFESSIONAL ASSOCIATIONS

There is a wide variety of private investigator, private detective, and related professional associations including national organizations, international associations, statewide associations, and local groups. In my opinion, professional people belong to professional associations. Doctors have the American Medical Association; lawyers have legal associations such as the National Association of Criminal Defense Attorneys (NACDL) and the American Trial Lawyers Association (ATLA). Likewise, investigators have numerous choices, related to their areas of expertise.

In addition to enhancing your stature as a professional by belonging to a professional association, it is also a great method of obtaining additional business. Networking with other investigators around the state or around the world will result in referrals to your business. I receive numerous new cases monthly from other investigative agencies throughout the United States as a result of my membership in professional associations. Membership also keeps me current on trends in the industry, legislation that may impact upon my business and training conferences and seminars.

NATIONAL ASSOCIATIONS

National Association of Legal Investigators, Inc. (NALI) —
www.nalionline.org
National Council of Investigation and Security Services (NCISS) —
www.NCISS.com
Association of Certified Fraud Examiners (ACFE) —
www.AFCE.org

National Association of Background Investigators —
www.background.org
National Association of Investigative Specialists (NAIS) —
www.PIMall.com/NAIS/home.html
Women Investigators Association —
www.TheGrid.net/rbacon/wiahome.html

INTERNATIONAL ASSOCIATIONS

Council of International Investigators (CII) —
www.CII@.org
Global Investigative Network (GIN) —
www.Ginetwork.com
World Association of Detectives (WAD) —
www.WAD.net

STATE ASSOCIATIONS

Alabama

Northern Alabama Investigators Association (NAIA)
Alabama Professional Investigators Association (APIA)

Alaska

Alaska Investigators Association (AIA) —
www.akcache.com/alaskapi/AIA/index.htm

Arizona

Arizona Association of Licensed Private Investigators (AALPI)

Arkansas

Private Investigators Association of Arkansas (PIAA)

California

California Association of Licensed Investigators (CALI) —
www.cali-pi.org/

Colorado

Professional Private Investigators Association of Colorado (PPIAC) — www.ppiac.org/

Connecticut

Connecticut Association of Licensed Private Investigators (CALPI)

Delaware

Delaware Association of Detective Agencies (DADA)

Florida

Florida Association of Licensed Investigators (FALI) — www.fali.com

Georgia

Georgia Association of Professional Private Investigators

Idaho

Idaho Private Investigators Association (IPIA)

Illinois

Associated Detectives of Illinois, Inc. (ADI) — www.pimall.com/adi/index.html

Indiana

Indiana Society of Professional Investigators (INSPI) — www.state.in.us/inspi/profile.html
Indiana Association of Private Detectives (IAPD) — www.pimall.com/iapd/

Iowa

Iowa Association of Private Investigators (IAPI) — www.iowa-investigators.com

Kansas

Kansas Association of Private Investigators (KAPI) — www.kapi.org/assites.html

Kentucky

Kentucky Professional Investigators Association, Inc. (KPIA)

Louisiana

Louisiana Private Investigators Association, Inc. (LPIA) — www.lpia.net

Maine

Maine Licensed Private Investigators Association (MLPIA)

Maryland

Professional Investigators Alliance of Maryland (PIAM) — www.olg.com/piam
Maryland Investigators and Security Association (MISA) — www.spybbs.com/misa/

Massachusetts

Licensed Private Detectives Association of Massachusetts (LPDAM) — www.lpdam.com

Michigan

Michigan Council of Private Investigators (MCPI) — www.mcpihome.com
Michigan Association of Private Detectives (MAPD)

Minnesota

Minnesota Association of Private Investigators (MAPI)

Mississippi

Mississippi Professional Investigators Association (MPIA) — www.mpia.com

Missouri

Missouri Association of Private Investigators (MPIA)

Montana

Montana Association of Private Investigators (MAPI)

Nebraska

Nebraska Association of Professional Investigators (NAPI) — www.napi.org/

Nevada

Nevada Investigators Association (NIA)

New Hampshire

New Hampshire League of Investigators (NHLI) — www.mv.com/ipusers/magee/

New Jersey

New Jersey Licensed Private Investigators Association, Inc. (NJLPIA) — www.njlpia.com

New Mexico

New Mexico Private Investigators Association (NMIA)

New York

Associated Licensed Detectives of New York State (ALDONYS) — www.aldonys.org/
Society of Professional Investigators (SPI) — www.spionline.org/

North Carolina

North Carolina Association of Private Investigators (NCAPI) — www.ncapi.org/

Ohio

Ohio Association of Security and Investigation Services (OASIS) — www.jhanda.com/oasis/

Oklahoma

Oklahoma Private Investigators Association (OPIA) — www.opia.com

Oregon

Oregon Association of Licensed Investigators (OALI) — www.oali.org/

Pennsylvania

Pennsylvania Association of Licensed Investigators, Inc. (PALI) — www.pali.org/

Puerto Rico

Society of Private Investigators of Puerto Rico

Rhode Island

Licensed Private Detectives Association of Rhode Island

South Carolina

South Carolina Association of Legal Investigators (SCALI) — www.pimall.com/scali/index.html
South Carolina Association of Private Investigators

Tennessee

Tennessee Professional Investigators Association (TPIA) — www.tpia.com

Texas

Texas Association of Legal Investigators (TALI) — www.tali.org/

Utah

Private Investigators Association of Utah, Inc. (PIAU) — www.webcircle.com/users/piau

Vermont

Vermont Association of Licensed Detectives and Security Services

Virginia

Private Investigators Association of Virginia, Inc. (PIAVA) — www.pimall.com/piav/

Washington

Washington Association of Legal Investigators (WALI) — www.wali.org/
Pacific Northwest Association of Investigators (PNAI) — www.pnai.com

West Virginia

Private Investigators and Security Professionals of West Virginia

Wisconsin

Wisconsin Association of Professional Private Investigators (WAPPI)
Professional Association of Wisconsin Licensed Investigators (PAWLI)

20

GETTING LICENSED

In most states, it is mandatory to obtain licensing in order to become a private investigator. In Florida, for instance, there is a double requirement; the applicant be sponsored by a private investigator (C license holder) who works for a private investigative agency (A license holder). The agency is required to maintain liability insurance. In Florida, you are eligible to obtain a C license if you have two years provable investigative experience (e.g., a prior law enforcement officer). If not, then you may apply for a CC license (intern), where you will be required to work under a C license holder for two years, and will then become eligible to obtain a C license.

Each state has its own requirements, although some states do not license investigators. There is a wide disparity in requirements, from mandatory background checks and insurance bonding to training requirements and testing prior to license issuance. However, there has been an increasing trend to require prior training and/or testing to become licensed and to attend continuing education to maintain the license.

All states that require licensing have a regulatory authority charged with license issuance, regulation, and enforcement. Some states such as Pennsylvania have licensing on the county level. The eight states that do not require licensure recommend that applicants contact local and county municipalities for possible business license requirements.

A number of books are available that provide information on obtaining licenses in all states. I recommend *Learn How to Become a Private Investigator ... in a 6 Billion Dollar Industry!*, by John M. Lajoie, a fellow certified legal investigator. This book is available through his web site at www.privateinvestigator.com. Needless to say, John has a veritable gold mine in owning that domain name.

Good luck to all of you who have read this book and aspire to be private investigators. I can tell you that it is a great job, seldom boring, and can be a very profitable business.

BIBLIOGRAPHY

Ciolino, P.J. and Castle, G.E., *Advanced Forensic Civil Investigations*, Lawyers and Judges Publishing, Tucson, AZ, 1997.

Golec, A., *Techniques of Legal Investigation*, Charles C. Thomas, Springfield, IL, 1995.

Kwitney, J., *The Fountain Pen Conspiracy*, Alfred A. Knopf, New York, 1983.

Lajoie, J.M., *Learn How to Become a Private Investigator in a 6 Billion Dollar Industry*, Boston, MA, 2000.

McMahon, R.J., *Criminal Investigations,* 1995.

McMahon, R.J., *Fraud Investigations,* 1995.

McMahon, R.J., *Fraud Investigations: A Textbook on How to Conduct White Collar Crime and Criminal Fraud Investigations,* 1999.

McMahon, R.J., *Insurance Investigations,* 1995.

McMahon, R.J., *Interviews, Interrogation, and Statements,* 1995.

McMahon, R.J., *Law, Lawyers, and the Courts,* 1995.

McMahon, R.J., *Principles of Investigation,* 1995.

Occupational Outlook Handbook, 1998-1999, U.S. Bureau of Labor Statistics, UM-St. Louis Libraries Edition, 1998.

Perron, B.A., *Uncovering Reasonable Doubt: The Component Method – A Comprensive Guide for the Criminal Defense Investigator*, Morris Publishing, Kearney, NE, 1998.

INDEX